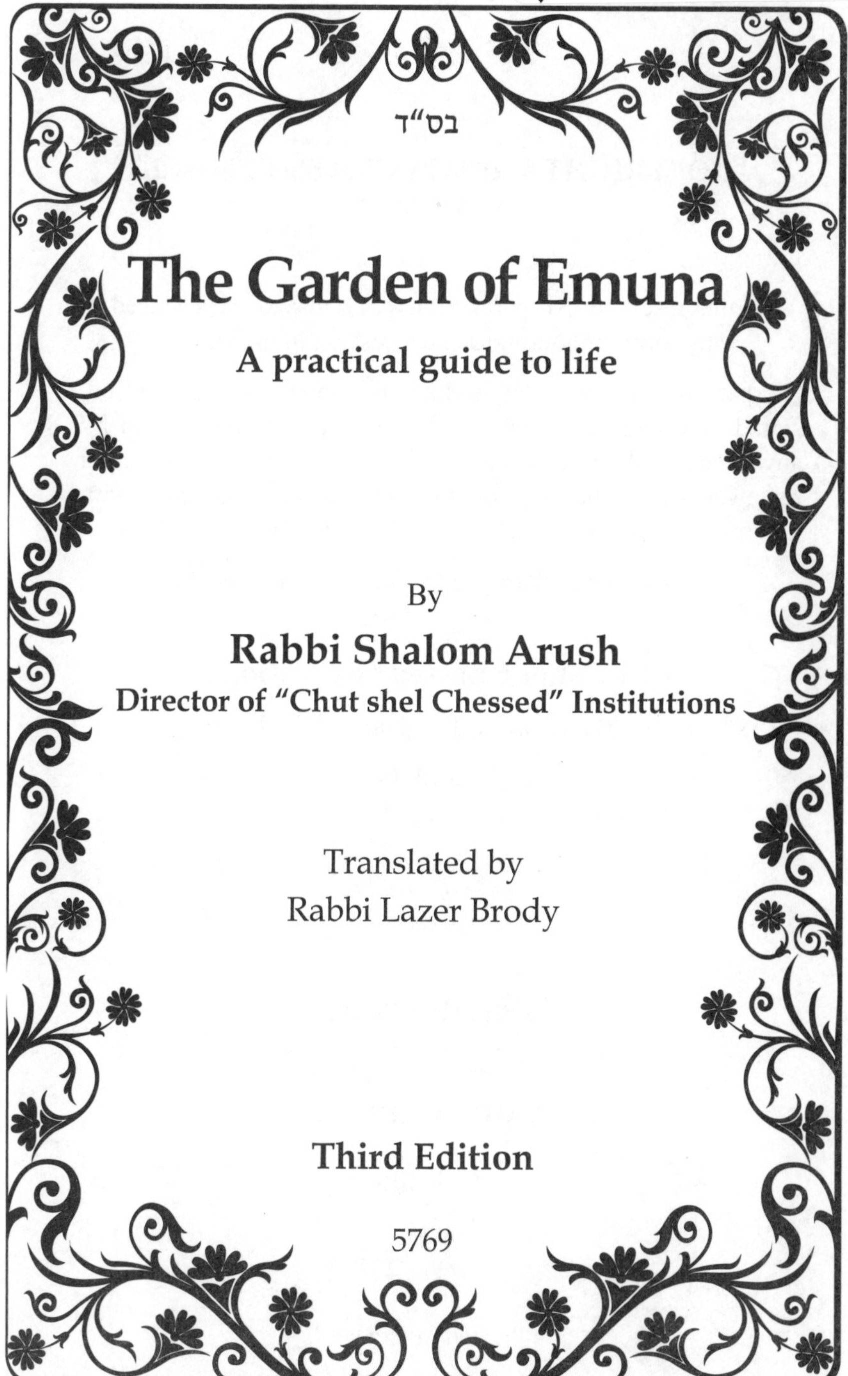

בס"ד

The Garden of Emuna

A practical guide to life

By

Rabbi Shalom Arush

Director of "Chut shel Chessed" Institutions

Translated by

Rabbi Lazer Brody

Third Edition

5769

In all matters relating to this book, please contact:

Chut Shel Chessed Institutions

POB 50226, Jerusalem, Israel

972-52-2240696

Design and Layout:
Eye See Productions
972-2-5821453

Distribution:
Tel: 972-52-2240696
www.myemuna.com

Third Edition

ISBN
978-965-91342-1-2

Printed in Israel

Contents

Chapter Five: Emuna and Emotions 211

Translator's Foreword - Third Edition

Rabbi Shalom Arush has helped more people overcome more problems in stress-ridden Israel than anyone alive. His smile is a sunburst through thick gray clouds and his words are a cool drink on a parched soul. He is the master physician of the soul who adeptly cures all people's ills with one secret spiritual remedy – ***emuna***, the pure and complete faith in The Almighty.

Over a decade ago, Rabbi Shalom Arush hired me to become the dean of the Ashdod branch of his renowned rabbinical seminary, "Chut Shel Chessed". My task was to teach rabbinical law to a group of aspiring young men. Little did I realize that my teaching career would become the greatest learning experience of my life.

Rabbi Shalom was never satisfied with building a student's mind. He stressed that a healthy soul is the only worthy spiritual receptacle for the wisdom of Torah. He encouraged me to augment our daily studies in Talmud and religious law with ethics and the works of the great Chassidic masters, particularly those of history's greatest doctor of the soul, our revered master Rebbe Nachman of Breslev (1772 – 1810), of saintly and blessed memory.

Once a week, Rabbi Shalom would come from Jerusalem to Ashdod and deliver a talk to the seminary students. He'd elaborate on Rebbe Nachman's teachings and their practical applications in our daily lives. Wide-eyed and dumbstruck, I would sit open-mouthed in the first row, savoring each syllable. Listening to Rabbi Shalom, the Dean felt like an empty-headed little boy.

My feeling of empty-headedness proved to be a blessing. By casting aside my preconceptions and my sorely limited intellect, I made room in my head for Rabbi Shalom's wisdom. Fine wine tastes best when poured into a clean and empty glass. From the moment I nullified my own brain and internalized Rabbi Shalom's teachings, I experienced enhanced blessings of success in virtually every area of my life. Every word of his lessons was spiritual money in the bank. But better than money, the lessons I've learned from Rabbi Shalom have become a priceless asset for posterity that I hope to share with you, dear reader.

One can easily fill an entire separate volume with praises of Rabbi Shalom. Notwithstanding, his five greatest attributes are his phenomenal humility, his ability to bring the lofty teachings of Rebbe Nachman of to the eye-level of this generation, his practice of every iota of what he teaches, his unshakeable emuna, and his smile.

Rabbi Shalom's popularity has mushroomed all over Israel, spilling outside of Israel's borders as well. In answering the overseas demand for his teachings, Rabbi Shalom called on me to translate his lectures and books to English. **The Garden of Emuna** was our first project after its Hebrew forefather, ***B'Gan He'Emuna***, took Israel by storm. Since then, Rabbi Shalom's books have become bestsellers in the English-speaking world as well.

Two years have transpired since we came out with the first edition of **The Garden of Emuna.** With Hashem's loving grace, the book's momentum continues to grow. We've received amazing feedback from across the globe. People from all walks of life have attested that this book has dramatically changed their lives for the best. Throughout the original translation and the two subsequent revisions of this book, Rabbi Shalom has implored me to make sure that **The Garden of Emuna** retains its universal nature. As such, the book has been just as popular in the general public as among its Jewish readers.

This third edition contains important additions that Rabbi Shalom felt necessary to include. He stresses that this is not a one-shot pleasure-reading book, but a guidebook for life that one must read over and over until the contents become completely internalized and second nature.

With Hashem's loving guidance, I have tried my utmost to preserve the flavor and intent of Rabbi Shalom's original sweet words. Even so, any deficiency in this book is surely that of the translator and not of the author.

Grand Rabbi Naftali Moscowitz of Melitz has been a beacon of advice and encouragement whose guidance has been vital to the publication of this book. The moving force behind this project is Rabbi Shalom Arush himself, who so selflessly has illuminated my mind and soul with his noble teachings. To them, my esteemed teachers and spiritual guides, I express my deepest gratitude. May Hashem bless them and their families with the very best of spiritual and material abundance always.

Shelly Perluss of Los Angeles has devoted his valuable talents and time in proofreading this edition. May Hashem bless him with all his heart's wishes for the very best always.

To my cherished wife Yehudit, we both know that the credit for this book – and everything else I do - belongs exclusively to you. May Hashem bless you with long and happy days, success, and joy from all your offspring. May they walk courageously in the path of Torah and emuna until the end of time, amen.

Three times a day, at the conclusion of the "Aleinu" prayer, we express our yearning for the day when "all flesh shall call Your name." Our hope and prayer is that The Garden of Emuna shall do its part to hasten that glorious day.

With a song of thanks to The Almighty and a prayer for the full and speedy redemption of our people Israel,

Lazer Brody, Ashdod, Tishrei 5769

A Personal Request from the Author

Dear Reader,

During the course of my work and my daily contact with people from around the world who seek my advice and help, I've come to the clear conclusion that the root of all human suffering is none other than a lack of ***emuna***, the pure and unshakable faith in The Almighty. Time and again, I've witnessed how people have overcome seemingly insurmountable personal problems by strengthening emuna; this was my motivation in writing a book that dealt exclusively with emuna.

If my sole desire was to write a book that defines emuna and lauds its virtues, I wouldn't bother; thank G-d, there are plenty of books on the market that do so already, better than what I could do. But, my entire objective in this modest volume is to bring the reader to the unequivocal conclusion that he or she needs to strengthen their emuna, and by doing so, the reader can look forward to a new, happier, and more fulfilling life – in this world and in the next.

For example, do you have financial problems? Your emuna needs reinforcement! You don't even have to pray for a better income; pray for emuna, and your income will improve automatically. Is your marriage on the rocks? Pray for emuna, and you'll have marital bliss, too. Do you suffer from emotional problems? Strengthening emuna is the best assurance in the world for emotional health. The same goes for *every* other problem in life.

Those fortunate individuals who succeed in learning that emuna is the master key to opening any door in life devote their principal time and efforts to attaining emuna. With emuna, you'll see how stress and despair become a life of satisfaction, challenge, and accomplishment. More than anything, emuna will grant you happiness and inner peace. What could be better?

My humble request is that you read this book carefully, while trying your best to apply its advice to your daily routine. I'm sure that this book will help you attain an enhanced measure of emuna in your life; if so, then all my efforts have been worthwhile.

I entitled this book **The Garden of Emuna**, alluding to the fact that emuna leads to a life as beautiful as a stroll down the enchanted paths of a lush exotic garden. In fact, emuna has the power to help a person blossom into his or her very best. Rebbe Nachman of Breslev calls emuna, "The power of growth"; nothing in the world is as conducive to one's personal growth and development as emuna.

I dedicate this book to my honored father, Machluf Arush, of blessed memory, whose pure and simple faith and impeccable character forever remain a shining beacon that illuminates my path.

My sincere thanks go to my esteemed teacher and spiritual guide, Rabbi Eliezer Burland, may Hashem grant him long and happy days, from whose sweet waters I drink and from whose magnificent spirit I draw the strength to spread the message of Jewish outreach around the world. The wisdom in this book can be traced directly to Rabbi Burland's phenomenal teachings.

A special note of gratitude goes to my wife - Miriam Varda, may Hashem bless her with a long, happy and healthy life, joy from her offspring and success in all her endeavors. She stands by my side always and deserves all the credit for my accomplishments. Her dedication to Jewish outreach knows no bounds, and surely her rewards shall be great, both in this world and in the next. May we see joy from our offspring, and may they, their children, and their children's children sincerely devote their lives to Torah and emuna until the end of days, amen.

My dear mother toiled selflessly to raise her children with love and compassion. May it be Hashem's will that she merit continued long, healthy, and happy years, seeing all her offspring growing to be upright and glorious trees in Hashem's lovely orchard, until the full redemption of our people, amen.

My appreciation and blessings go out to the distinguished scholar Rabbi Yehoshua Cohen, author of "Kerem Yehoshua", who so graciously assisted with his comments, suggestions, and critiques on the original Hebrew version of this book.

The original Hebrew version of this book would never have seen the light of day without the trusty help of Rabbi Yaakov Hertzberg, who has toiled days and nights in getting all of my ideas down on paper. May the merit of this project stand to his credit always, and may he see joy from his offspring and success in all his endeavors.

The English edition of this book became a reality thanks to the steadfast support of my very dear friend Mr. Leor Tamir of Los Angeles, California. May Hashem bless him with the very best of spiritual and material blessings always.

My heartfelt gratitude goes to Rabbi Eliezer Raphael (Lazer) Brody, the dynamic author of "Pi HaBe'er", "Nafshi Tidom", "The Trail to Tranquility", and the "Lazer Beams" web journal, who has so selflessly dedicated himself to spreading my teachings across the four corners of the English-speaking earth, and particularly for the translation and adaptation of **The Garden of Emuna**. May Hashem grant him strength for his continued efforts in Jewish outreach, success in all his endeavors, and joy from his offspring.

Last but certainly not least are my thanks to Rabbi Eitan Tzofiof and Rabbi Yosef Nechama who toiled tirelessly so that this book would become a reality. May Hashem bless them and theirs with all the very best in spiritual and material abundance.

I cast my prayer to The Living G-d, that He shall fulfill my wish: May all who read this book strive for emuna. I bless all of you, dear readers, that your learning of this book will help you cling to

Hashem. May your troubles disappear and may you merit a personal redemption of body and soul as well as long and happy lives. May we witness the ingathering of the exiles and the rebuilding of the Holy Temple in Jerusalem, speedily and in our days, amen.

Shalom Arush, Jerusalem, Elul 5766

The following are excerpts from the approbations that this generation's leading rabbinical figures wrote for the original Hebrew version of **The Garden of Emuna**:

Rabbi Ovadia Yossef, Rishon Letzion and President of The Councel of Torah Sages:

"**The Garden of Emuna** is the work of an artist, the Prince of Torah, the brilliant and pious Rabbi Shalom Arush, may he merit long and happy days, who has assembled in his purity a golden treasure of wonderful spiritual arousal..."

Grand Rabbi Naftali Moscowitz, the Melitzer Rebbe:

"The Divine Presence glistens from the pages of **The Garden of Emuna,** which is full of spiritual arousal and practical advice for the strengthening of emuna in everyday life, all derived from reliable sources that walk in the path of holiness... Every person will derive benefit from this book, for there is no limit to the obligation to learn and relearn about emuna until it becomes internalized in the heart..."

Rabbi Eliezer Berland, Rosh Yeshiva of Shuvu Banim Breslov, Jerusalem

"I have been moved to the core of my soul by reading **The Garden of Emuna**...a book that's a necessity for every Jew in every place... whoever learns this book will merit every good in this world and in the next!"

Chater One

Foundations of Emuna

Life's Riddles

This world is full of questions: What's the meaning of life? Where am I going? What will be in the end? How should I live my life? Will I ever be happy? The list is endless…

The drastic and seemingly unfair differences between one person's life and another's frequently perplex us. One person seems to glide on easy street while another person lives a life of excruciating hardships. One person is born with strength and perfect health while another is feeble and crippled. One is rich, yet another is poor. A kind person that never harmed a flea dies young, while a ruthless tyrant reigns until a ripe old age. Why?

Those who ask the most questions are the ones who suffer the most.

The person with a limited income asks, "Why does so-and-so have plenty of money, and even though I work just as hard, I go crazy trying to make ends meet?"

The parent of a sickly child asks, "Why does everyone have strong and healthy children, and I have the hard luck of raising a child that needs round-the-clock medical supervision?"

The handicapped person asks, "Why is everyone so beautifully free and agile while I'm so repulsively limited and impaired?"

The poor look at the rich and ask, "Why do they deserve a silver spoon, when our lives are a never-ending war with poverty and deprivation?"

The lonely individual that can't seem to find a spouse asks, "Why am I – with all my good qualities – unable to get married, yet others, with all their faults, find perfect spouses at a young age?"

That's not all...

Changing Times

We have an additional array of questions about the changes in our lives from day to day. Here are a few familiar examples:

- Why was yesterday such a splendid day, when everything went according to plan, while today – for no apparent reason – everything's a disaster and I feel nothing but pain and sorrow?
- Why did I have plenty of money in my pocket last week, yet this week's unexpected expenses have left me without enough to buy a loaf of bread?
- Why did I glean phenomenal joy from my children yesterday, who were the epitome of respect and deportment, yet today they've become miniature terrorists, driving me up a wall?

The list is endless, as we all know.

The Universal Answer

All of life's questions have one universal answer – **emuna**. Emuna is like a master key to life's locked dilemmas.

Emuna is the original biblical Hebrew term for a firm belief in a single, supreme, omniscient, benevolent, spiritual, supernatural, and all-powerful Creator of the universe, which we refer to as God (or **Hashem**, which literally means "the name", so that we don't risk using God's name in vain). He alone cares for each of us in a unique, tailor-made fashion according to our own individual needs.

As we shall see throughout this book, everything that happens to us in life is the product of Hashem's will and personal intervention in our lives, which we shall often refer to as Divine Providence. Divine Providence is designed to help us perform our task in life.

Divine Providence not only determines events on a global scale, it dictates the tiniest details in the universe, such as the evening meal of a worm. Our lives in their entirety – including each individual moment – are the outcome of Hashem's Divine Providence-oriented decisions. Hashem decides when we succeed and when we fail, when times are easy and when they're hard.

According to Kabbala, or Jewish esoteric thought, completing one's soul correction, or ***tikkun***, is the loftiest achievement a person can accomplish in this material world. Oftentimes, we must suffer or experience hardship in order to attain a higher spiritual level or a correction to the soul, just like a champion athlete must withstand excruciating training sessions to reach higher achievements and peak performance.

Once we develop a deep sense of emuna that Hashem, by way of Divine Providence, does everything for our ultimate benefit to guide us on the path of our needed soul correction, then the puzzle-pieces of life suddenly come together in a picture of striking clarity. With these principles in mind, emuna becomes the universal answer to all of life's questions.

Getting to Know Hashem

Essentially, Hashem has only one simple request from each of us – that we get to know Him. According to the holy Zohar, the 2nd-Century C.E. esoteric interpretation of the Torah by Rebbe Shimon Bar Yochai and his disciples, Hashem created us for the soul purpose of getting to know Him. As such, the daily events and experiences of our lives are none other than personal messages from Hashem, designed to stimulate our emuna, encourage us to speak to Him, and thereby facilitate our efforts to get close to Him. Why? The closer one gets to Hashem, the better one gets to know Him.

Achieving proximity to Hashem and thereby getting to know Him are the ultimate soul correction, our individual goal and mission on this earth. Hashem, in His limitless love for each of us, directs our lives in a manner that helps us to successfully achieve this goal. Understanding the vital fact that everything in our lives is for our own ultimate good, that is, to help us achieve our soul correction, enables us to cope with all types of situations – whether good or seemingly bad – happily and without stress, worry, and anxiety.

Consequently, when people ignore Hashem's personal messages, Hashem is compelled to send "louder" messages, in other words, situations of greater difficulty. Those who fail to get to know Hashem in good times risk being placed in predicaments devoid of any natural or logical solution, where the only remaining alternative is to cry out to Hashem. In this manner, Hashem – in His infinite lovingkindness - helps each of us reach Him and thereby achieve our ultimate soul correction. The more we cooperate, the easier our lives become.

Hashem Reproves Those that He Loves

The Zohar (*Bechukotai, 114*) states: "How beloved are the children of Israel before the Holy One, blessed be He! He desires to reprove them and to lead them on the straight path, like a loving father who wields a rod in hand in order to lead the son on the straight path, so that the son shall not stray to the right or to the left, as it is written (*Proverbs, 3:12*), "Hashem reproves those that He loves, and like a father, mollifies the child."

Ponder the above proverb for a moment. If Hashem reproves those that He loves, inversely, He doesn't reprove those that He hates! If so, a life devoid of trials and tribulations is not a very good sign!

Our Talmudic sages warned (*tractate Arachin, 16b*) that if a person has forty consecutive days free of tribulations, he or she forfeits their share in the world to come! They also stated specifically (*tractate Kiddushin, 40b*) that the righteous receive tribulations in order to merit a lofty place in the world to come.

So, when we experience difficulties in life, it's a clear sign that we're a beloved son or daughter of Hashem. Knowing that Hashem loves us and does everything for our benefit makes life not only bearable, but gratifying. The contrary also holds true - ignorance of the fact that Hashem loves us and is helping us to attain our needed *tikkun* is the root of all suffering, worry, and anxiety.

Those with emuna therefore direct their efforts to achieving their tikkun, and focus on getting to know Hashem. Such individuals are constantly seeking Hashem. As a result, Hashem doesn't need to send them superfluous "wake-up calls" that manifest themselves in the form of extreme tribulations. "Emuna" people consequently live happy and tranquil lives, regardless of their life's trials and challenges.

So many people in modern society entertain the folly that they alone control their own fate; these people are prime candidates for suffering and emotional ills. Hashem – our loving Father – uses the rod of tribulations as an expression of love, to teach us that we're not "calling the shots", but subservient to a higher authority. Also, to awaken His beloved children from their spiritual slumber, Hashem oftentimes gives us a "jolt" in the form of some difficulty or challenge that forces us to seek His help. As we said earlier, Hashem doesn't send difficulties to those that He disdains.

The Rod and the Staff

Rebbe Nachman of Breslev teaches (*Likutei Moharan I: 206*) that Hashem immediately calls out to a person that strays from the proper path, beckoning that individual to return. Hashem summons each person in a tailor-made fashion and in accordance with that person's needs. For some, Hashem's call may be a subtle hint for one person yet a vocal reprimand for others. A "louder" call might assume the form of physical punishment; in the jargon of our sages (*Midrash Mishli, 22*), "A whisper suffices for the wise, but a fool needs flagellation."

Even extreme handicaps are for a person's own good. Hashem alone knows what a soul must correct, and thereby places each soul in a circumstance that is conducive for its necessary *tikkun*, or soul correction. As we are usually unaware of our needed tikkun, we sometimes make wrong choices or entertain useless aspirations; Hashem helps us modify our plans to prevent us from wasting our lives on folly and fantasy.

For example, let's suppose that a person – left to his or her own will - would have aspired to be a professional singer. But, as a singer, that person wouldn't possibly achieve his or her required tikkun. As such, Hashem causes that person to be born with a raspy voice. Yet, the raspy voice doesn't hamper that person from becoming an outstanding teacher or spiritual leader that inspires thousands of people (*their real tikkun!*).

Hashem closes those doors that aren't beneficial to our souls, yet opens the doors that lead to what's best for each of us, to keep us on a focused and directed path in life. Without His Divine guidance, we'd be totally lost.

At this point, people usually ask, "If everything is in Hashem's hands, then what's *my* job on this earth?" Good question.

Our task is to develop our spiritual antennae and to discern – by correctly processing Hashem's personal messages to us – what Hashem wants from each of us. Hashem constantly communicates with us via our environment, telling us where He desires to take us and to what objective. Even though these "hints" - or Heavenly messages - are frequently clothed in sorrow, hardship, and deprivation, they are actually the epitome of perfect lovingkindness. How?

Sorrow, hardship, and deprivation are perfect lovingkindness when they are the agents that bring about one's tikkun – the correction and perfection of the soul, the greatest achievement on earth. When we accept life's difficulties with emuna – calmly and happily, knowing that Hashem is doing everything to help us achieve the loftiest of aspirations – we become candidates for eternal happiness and inner peace, in this world and in the next.

An athlete is prepared to implement grueling demands from a seemingly-merciless coach; not only that, but a top athlete usually loves and respects his or her coach. Why? The athlete *knows* the coach, and trusts that the coach wants to build him or her into a winner and champion. We should have the same knowledge of and trust in Hashem.

Imagine that we're driving a car and want to make a right turn, but Hashem blocks the way; we decide to make a left turn, but Hashem has set up an obstacle to block that way also. Without emuna, we'd be subject to anger, frustration, and disappointment.

But, with emuna, we believe that life's stumbling blocks, barriers, and hindrances are agents of Hashem's Divine Providence. We don't sink to frustration, anger, and depression when armed with the knowledge that life's setbacks are milestones, guiding lights, and personal gifts from Hashem.

Suppose that the ticket agent at the airport informs us that our flight has been overbooked, and that we must wait until the next flight. We ask, "Why me - can't you bump one of the other three hundred people on the list?" The ticket agent doesn't budge; he doesn't bother listening to what we have to say. We react with anger; our heart beats faster, we clench our fists and feel the blood rushing to our cheeks. Stressed and bewildered, we don't know whether to call our lawyer, bang on the counter, or create a scene.

Hold on a second! Suppose the flight took off – without us – and developed engine trouble, crashing into the sea with no survivors. Would we still be angry that we missed the flight? Of course not! With hindsight, we'd understand that Hashem did something that seemed harsh at the time, for our ultimate good – to save our life!

Emuna turns hindsight, as in the above example, into the foresighted knowledge that Hashem is leading each of us on the very best path. With emuna, we roll with life's punches, knowing that difficulties – even failure – are loving expressions of Divine Providence to help us attain the perfection of our individual souls.

Without emuna, a person is doomed to a life of confusion, frustration, and costly mistakes that could have been avoided, had that person heeded Hashem's messages. Emuna is our best tool – if not our only tool - for attaining a soul correction and completing our designated mission in life.

Lack of Communication

In light of what we've learned until now, a person that ignores Hashem's messages creates a lack of communication with Hashem. Hashem's loving hand tries to direct a mule-headed individual on the right path – for his or her own good – but the mule head stubbornly insists on taking a different road, a detrimental one.

Stubborn people that lack emuna force Hashem to send them all types of obstacles and hindrances – human or otherwise – to prevent them from wasting their lives or doing damage to themselves. Usually the mule heads continue to ignore Hashem's messages, only adding more bitterness and frustration to their lives, oftentimes driving themselves – with their own two hands - to pills and to psychiatrists. Even more alarming, the mule head fails to understand why he or she lives a life of so much pain and bitterness.

Those who squander their days trying to satisfy physical appetites - while ignoring Hashem's commandments - can expect a fate of misery and hard knocks. Why? A human driven by lust and bodily desires is inferior to an animal. Such people lack the spiritual refinement required to discern the delicate signals from Hashem that say, "My son or daughter, you're walking down a dangerous path!" When people ignore the delicate signals, Hashem is forced to catch their attention with louder and much more severe signals. In short, when they don't hear the gentle whisper, they risk the ear-splitting wail of a police or ambulance siren.

King David teaches us to seek Hashem's guidance, when he pleads (*Psalms 25:5*), "Lead me in Your truth," *Your* truth, and not mine, for only You, Hashem, know what's best for me. He also prays (*ibid. 73:24*), "May You guide me in Your counsel," *Your* counsel, Hashem, and not the counsel of my limited human brain.

Maybe you're asking yourself at this point, "How do I discern Hashem's messages? How do I know what Hashem really wants from me?" With Hashem's loving help, this book will answer these questions, and help you successfully complete your mission on earth. In addition, this book will save you untold headaches and misery, and help you achieve life's rarest commodity - genuine happiness and satisfaction.

A Reason for Living

Without emuna, what's life all about? If mortals are destined to die, then their entire lives of strain, suffering, effort, and aspirations are rendered meaningless. Even if a person succeeds in realizing a dream or a goal, he or she won't enjoy the fruits of reward for long, because the last stop on the train of life is the graveyard. Most people leave this earth before they've accomplished what they set out to do. So, what's a life full of suffering, trials, and tribulations for?

> A hobo's wife had a tantrum about her husband's laziness. She threw a frying pan at him and yelled, "Go get a proper job, you good-for-nothing!!"
>
> The hobo ducked in time, and the frying pan broke the only window in their dilapidated shack. With a grin, he raised his head and replied, "So that your next husband will inherit my hard-earned riches? No way!"

Let's take a look around us; as soon as we get past the "mask", the plastic smiles and the cosmetic façade that people hide behind, we almost always find that our neighbors, friends, and relatives *all* have a generous portion of hardship, pain, and suffering. Even the enormously successful - the glamorous, the rich, and the famous - live nightmarish lives that often terminate in bankruptcy, broken marriages, substance addiction, and suicide. All the fame and fortune in the world – when devoid of emuna – is none other than a dismal, dead-end path.

Emuna provides a reason for everything on earth. Emuna is the only effective consolation for the pain and sorrow that we all encounter from time to time. Hashem doesn't want to torment us, Heaven forbid, but to stimulate our soul-searching and ***teshuva***, or penitence - for our own benefit – to add meaning to our lives and to correct our souls. With a genuine reason for living, life takes on a whole new dimension of purpose and lasting gratification. With a corrected soul, we can achieve true happiness.

Peace and Tranquility

The outside world is a stage of tension, stress, and anger. Modern man is always on the run and under the gun; he finds no relief from emotional unrest, financial insecurity, and cut-throat competition, the results of a society that lacks emuna.

If the inhabitants of this earth had emuna, then they'd be relaxed and contented. Knowing that their lives are in the hands of a loving Creator - anxiety, worry, and stress would become superfluous. A world with an emuna-oriented populace would become a Heaven-on-earth haven of peace, justice, and compassion. Essentially, this is the world we hope for in our anticipation of ***Geula*** and ***Moshiach***, the redemption of our people and the coming of the messiah.

War and strife among nations are impossible in a world of emuna, for each nation would realize that it has its own specific task in the global scheme of things. Just as a carpenter doesn't compete with a butcher – on the contrary, each requires the services of the other – the nations of the world would cooperate in peace rather than bicker in constant conflict.

The prophet speaks about the messianic era's world of emuna when he says (*Isaiah 11:6-9*), "The wolf will dwell with the sheep and the leopard will lie next to the kid goat...they will neither injure nor destroy in all of My sacred mountain, for **the earth will be filled with knowledge of Hashem** as water covers the ocean floor." Only emuna leads to the knowledge of Hashem that will pave the way to a wonderful world of peace and tranquility.

Rebbe Nachman of Breslev writes (*Likutei Moharan II: 8*), "In the future, as the knowledge of Hashem increases, there will be no more damage and cruelty. Mercy and compassion will spread, since they are the outcome of the knowledge of Hashem."

Preventing Doomsday

Without emuna, one can likely ask, "Why should I be a goody-goody? Why can't I have a good time? Why get married when I can take whatever I want whenever I want? Who needs ethics and morality? I'm going to die anyway, so why not go for the gusto while I'm here?"

Only the fear of getting caught and punished deters such a person from committing grand larceny, embezzlement, murder, and adultery.

Emuna - the faith and knowledge that the Creator sees all, rewards, and punishes - uplifts the human from the state of a vicious, wild monster.

Where there's no emuna, there's corruption and anarchy. Injustice becomes the norm and humans become heartless. A man with no emuna can covet his best friend's wife with no qualms, or lie, kill, and steal for his own personal interests. Only emuna restrains and refines a person, by teaching him or her to be satisfied with their lot in life and not to covet what Hashem gives their neighbor.

People without emuna develop weird, warped, and destructive ideologies. For example, the Nazis had strict laws against cruelty to animals, yet murdered millions of human beings with no remorse. Society even glorifies twisted thinking, such as making a hero out of the legendary thief Robin Hood, who robbed the rich to give to the poor. With emuna, they would have never idealized thievery in any shape or form. Why? Only Hashem decides who'll be rich and who'll be poor, and no one has the right to invent laws that negate Hashem's commandments, such as the prohibition against stealing.

A world void of emuna is full of twisted notions and warped ideologies. A long list of false "truths" threatens the continued existence of the world. These "truths" – fascism, communism, socialism, capitalism, or whatever "ism" a given society chooses – are simply different forms of lies. Even the revolutions and counter-revolutions are simply substitutions of one lie for another.

Emuna connects a person, a nation, or a society to Hashem's one and only absolute truth. Truth, like Hashem, is eternal – it never changes. The world can ultimately continue only on the basis of truth; without truth, we can only see the bleakest prospects of a nuclear Armageddon and mass destruction.

Since truth prevents conflict and mass destruction, and one can obtain truth only by means of emuna, then emuna is the necessary requisite for the world's continued existence.

The Power of Emuna

Emuna not only helps us to understand the world around us, it is essentially our most powerful asset. Emuna girds us with phenomenal inner strength and enables us to successfully weather any and all of life's difficult tests and challenges, whatever they may be. Ups and downs, life's bumpy transitional periods, and times of turbulence all become easier when a person relies on emuna.

Emotional breakdowns and despair all result from a lack of emuna. Life is unbearable when one loses hope. The dead end that a person reaches when he or she can't believe that there's a solution to their tribulations is tantamount to a foot in the grave – a living death.

With emuna, we know that there's no situation on earth – no matter how seemingly dismal – where Hashem can't come to our rescue.

Isaiah the prophet informed King Hezekiah that the latter had been sentenced by Heavenly edict to death. The king answered the prophet, "Ben Amotz – belay your prophecies and leave! I have a tradition from my great-grandfather King David that even if a sharp sword comes to rest on a person's throat, he should not lose hope in Divine mercy (*see Gemorra, tractate Berachot, 10a*)."

Rebbe Nachman of Breslev teaches, "One who has emuna is truly alive, and his days are always filled with good. When things go well, it is certainly good. But when one has troubles, it is also good, for one knows that Hashem will eventually have mercy, and make the outcome good. Since everything comes from Hashem, it's definitely for the best. But, Heaven forbid, a man without faith is not really alive. Evil befalls him and he loses all hope. There is nothing to cheer or comfort him, for he has no emuna. He is outside of Hashem's providence, and has no good at all. But with emuna, life is good and pleasant. (*Sichos HaRan, 53*)."

Everyone has Emuna

In reality, all of us have emuna; most people simply fail to "live" their emuna. In other words, they don't know how to apply the powerful concept of emuna to daily practice. We tap our cogent resources of emuna once we begin speaking to Hashem and asking for all of our needs. Emuna isn't activated in its entirety until a person begins a daily personal dialog with Hashem. As such, whenever we speak about emuna, we intrinsically refer to prayer.

Let's examine five principle doubts that prevent us from "living" our emuna:

- Doubt that Hashem is constantly within our midst, watching over us and managing the minutest details of our lives: If we don't believe in Hashem at all, or believe that He created the world but leaves everything to the course of nature, then we won't consider the option of turning to Hashem for all of our needs.

- Doubt that we have the power and privilege to speak to Hashem – in our own language and in our own words – whenever we wish.

- Doubt that Hashem listens to us, heeds our prayers and the prayers of every creation.

- Doubt that Hashem loves each of us and desires to help us, especially those that turn to Him and speak to Him.

- Doubt that Hashem's power, mercy, and compassion are

limitless, and that He possesses the resources and the ability to help us in *any* situation, even when we don't deserve His help.

The Power of Prayer

Internalize this golden rule: **With true emuna, any person – by means of simple personal prayer and dialog with Hashem – can transcend any natural limitation and work wonders!**

Prayer has the capability of altering nature. Since Hashem is above nature, those who turn to Him raise themselves above the limitations of nature. Jewish tradition is full of stories about how our sages initiated nature-defying miracles with the power of their prayers. The list is long and exhaustive.

Don't ever forget that Hashem listens to, sees, and personally provides for the lowest and simplest creatures in the universe. It therefore goes without saying that Hashem is always ready to help one of His beloved sons or daughters, the highest order of creation.

As soon as we activate our emuna and turn to Hashem – in our own words, like speaking to a beloved parent or best friend – we can achieve literally anything, such as a remedy for our ills or the fulfillment of all our needs.

Rabbi Nathan of Breslev, Rebbe Nachman's prime disciple, always used to say, "Wherever I see deficiency, either there was no prayer or insufficient prayer." Consequently, sufficient prayer can invoke a solution to any problem.

A sure-fire spiritual law says that each prayer has its power, and that each request requires a certain amount of prayer - or spiritual power – to bring about its manifestation. Just as an ounce of dynamite is enough to put a hole in a laboratory table, one might need a ton of dynamite to blow a hole in a mountain. By the same token, the greater the request, the more prayer – or spiritual dynamite – is required. Remember, **sufficient prayer invokes a solution to any problem.**

By believing in the power of prayer, we are able to keep praying until our request is fulfilled. The Talmud testifies (*tractate Berachot 32b*), "Rabbi Chanina says, anyone who prays long enough doesn't go away empty-handed!"

The Midrash explains (*Yalkut Shimoni, 31*) that when Hashem decreed that Moses wouldn't be allowed to enter the Land of Israel, Moses prayed 515 prayers, until Hashem commanded him to stop praying! Why? With one more prayer, Hashem would have been obligated to rescind the decree.

We learn from the above Midrash that when we meet the required prayer quota for a given request, the request is filled! As long as Hashem doesn't command us to stop praying, we can - and must – continue to pray until our prayer is answered!

Hashem Favors Those who Seek Him

Clearly, people don't take advantage of emuna and prayer - the tremendous power that's always at their disposal – simply because they're unaware of their own potential.

Some believe in a faraway Creator, or a Creator that has some undefined, removed, and minor influence on their lives. Few fully connect the tiny and mundane details of their daily lives to emuna and to Divine Providence. ***Emuna shlema*, or complete emuna, means that one relates every single happening in life to Divine will and providence.** For example, when a wife scolds her husband, the husband – with proper emuna - doesn't lose his temper because he knows that Hashem decreed that she scold him. The same goes for more difficult situations, such as health and financial problems.

Emuna means that we accept everything that happens to us as Hashem's will. And, when we need help, a solution to a problem, our daily needs, or whatever we desire, we speak to Hashem.

Dear reader, I know that you believe in Hashem, so why don't you talk to Him? If you don't speak to Him, it's a sign that you don't believe that Hashem can help you; in that case, you must strengthen your emuna.

Hashem wants us to turn to Him for *all* our needs, big or small. Hashem doesn't care about how much power, money and influence we have. He loves each of us whether or not we have a university degree, and really doesn't care if we're a Phi Beta Kappa or not. King David said (*Psalms 147:10-11*), "Not in the strength of the horse does He desire, nor in the thigh of man does He favor; Hashem favors those who fear Him, those who long for His lovingkindness."

In contemporary jargon, Hashem doesn't need us to show off the "horses" in our fancy stable – military might, technological achievements, or a Swiss bank account. He also isn't impressed by the "thighs" we've developed in our weightlifting, aerobics, or judo workouts. He wants us to pray to Him, to be one of those who "long for His lovingkindness."

Once we become accustomed to praying in every situation, we develop a spiritual sensitivity that is conducive to feeling Hashem's constant presence. When we feel Hashem's presence, we willfully and happily thank Him, speak to Him, and pray to Him all the time. When we're constantly seeking Hashem, He doesn't need to send us wake-up calls of troubles, trials, and tribulations.

Beyond the Material World

The Zohar explains that entrance-level emuna is the cognizance of a world to come, far beyond the limited material world.

An emotionally healthy person isn't prepared to do anything that is not beneficial or that doesn't serve a purpose. For example, if you ask someone to raise and lower their hand for sixty minutes for no apparent reason, they'll certainly refuse. Even if you offer them a fair hourly wage to fulfill your request, they still might not consent if they don't see a purpose to what they're doing.

If a human does things for a purpose only, then you can rest assured that Hashem does nothing without a specific and very good purpose.

Did Hashem create such a magnificent universe – from the tiniest one-celled amoeba to the greatest galaxies – just for the fun of it? Of course, not! Every mineral, plant, animal, and human has an important task to perform in the overall scheme of creation. Hashem gave the human fabulously sophisticated components - intellectual potential, physical capabilities, and spiritual power – for a definite purpose.

We must therefore ask ourselves: "Am I here for the gratification of my body! The body is destined to ultimate decay in the grave! Why would Hashem create me with such a sophisticated spiritual and emotional apparatus if I were meant just to work like a mule all my life, then die, and then become dinner for the worms? My body, with all that I've invested in it – the spa, the hairdresser, the massages, the beauty treatments – ends up as fertilizer for the flowers. It's a harsh realization, but it's true. Is that all there is to life?

Certainly not. Hashem wouldn't have given us a soul – our spiritual self – without a purpose. We can therefore surmise that there must be a continuation of spiritual life far beyond physical demise. We toil in this world, and reap the rewards in the world to come.

Reward and punishment manifest themselves in this world as well. We achieve a sense of content, fulfillment, and inner peace when we perform Hashem's will. Inversely, transgressions of Hashem's will lead to tribulations in life – not as punishment per se, but to stimulate soul-searching and to help us make the right choices – for the ultimate and eternal benefit of our soul. Without a post-physical world, a grand scheme of reward and punishment is superfluous.

Tikkunim: Soul Corrections

The belief in a world to come is the basis of genuine emuna, providing an explanation to many of life's perplexities. Our powers of comprehension and cognizance become greatly enhanced when we realize that our lives began long before we're born and continue long after we die.

Here's a true story about a tragedy that jolted the very foundation of an entire Jewish community's emuna in Hashem:

> A beautiful young lady - daughter of one of the community's most prestigious and respected families - married a righteous merchant, a man of charity and compassion. The early years of their marriage were blessed with happiness, abundance, and children. The modest wife became a wonderful mother, utilizing every free minute from her busy schedule to recite Psalms or to care for the community's poor and underprivileged. The husband, whose successful commerce carried him to surrounding cities and hamlets, never failed to fulfill a strict daily quota of prayer and Torah learning. In addition, he gave enormous amounts to charities all across the country, easing the suffering of thousands of impoverished people.
>
> Suddenly, disaster struck. Their home - a bright beacon of charity, good deeds, and lovingkindness - became the scene of agony. A drunken soldier viciously abused, mutilated, and murdered the couple's three-year-old son!

The entire community was appalled. Thousands joined in the mourning, including the nation's leading sages and spiritual leaders. No one understood. Many vocalized the doubts in their hearts in public: Is this the reward that such a righteous couple deserves? Why did Hashem do something so horrendous like that to them? Why did the poor little toddler have to suffer so severely? Others harbored malice in their hearts against Hashem that weakened their emuna and distanced them from Torah.

The couple reacted with total emuna, capitulation, and loving acceptance of the Divine decree. They continued with their righteous lifestyle as if nothing had changed - the wife with her acts of lovingkindness and the husband with his Torah learning and magnificent charity.

Shortly thereafter, tragedy struck again: Like wildfire, word spread around the town that the righteous merchant had fallen deathly ill. All of the local synagogues mobilized their members in round-the-clock prayer vigils. Everyone loved the merchant. Almost every person in town had benefited from his generosity at one time or another. Understandably, the cries of the community pierced the very thresholds of the Heavens.

The community beadle ran breathlessly into the town's main synagogue, where the head rabbi prayed, and shouted, "The doctors have given up hope! They say the end is near!"

The head rabbi, himself a pillar of righteousness and a learned master of Talmudic law, declared forcefully but calmly, "It shall not happen! No evil shall befall our brother the righteous merchant!"

The pain and bewilderment of the entire town reached new heights when the word of the righteous merchant's death became common knowledge. Such a young man, at the prime of life - didn't he suffer enough? He did nothing but good deeds his entire life, is this what he deserved? The tears of the young, barely thirty five-year-old widow tore at the community's already perplexed and agonized heart.

A few years passed. One Friday afternoon, the newly-married son of the young widow came to wish his mother "Shabbat Shalom"; she tried to smile, but burst into tears.

"Mama," the young man pleaded, "three years have passed already. You've cried enough! Our sages prescribed set times for mourning. If someone cries more than they should, then sorrow never leaves them! We are believers; none of us can know Hashem's considerations. Everything Hashem does is for the very best! Mama, your crying not only saddens us - your children - but it saddens Papa's soul, too. The matchmakers have been chasing after you with several good proposals, and you've been avoiding them. Mama, please, you must continue on with your life."

The young widow took a deep breath. Enough! She made a firm resolve to overcome the sorrow. An encouraging thought flashed across her mind: "Am I more merciful than Hashem? Of course, not! I've always trusted Hashem, so why shouldn't I be happy?!" To the relief of her worried children - that very Shabbat - Mama became a new person.

For the first time in years, the widow slept soundly and peacefully. She realized that a lack of emuna - not her husband's absence - was responsible for the gap in her heart. Now, that gap was filled again.

She had a dream... *She saw herself standing in an exotic garden of supernatural beauty, and she understood that this must be the next world. Standing among the aromatic flowering trees, she saw an image of an old man with a long beard, who radiated brilliantly. He approached her, and asked if she'd like to see her deceased husband. She nodded in the affirmative. He led her to a magnificent palace where a young man was giving a Torah lecture to thousands of elderly righteous souls. When the lecture was over, the lecturer approached her – it was her husband!*

"Dearest husband," she exclaimed, "why did you leave me alone at such an early stage in our lives? How have you become the teacher of so many tzaddikim? You were a merchant and an upright man, but you were never a Torah scholar."

The husband smiled. "In my former life, I was a great scholar, but I never married. When I died, I was told that I can't assume my designated place in the upper palaces of Heaven because I never fulfilled the first commandment of the Torah, namely, that one must be fruitful and multiply. Therefore, I was reincarnated again for the sole purpose of marrying and having children, and to raise them in the path of Torah. That's exactly what I did. As soon as I completed my tikkun – my soul correction and my mission on earth – I no longer had to remain down there. Now, as you see, I live a life of eternal bliss..."

"Then why did our little son die?" probed the wife.

The husband answered, "He is the lofty soul of a holy tzaddik, an extremely righteous individual. In his previous life, he was kidnapped at birth and raised on the milk of a gentile surrogate mother. Finally, at age three, he was redeemed by the Jewish community and subsequently became a sage of enormous spiritual proportions. After his death, he was denied his rightful place in Heaven since his early childhood had left a tiny blemish on his soul. His sole tikkun was to return to earth, to be born, nursed, and raised for three years by an upright Jewish woman; you, dear wife, were granted the privilege of being that woman!"

"But why was his death so horrible?"

"Know," continued the husband, that since our toddler son had completed his tikkun, he was destined to die anyway. At the same time, the Heavenly Court had decreed - in light of the dire sins between man and fellow man in our town – that all its inhabitants be destroyed in a catastrophic pogrom. The righteous soul of our little one volunteered to die a terrible death as atonement for the entire town. He became a holy martyr and sanctified himself as a public sacrifice. No one is allowed to reach his lofty abode except for me, since I was his father. When your time comes, you – as his mother – will also be allowed. You can't imagine the bliss of the Divine light that surrounds our son..."

The husband faded away. Before he departed, his voice reverberated, "Only by virtue of your reinforced emuna was I revealed to you! As long as you were in a cloud of sadness, you almost lost another child. All my requests to be revealed to you were refused... my tikkun is over, but you still have much to do. Go, remarry, and live a life of emuna and joy. Go with my blessing...farewell!" The husband's image disappeared completely.

The widow awakened. She felt like she was born anew. She realized that her questions – as well as the rest of the town's questions – were needless. If the Torah teaches that Hashem is righteous and just, then there's no need to wonder why Hashem does what He does.

Those of us who don't merit revelations in our sleep should strive to strengthen our emuna. The knowledge that Hashem does everything for our eternal benefit should be engraved on our hearts and minds.

The Mission

Each of us comes to this earth for the express purpose of fulfilling a mission. Longevity depends on the task we have to complete. One's death – even in a sudden tragedy or accident – is always the result of Hashem's personal decision. Some live for twenty years and others for one hundred years, but we all eventually leave this earth at the precise moment that Hashem decides. A mind-boggling set of Divine considerations influences the circumstances of a person's life and longevity – the person's deeds, former lives, public edicts, and other criteria that defy our understanding.

Some souls come to this earth for a short and specific tikkun, and then return to the upper worlds. Such souls are usually remarkably special people, with little or no evil inclination, gentle, kind, and pleasant. Therefore, don't be surprised when you hear of young, upright people that die suddenly; they've simply completed their tikkun - their soul correction and mission on this earth.

Rabbi Isaac Luria Ashkenazi, the famed "Arizal" and 17th Century C.E. father of Kabbala from Safed, teaches that we encounter most resistance in the area of our mission on earth, since the ***Yetzer Hara*** – the evil inclination – doesn't want us to complete our mission successfully. The more we're hampered by the *Yetzer Hora*, the more we have to accomplish on earth.

A Brief Visit

Sometimes, a soul makes a brief visit to this earth. One story tells about the Arizal who was the *sandek*, or godfather, at a *brit mila*; immediately after the circumcision, the baby died. When the baby's friends and relatives wailed like wounded animals, the Arizal said, "Why do you cry? You merited in hosting the soul of our master, Rebbe Joseph Karo (*a contemporary of the Arizal and author of the Shulchan Oruch, Code of Jewish Law*)!

With his holy spirit, the Arizal saw that Rabbi Joseph Karo died and arrived at the gates of Heaven. Rabbi Joseph had fulfilled every one of Hashem's commandments with didactic precision, except for one – circumcision. When he was born, he was jaundiced and therefore circumcised later than the prescribed age of eight days. His entire tikkun was to return to earth and be circumcised on the eighth day of his life; he had no further reason to remain on earth.

The Arizal knew every soul, its background, and its mission on earth. His testimony shows how our lack of even one small but critical detail makes Hashem's lovingkindness seem like cruelty, Heaven forbid. Like a gigantic jigsaw puzzle, if one piece is missing, the entire picture seems flawed. Emuna – our unshakable belief and trust in Hashem – fills in the missing pieces that our limited vision sometimes creates.

A Deposit for Safekeeping

The Midrash (*Mishli, 31*) relates a poignant story about the holy *Tanna* (2nd Century CE Mishnaic sage) from Tiberias, Rebbe Meir Baal HaNess:

> One Sabbath, Rebbe Meir sat in the house of study, unaware that both of his sons had died. Bruria, his wife, withheld the bitter news from him, covered the two bodies with a sheet, and moved them up to the attic. That evening, after

> Sabbath ended, Rebbe Meir returned home and asked, "Where are the two boys?" Bruria changed the subject and served her husband his evening meal.
>
> When Rebbe Meir finished his grace after the meal, his wife said, "Rebbe, I have a question."
>
> "Feel free to ask, my wife."
>
> "If a person gave me a deposit for safekeeping some while ago and now he has come to claim it, what should I do?"
>
> "Simple," replied Rebbe Meir, "you must return the deposit."
>
> Bruria took Rebbe Meir by the hand, led him up to the attic, and showed him his two lifeless sons. Rebbe Meir began to cry, lamenting his grievous loss. "Rebbe," his wife said, "didn't you just tell me that a deposit for safekeeping must be returned when the owner comes to claim it?"
>
> Rebbe Meir stopped crying immediately and quoted (*Job 1:21*), "Hashem has given, Hashem has taken, blessed be Hashem's name!"
>
> Rebbe Chanina, another holy sage and contemporary of Rebbe Meir, praised Bruria and her poignant consolation that so effectively relieved her husband's grief, and said (*Proverbs 31:10*), "A woman of valor, who shall find?"

The Talmud (*tractate Berachot, 5b*) tells of the renowned sage Rebbe Yochanan, who having lost all his ten sons, would walk around with the tooth of his tenth son in his pocket and declare, "This is the bone of my tenth son that died. See how I lost ten sons, but am still happy and smiling! I realize that this world is not our principle concern, and those holy souls that were my sons simply finished their tikkun and respective missions in this world, so why should I be sad? They are now in a world of eternal bliss, but we are still suffering on this lowly earth."

Rebbe Nachman of Breslev lost his only two sons, his first wife, and left this world at the young age of 38.

Many Tzaddikim buried loved ones and suffered other grueling tribulations, yet everyone knew that they were pillars of righteousness. Often, there's no connection between longevity and a person's good deeds. We shudder when hearing about the loss of a young person. Actually, the thought of an elderly person's death should jolt us even more, showing us that death is unavoidable.

Don't Forget the World to Come

Oftentimes a person takes his initial steps as a spiritually-awakened Jew, or *Baal Teshuva*, and suffers some form of damage – physical, financial, or otherwise. The resulting question usually sounds like this: "Why now, when I've chosen the path of Torah and have started to observe the Sabbath, do I deserve such punishment? Is this the reward of Torah?"

Still other times, a new Baal Teshuva dies a sudden, tragic death. People ask, "How is this possible? What's going on here? A new Baal Teshuva that left a life of glitter and good times to devote his life to Hashem…He should have lived forever! Why did Hashem take him so suddenly?"

The most famous question of the perplexed is: "What about the Holocaust? Why did Hashem allow six million Jews – many of whom were holy and righteous Torah scholars – to die in the gas chambers and concentration camps?"

People forget that this world is a place of temporary significance at best, where a soul assumes a bodily form to perform a mission and achieve a needed tikkun. But, if they'd remember that the life and health of the *soul* is our prime concern – and not the *body* - then their questions would fall by the wayside.

Mortal Man

We can't possibly know when our tikkun has been achieved. No one knows how they'll leave this world, either. Yet, we should always remember that we're mortal, and destined to die some day. King Solomon, the wisest of all men, advised (*Ecclesiastes 7:2*): "It is better to frequent the house of mourning than the house of feasting, for it signifies the end of all men - and the living should take it to heart!"

Apparently, the above advice to attend funerals and visit mourners is simple: By visiting mourners, we remember that someday, our lives will terminate also. Surprisingly though, certain professionals like doctors, nurses, and geriatric attendants see death all the time, yet how many of them are aroused to teshuva? Many of them remained bogged down in the pursuit of material amenities their entire lives. That's why King Solomon stressed:

"And the living should take it to heart!" All of us must remember that we're mere mortals, here today and gone tomorrow; if we forget, we're liable to fall into spiritual slumber. The fear and awe of our final day on earth and subsequent day of reckoning helps us monitor our thoughts, speech, and deeds. When establishing our list of priorities, we should remember that fame and fortune are worthless in the grave; this world's amenities are worthless in the next world. Our ultimate objective is the world to come, and emuna will get us there.

Truth

Now that we have a better understanding of our purpose on this earth, is it logical that Hashem would send us here without giving us an indication of what we're supposed to do? Would he distribute reward and punishment without informing us of what's permissible and what's not? Would Hashem let us all grope around in the dark with no direction? Of course not.

Hashem gave mankind, and the Jewish people in particular, clear instructions as to one's purpose in life. Not only do we have our holy Torah and its commandments; we have the great tzaddikim – the righteous sages and spiritual leaders of every generation – that lead us on the path of truth. The path of truth leads to genuine emuna.

Conversely, one cannot hope to achieve and internalize genuine emuna without Torah, for in the absence of Torah, humans – subjectively swayed by their own vested interests and appetites – decide their own truth. As mentioned earlier, nations and societies can arrive at utterly warped conclusions, such as genocide of another people, when forming their own "truths".

The Golden Path

Life is a labyrinth of utter chaos in the absence of Torah, where confused people live lives of folly and fantasy. Look around you: Neighbor A is on a mad chase after more money, Neighbor B thirsts for fame and recognition, Neighbor C never stops trying to allure Neighbor D's wife, Neighbor E can't stand Neighbor F, who's jealous of neighbor G's new car.

Without Torah, the world is a heartless, unbearable hothouse of strife, hatred, competition, slander, theft, revenge, cruelty, adultery, and injustice.

The world can be lovely, enjoyable, and tranquil. A life of Torah is like a smooth ride in a new car when the owner fulfills all the manufacturer's instructions as listed in the owner's manual. The Torah – the Creator's manual for our bodily and spiritual welfare

- shows us how to be happy, how to respect our fellow man, and how to raise our children. A true Torah observer deals honestly, helps others, and rejoices when they're happy. Such individuals wouldn't dream of touching something that didn't belong to them. They live worthy and fulfilled lives, and make the world a better place.

In short, the Torah is the venerable golden path to a good and meaningful life.

Unfortunately, if a person learns Torah without striving for emuna, then the power of Torah becomes lethal and damaging. For example, without emuna, Heaven forbid, a simple thief can utilize the wisdom of Torah to become a dangerous, sophisticated thief. Without the guidance of the generation's tzaddikim – our righteous spiritual guides – one cannot hope to attain truth and emuna. As such, many can be "religious", yet remain far from truth and from true emuna. Rather than appealing to Hashem for all their needs, they put their hopes in the hands of futile flesh and blood, become easily worried and upset, and quarrel with others.

A Man of Spirit

An unbroken chain of righteous tzaddikim extends from Moses to this very generation. The tzaddikim help us understand the Torah, its commandments, and our individual purpose in life.

Each of us must search for a genuine tzaddik of true spiritual stature that can help us find the way to applying the Torah to our daily lives. A random righteous person that hasn't been the understudy of a righteous spiritual guide before him will not suffice. The expert spiritual guide – whom the Torah calls "A man of spirit" (*Numbers 27:18*), knows how to apply the laws of Torah for the benefit of each individual's spirit.

For example, a qualified rabbinical authority who is also "a man of spirit" might permit a certain action under one circumstance, yet completely forbid it under another circumstance. He sees the unique needs of each individual, just as a shepherd knows the needs of each lamb and ewe. Such a rabbi, tzaddik, and spiritual guide knows how to arouse a person from spiritual slumber, strengthen souls, and show them the way to Hashem.

Without a qualified and righteous spiritual guide, a person might learn Torah for a lifetime, yet make tragic errors in spiritual navigation and never attain his or her tikkun. Two groups of people have difficulty finding their way in the world – those without Torah altogether, and those without a spiritual guide. "Blessed be He who separates us from the mistaken" (*Kedusha D'sidra, morning liturgy*); every day, we ask Hashem to save us from both groups.

Rebbe Nachman of Breslev writes (*Likutei Moharan I: 123*): "The foundation and most important principle – one's connection to the tzaddik of the generation, to accept his teachings about everything, big or small, without straying to the right or left, Heaven forbid, as our sages instructed (*Sifri, parshas Shoftim*): 'Even if you're told that right is left…', that one must cast aside his own wisdom, logic, and opinion as if there is no brainpower other than that what he receives from the tzaddik of the generation, and as long as one depends on one's own intellect, he is in a state of imperfection, not fully connected to the tzaddik."

Rebbe Nachman also writes (*Likutei Moharan II: 8*): "One must search and pray very hard for a true spiritual guide, and insistently request from Hashem that he merit to find a true leader, so he can attain true and complete emuna, for when one connects – Heaven forbid – to a false leader, one is exposed to false believes…therefore one must search and pray for a true leader to connect to."

Caution!

One can find a true spiritual guide and leader only by way of prayer, for most of us lack the tools to discern between an authentic tzaddik and a good imitation. Furthermore, we may find a tzaddik that may not be the right spiritual guide for us, or an individual of insufficient spiritual stature to guide us on the true path of emuna and tikkun. We must therefore exercise supreme caution in avoiding the pitfalls of criticizing a group or its leader, who doesn't seem to be the right leader for us. Why? Belittling a fellow Jew – let alone an entire group or its leader – is a severe transgression of Torah law.

Those who rely on their own intellectual prowess to search for a proper spiritual guide are prone to mistakes. Therefore, we must pray to find the true tzaddik that can show us the way to genuine emuna.

Now that we've learned the foundations of emuna, we're ready to proceed to our next chapter and learn the levels of emuna.

Chapter Two

The Levels of Emuna

Having learned the foundations of emuna in the first chapter, we're now ready to learn about the different levels of faith.

Emuna can be divided into three main levels:

1. Basic-level emuna: This is the firm belief that everything comes from Hashem by way of perfect Divine Providence, even the tiniest and most seemingly insignificant event.

2. Intermediate-level emuna: In addition to flawless basic emuna, the intermediate believes that everything Hashem does is for the very best.

3. Upper-level emuna: In addition to solid basic and intermediate level emuna, the upper-level individual believes that Hashem does everything for a specific purpose, and tries to understand the message within whatever Hashem does.

The above three levels are actually one intrinsic whole, since emuna itself is one entirety.

Emuna is the belief that there is none other than Hashem, whose Divine Providence is the root of all things and all events. Since the main reason for Hashem's creating the world is to bestow His lovingkindness on all His creations, everything He does is for our ultimate welfare. Hashem does nothing in random; all His workings have a specific rationale and purpose.

This chapter will discuss each level individually, and help us apply its principles to our daily lives.

Section One - Basic-level Emuna:

Belief in Divine Providence

This is what Hashem wants!

Basic-level emuna teaches that Hashem is the lone sovereign of the universe, whose surgically-precise Divine Providence is responsible for every single occurrence in the universe – big or small. The very first of the thirteen tenets of our faith (*see Maimonides, The Thirteen Tenets of Faith, appears in most prayer books at the end of Shacharit, the morning prayer service*) states: "I believe with complete emuna that the Creator, blessed be His name, is the Creator and Ruler of all the creations, and He **alone** did, does, and will do every single deed."

Simply speaking, everything that happens in the world – from the multiplication of a one-celled amoeba to the earth-shaking events that affect entire continents – all come from Hashem.

Let's bring the above principle down to a personal level: **Everything** that happens to us – spiritually or materially, accidental or intended, no matter who or what the catalyst seems to be – comes **exclusively** from Hashem.

Let Emuna precede intellect

The following salient rule of thumb enables us to begin applying emuna to our daily lives: **Anytime something happens that upsets us, we should let emuna precede our intellect**. Emuna must be our initial thought! Before the brain and intellect begin blaming our troubles on "natural" forces and phenomena, on others, or on ourselves, our emuna tells us that our particular predicament or situation is exactly what Hashem wants, otherwise it wouldn't have occurred.

Hashem alone assembles the multitude of "puzzle pieces" - the people, events, and influencing factors in our lives – to create a certain situation in our lives or in the world around us.

To effectively use our intellectual powers, we must first remember that anyone or anything that influences our lives - for better or for worse - is merely Hashem's messenger and an agent of Divine will. Once we stand firmly on this basic tenet of emuna, we're ready to activate our intellectual prowess – according to Torah, of course – and attempt to understand Hashem's message that's cloaked within a given occurrence.

For example, someone that forgets to let emuna precede intellect might blame his or her feet pains on the "natural phenomenon" of a bad pair of shoes. Others might attribute their lack of career success to a tyrannical boss, or torment themselves for losing money in a bad investment. Even though the shoes were really poorly made, or the boss is truly a tyrant, or the investment was surely a silly mistake, Hashem is right there on the scene, hiding behind all the events that He causes to create a certain situation. Life's situations are none other than personal messages for our ultimate benefit.

Letting emuna precede intellect is the proper way to react in any situation. We say to ourselves, "Hashem is making me lose money; Hashem is blocking my career advancement; Hashem gave me the bad shoes!" When we remind ourselves that a given situation comes from Hashem, we're comforted, knowing that everything Hashem does is for the very best, as we'll see in the second section of this chapter. Once emuna precedes intellect, then we're ready to utilize our brainpower in order to understand what Hashem wants from us.

Who wields the stick?

At this point, we need to learn **two important laws of spirituality**:

Law #1: **Hashem is the cause of every catalyst**. The old adage tells of a master that uses a stick to clout a slave; the unfortunate slave certainly doesn't blame the stick for his troubles, nor is he angry at the stick, nor does he try to appease the stick.

Do we have less common sense than the simple slave of the adage? How can we forget that any situation, person, object, or animal that saddens us is none other than a "stick" in Hashem's hands? Would we try to reason or negotiate with a stick? Certainly not! Just as the slave turns to his master, we must turn to Hashem whenever we seek to understand what's happening in our lives. So, with the slave-and-stick adage in mind, we're now ready to learn Law #2:

Law #2: **Any situation of tension, stress, or sorrow is none other than a test of faith**. As such, we need to put our intellect on the shelf, for the following reasons:

- The intellect doesn't have the emuna that everything comes from Hashem.

- The intellect tries to grasp "rationale" straws that lead to sorrow, anger, and frustration – all of which cause depression and despair.

- The intellect looks for a "culprit" at fault, and therefore leads to feelings of resentment and revenge.

Negative emotions literally destroy people's lives. To avoid them, we need to put our intellects aside temporarily and reinforce our emuna that everything comes from Hashem! There is none other than Hashem! Everything that happens to us is His Divine will! Man *and* nature are nothing more than mere agents, sticks in Hashem's hands. Rather than looking at the stick, we should always remember to look at who's swinging it – Hashem! Appealing to Hashem is the only way to solve a problem.

Free will

Most of the things that sadden us fall into one of three categories:

- **Nature**, such as a virus or bacteria;
- **Fellow human** with his or her own free will;
- **Ourselves**, what we often call our own stupid mistakes.

People normally understand that naturally-caused tribulations – such as sickness, Heaven forbid – come from Hashem. Sometimes, the same people mistakenly put their trust in doctors and medicines. When the doctors and medicines fail, the sick and their loved ones ultimately turn to Hashem for help. You've never seen or heard anyone asking for mercy from a bacteria or virus.

Since we know that Hashem gives humans free will to do good or evil, many of us think that man's actions are beyond Hashem's control. Our intellect tells us to take issue with the individual that torments us, and attempt to effect a change in his or her behavior. At a superficial glance, the intellect is correct: Why pray to Hashem when here, standing in front of me, is the person that's making me miserable? This person possesses free will, so why not appeal to him or her? Maybe I should just hit them in the face! Who needs prayer?

The truth is that we *all* need prayer, for everything that happens to us comes from Hashem; He **alone** did, does, and will do every single deed.

Remember this very important principle: **Hashem's personal Divine Providence over our lives is responsible for any person that brings us pain or pleasure.** Here's how:

Granted, the person that's causing us pain possesses free will. Yet, any person who torments or saddens someone else – whether physically, verbally, or emotionally – is ultimately punished.

Now, imagine that Hashem has decided that you must be insulted today, for any number of reasons; Hashem simply utilizes the free will of an abrasive person who's going to be punished anyway, to do the "dirty work" of insulting you. The person in front of you is merely a stick in Hashem's hands.

Other people's free will is not our issue! Whenever Hashem is manipulating them to cause us pain, we're always better off by appealing to Hashem. Most victims suffer tremendous anguish when they try to cope with tormentors on their own.

Blaming others for our suffering is the world's most tragic mistake. One who blames another – no matter who – not only blemishes emuna, but forfeits the Divine intervention that he or she would have received had they appealed to Hashem. Once a victim forfeits Divine intervention, he or she falls into the hands of the tormentor!

Any purgatory is paradise compared to falling into the hands of a cruel human. When we realize that we've been suffering because we haven't appealed to Hashem, and when we begin a process of prayer, soul-searching, and teshuva, we often see miracles. Not only will a tormentor stop causing us anguish, he or she will become our loyal friend. Sound far-fetched? King Solomon, the wisest of all men, said (*Proverbs 16:7*), "When Hashem favors a man's ways, even his enemies shall make peace with him."

Those who consider themselves righteous martyrs that are suffering for no reason are prime candidates for continued suffering.

Those who suffer, yet fail to activate their emuna and turn to Hashem, fall into one of three categories:

1. The helpless – these are the folks that must deal with elements more powerful than themselves, such as police, judges, tax authorities, bank managers, or employers. Their lack of emuna leads them to believe that they are helpless victims, and are

therefore prone to frustration, despair, depression, and in extreme cases, suicide.

2. The equals – these are the victims that consider themselves equal to their tormentors. In such instances, feelings of hate occupy a victim's thoughts constantly, day and night. Such people can lose sleep for days, weeks, and even months plotting their revenge. In other instances, they degrade themselves by flattering or groveling before their tormentor.

3. The lip servants – these are the folks that pay lip service to Hashem, and say, "Yes, I believe that everything's from Hashem, but I don't deserve this," and so forth.

A person truly remains helpless until he or she internalizes the fact that there is none other than Hashem! Once we understand that we have the free choice of appealing to Hashem, we actually take our fate into our own hands, rather than continuing to suffer at the insensitive and often cruel hands of others.

May I never fall into the hands of others!

King David, when faced with a choice between falling into the hands of a human with free choice and falling at the mercy of Hashem, said (*Samuel II 24:14*): "Let us fall into the hand of Hashem, for His mercies are abundant; but let me not fall into human hands." King David wanted no dependence whatsoever on people; he placed his entire life in Hashem's loving hands.

No matter how dismal a particular predicament may seem, when we gird ourselves with complete emuna, lean on Hashem only, and cry out to Him from the inner depths of our soul, Hashem uplifts us far beyond the limitations of nature. Miraculously, often suddenly and unexpectedly, we see a solution to what could have been – without emuna, Heaven forbid - a hopeless situation.

How unfortunate are those who turn to flesh and blood for relief! When someone trusts anything or anyone other than Hashem, Hashem turns away from that person, leaving him or her at the mercy of the futile object of their trust; then, they're really in trouble!

People or poisonous snakes

Joseph's brothers despised and resented him, and decided to kill him (*see Genesis 37: 18-24*). When Reuven, the eldest brother, saw that the other brothers were firm in their decision, he cleverly saved Joseph by suggesting that the brothers refrain from murder, and cast Joseph into a pit of poisonous snakes and scorpions instead.

Strange, how can this be termed, "saving Joseph"? A pit full of poisonous snakes and scorpions is a certain death! What kind of favor did Reuven do for his brother Joseph? Wouldn't throwing himself at the mercy of his brothers be better than the nightmare of nature's most heinous killing creatures?

The answer to the above dilemma is surprisingly simple: Reuven knew that Joseph was a tzaddik with complete emuna. He knew that the instant that Joseph would be exposed to the poisonous snakes and scorpions, he'd pierce the Heavens with his prayers to Hashem. Reuven knew that Joseph would cry out with every last ounce of his physical, emotional, and spiritual strength; Reuven also knew that Hashem answers such prayers, and would surely rescue Joseph.

Rebbe Nathan of Breslev explains (*Likutei Halachos, Birkot HaShachar, 5*), that Hashem designed the universe in such a way that prayer can effect a change in nature. When the Children of Israel cried out to Hashem, the Red Sea was required to split its waters (*Exodus 14:10*). When Joshua was in hot pursuit of his enemies, he commanded the sun to stand still (*see Joshua 10:6–16*). The prayers of tzaddikim can cool the intense heat of fire (see

Daniel 3:10–26), or placate hungry lions (*ibid 6: 17-24*). In every generation, the true tzaddikim are bestowed with the power to alter the course of nature with their prayers; this power is a condition that The Creator instilled within all of creation."

Yet, Reuven wasn't fully confidant how his brother Joseph, the tzaddik, would perform in a test of emuna against a human of free choice in general, and against his brothers in particular. Reuven knew how difficult such tests of emuna can be. Would Joseph bend under pressure, plead and grovel before his brothers? Would he beg for his life, as if they were responsible for his fate?

Reuven was concerned that if Joseph would depend on logic in the slightest and appeal to the mercy of his brothers, then his complete emuna in Hashem might be compromised. As complete emuna enhances a person's chances to be saved from any peril, a breach in emuna is the gravest danger of all.

Reuven's concerns were well-founded. In the end, Joseph pleaded for mercy, as the brothers later testified (*Genesis 42: 21*): "Indeed we are guilty about our brother, for we saw his deep anguish when he pleaded to us, and we paid no attention." Reuven's gamble therefore paid off, by throwing Joseph at the complete mercy of Hashem. Joseph cried out for help, and Hashem rescued him.

Focus on Hashem

Let's apply the above lessons in practical terms. From time to time, all of us are faced with a human of free will that's causing us pain or anguish, such as a policeman who pulls us aside, a spouse that's scolding us, or a child that's misbehaving. In any similar situation where another person is causing us grief, we must decide conclusively to focus on Hashem and *not* on whoever's causing us pain or anguish.

When we focus on Hashem, we need not flatter or plead to other people. We don't have to crawl on our knees or talk until we're blue in the face to try and convince others to refrain from hurting us, and we certainly don't need to react violently toward them. Emuna means that we focus on "The Master" – Hashem - and not the stick in His hand.

Breaches in pure emuna range from the outright to the very subtle, with many levels in between. For example, one who suffers from another person might accept the plight with emuna, speak to Hashem, do some serious soul-searching and teshuva, and yet ultimately appeal to the tormentor and request mercy or consideration. Such an attempt is a flaw in emuna, since the victim attaches importance – even in the slightest – to the flesh-and-blood "stick" rather than to The Almighty's hand that swings it.

Those who place their fate in the hands of humans blemish the very Divine Providence that's designed to guard over them. Conversely, the more we place ourselves in Hashem's loving hands, the more we amplify the Divine Providence that delivers us from any evil.

"I'm a failure!" is a declaration of arrogance

Sometimes people suffer from mistakes or failures that apparently seem to be their own fault. In such a case, we need to remember another important rule: **Before making a mistake, a person has apparent free choice not to make a mistake. But, after the fact, one must believe that Hashem willed the mistake!** Knowing that Hashem willed the mistake, a person has no reason to be disappointed, depressed, disheartened, and certainly not self-flagellating or guilt-ridden.

With emuna, we attribute our successes to Hashem's Divine assistance.

One who fails to acknowledge Hashem's assistance is – without mincing words – arrogant, for he or she declares, "**I** succeeded!" To avoid arrogance, we therefore frequently use such terms as "God willing", "with Hashem's help", or "if Hashem so desires". So, if our successes are a result of Hashem's intervention in our lives, then our failures are also the result of Hashem's intervention in our lives. As Hashem knows what's best for us, we should accept our failures lovingly and with emuna, just as we accept our successes.

Those who fail to accept mistakes and setbacks lovingly are angry and disappointed in themselves; the same people pride themselves in their successes. Either way is a clear sign of arrogance, since they attribute their fate to themselves.

Failure is the true test of emuna; by virtue of emuna, we acknowledge that our mistake in judgment, bad decision, or any other setback was Hashem's will. With emuna, we refrain from persecuting ourselves day and night and therefore spare ourselves from untold emotional wear and tear. We can console ourselves that Hashem didn't want us to win the gold medal or the semifinals game. But, we can always take to heart that after any fall, all we have to do is to put a smile on our face, brush ourselves off, pick ourselves up, and start anew with a better effort, as we'll see later in this book.

A person must believe that any sorrow or deficiency in life is the sole product of Hashem's will!

Why?

One who achieves basic-level emuna – the belief in Divine Providence – is well on the way to a life of happiness. Yet, limited basic-level emuna is deficient; although the basic-level believer attributes everything to Hashem, he or she is still susceptible to questions and complaints about how Hashem runs the world. They're likely to ask, "Why did Hashem do such-and-such to me? I don't deserve this! Why must I suffer?" The grievance list is long.

Any questions and grievances against Hashem are blatant breaches in emuna. The true belief that everything comes from Hashem must go hand-in-hand with the next level of emuna, namely, that Hashem does everything for the very best. King David says (*Psalms 145:9*), "Hashem is good to all, and merciful on all his handiworks". Since everything that Hashem does is good, one cannot say that he or she believes in Hashem while complaining about their lot in life – such is a contradiction of terms. So, to achieve complete emuna, we must graduate to the next level.

Section Two – Intermediate-level Emuna:

Everything Hashem Does is for the Very Best

Intermediate-level emuna is the belief that everything Hashem does is for the very best, even though it may appear otherwise.

Many are the cases where we see how seemingly bad situations are for the ultimate good. We all have scores of experiences in our own lives. For example, somebody's in a tremendous rush to get to work or to school on time. They sprint to the bus station just as the bus is pulling away from the curb, shouting at the driver to stop and let them board. The driver ignores them.

In the above situation, we might succumb to anger, either humiliated by the driver's lack of regard or frustrated by the impending tardiness to work or to school.

Let's add one missing piece to the above incomplete picture: Suppose that *we* missed the bus; a minute later, we hear a tremendous crash or explosion and discover that the very same bus has been involved in a fatal accident or terrorist attack, leaving many of its passengers maimed or wounded. Would we still be angry at the driver for leaving us behind? Would we still have complaints against Hashem? The answer is an obvious no.

A mortal can't possibly see or understand all the variables that Hashem takes into account. Just as a courtroom judge can't try a case – or comes to a mistaken verdict – with incomplete or insufficient facts, none of us are in a position to conclude that a particular situation is bad, without seeing what the future holds in store.

Oftentimes, as time passes, we see in retrospect how a particular seemingly-bad situation turned out for the very best. At other times, we never become privy to Hashem's considerations, calculations, and motivation for putting us through a certain trying and rigorous situation. Such things will remain concealed from our eyes until *Moshiach* comes; until then, emuna gives us the strength and peace of mind in knowing that everything Hashem does is for the very best.

Only Hashem knows the optimum, tailor-made path in life that is perfect for each individual. Sometimes we see the purpose of our suffering, and other times we don't. When we don't understand why we suffer, life's ups and downs can be an insufferable roller coaster; only emuna can put life on an even keel.

"Under fire" – in the midst of a difficult tribulation – we can't *see* how our current predicament is for our own good. But with emuna, we *believe* that our current predicament is for our own good. Our faith gives us the strength to cope and to function at our best under any situation.

Everything, not "almost" everything

Intermediate-level emuna isn't separate from basic-level emuna, only a stronger cognizance that everything comes from Hashem's Divine Providence; **everything** is for the best, not "nearly" everything.

Everything is for the best – this level of emuna is not some spiritual plateau that few can obtain. The Code of Jewish Law (*Shulchan Oruch, Orach Chaim 230:5*) requires each of us to believe that everything Hashem does is for the very best. Just as every Jew has the obligation to eat kosher food, to observe the Sabbath, and to comply with any other statute in the Code of Jewish Law, he or she is required to fulfill the above statute OC 230:5 as well.

Jewish law in general and the belief that Hashem does everything for the very best in particular, is designed for everyone. Hashem doesn't make demands that we can't fulfill.

The Code of Jewish Law is exacting about every single syllable; close inspection reveals that the aforementioned clause states that **everything** Hashem does is for the best, not "nearly" everything. Even if a soldier is surrounded, being attacked and bombarded from all directions, he mustn't say, "I believe that Hashem does everything for the best except for *this*!"

"Almost everything" is the mistake that most people make, even when in principle, they accept the notion that everything Hashem does is for the very best. Their "almost emuna" is fine, as long as it's not tested beyond their maximum comfort level. As soon as a tribulation pinches their prestige or income, ruins their plans, or makes life uncomfortable, their incomplete emuna crumbles. 99% emuna is in effect 100% lack of emuna, since **everything** comes from Hashem – with no exceptions and for the ultimate good - and not *almost* everything.

When the brain kicks out

Understanding that a given situation is for the best is not *emuna* that everything is for the best. From a spiritual standpoint, comprehension is a much lower level than emuna. At the point where the brain no longer understands how Hashem is doing everything for the very best, emuna begins. In other words, emuna kicks in when the brain kicks out.

In trying times, whenever the brain complains that a certain situation is bad, we do ourselves a tremendous favor by putting our brains aside and by activating our emuna that everything Hashem does is for the very best. With emuna, we rejoice rather than succumbing to despair and depression. When we're happy, our brains operate much more efficiently. Therefore, emuna actually enhances our brain power and our ability to cope under any situation.

Even if something distasteful happens to us, and we wish that life would be different, we still must subjugate our will to Hashem's will. Reconciling oneself with Hashem's will is virtually impossible without emuna, for if a person doesn't believe that Hashem is doing everything for the ultimate best, then why accept Hashem's will? Who wants a life of "bad"?

Emuna illuminates our hearts with the confidence that Hashem has a good reason for everything He does, and that the currently rocky roads will eventually lead to smooth and peaceful paths. By letting our emuna override our brains, we can readily rise to any challenge that life throws our way.

Our sages teach that when a person thanks Hashem and is happy under *any* circumstance – relying on the emuna that everything Hashem does is for the very best – he or she will see the most trying situations in life make complete turnarounds for the better. Emuna is therefore the best way out of any difficulty.

Rebbe Nathan of Breslev writes (*Likutei Halachos, Choshen Mishpat, Hilchos Prika V'taina 4*), "If people would truly heed the tzaddikim and always believe in Hashem that everything is for the best, and if they'd give thanks and praise to Hashem always, whether in good times or in bad times, then all their troubles and all the suffering of the Diaspora would completely become null and void, and our people would be redeemed."

A turnaround for the better

A person that doesn't yet observe all of the Torah's laws is probably liable for any number of transgressions. One's transgressions incur spiritual debits that our sages term "severe judgments", the root cause of much of life's suffering. Yet, if the same person believes that Hashem does everything for the best and thanks Hashem under any circumstance, he or she will most likely be spared of most severe judgments. How? Simple and pure emuna neutralizes severe judgments, just like an alkaline neutralizes an acid.

If the emuna of a non-observant person has the power to neutralize, or "sweeten" severe judgments, then surely the complete and simple emuna of a person that tries his or her best to fulfill the Torah's laws will lead to a life of gratifying sweetness.

An ostensibly non-observant young man once attended a lecture presented by the author of this book. After the lecture, he approached the author, and recounted the following experience:

"By chance, I happened to obtain a CD of Rabbi Arush's lecture about emuna and giving thanks to Hashem. I wanted to meet the rabbi in person just to say – from my own personal experience - that every single word is true!"

The young man continued, "The day after the lecture, I opened up a Bible to The Book of Job. I read the part where Job's wife tries to incite him against Hashem because of all the troubles in their life, and Job answers (*Job 2:10*), 'You talk as any impious woman might talk; shall we accept the good from Hashem and not accept the bad?' These words penetrated my heart; I knew that I was hearing pure truth. I decided - no matter what – that I'd thank Hashem for everything in my life, the better and the worse, and bingo! My life has taken a complete turnaround for the better!"

With animation, the young man related a series of miraculous solutions he had received - by Divine Providence and not by his own efforts - to some seemingly-hopeless predicaments that had made his life unbearable. Emuna had triggered a one-hundred-eighty degree improvement in his faltering marriage and floundering career. He tasted happiness and optimism for the first time. "I just wanted to thank Rabbi Arush and to reinforce his teachings", concluded the young man. "Emuna that Hashem does everything for the best really gave my life a turnaround for the better!"

An unhappy Jew?!

The same non-observant young man attended another one of the author's lectures, and this time brought his brother, an observant Jew that learns Torah all day long. While former was pleasantly optimistic, the latter was depressed, complaining about a long list of worries and tribulations. "Nothing goes right in my life," he mumbled. "Were it not for my brother, who lately has been a source of strength and encouragement for me, I don't know what would become of me!"

The melancholy brother complained about the "illogical" and "unfair" way that Hashem runs the world. "I observe all the commandments and learn Torah all day long. Why is my life so bitter? Yet, my brother observes almost nothing, and everything seems to be going his way. What's going on here?"

The author cited a passage from the Talmud (*tractate Shabbat 55a*) that sin causes tribulations, suggesting that the brother do some soul-searching and teshuva.

"What do I need to do teshuva for?" argued the brother. "I observe the Sabbath, eat kosher food, give charity, send my children to religious schools, and live a life of poverty and deprivation. What's wrong with me? I understand that even the biggest tzaddik can commit a small sin from time to time; but, tell me - how on earth do I deserve such unbearable troubles?"

The author replied, "You obviously think that as long as you don't break any laws, you don't deserve any troubles in life. But, you're missing the main point: Torah and mitzvoth should be bringing you to emuna. You should be thanking Hashem for what you have – such as your wife and your children - and accept the rest of Hashem's Divine Providence happily and with love. Failing to do so invokes severe judgments that manifest themselves in all sorts of suffering and tribulations. Hashem has no joy from the Torah and mitzvoth of a person with a sour attitude."

"Look at your brother," the author continued. "Despite his non-observant lifestyle, he's all smiles and you're not; he thanks Hashem for what he has, and you don't. He's become a winner, while your life is unbearable. Emuna alone is enough to sweeten a person's life. And guess what;" concluded the author, "your brother – with all his shortcomings – brings a lot more joy to Hashem than you do with all your Torah. Emuna tips the scales in his favor!"

"How can that be?" protested the observant brother. "My brother breaks nearly every law in the Torah!"

The author removed a book from his briefcase, The Ramban's classic commentary on the Torah, and opened it to portion "Bo". He read out loud, "The intent of all the mitzvoth are that we believe in Hashem and thank Him for being our Creator; this is the purpose of all creation. The sole request of the upper worlds from the nether worlds is that man should thank and get to know his Lord that created him."

Rabbi BenTzion Halevi Bamberger, author of *Ginzei Shaarei Tzion*, elaborates on the Ramban's principle, namely, that knowing The Creator, accepting His dominion with emuna, and thanking Hashem as a result of getting to know Him is the very purpose of creation, and without this, all of creation is superfluous."

A new light

The observant brother was stunned. He realized that he was further away from truth than his non-observant brother, whom he previously held in disdain. He suddenly realized that Torah learning and mitzvah observance alone are sorely incomplete without emuna.

The author continued, "Now you understand how your brother – who you always thought was so far away from Hashem – is actually closer to Hashem than you are, even though you're the one that's observant! He believes that everything's for the best, and welcomes whatever Hashem does. He thanks Hashem for what he has, and consequently fulfills one of the main purposes of creation, that of recognizing the Creator! You might be an Orthodox Jew, but you don't live your emuna like your brother does. Anytime things don't go your way, you complain and become depressed. Even though you're accustomed to saying 'thank G-d' and the like, you're never happy with your lot in life. As a result, *you* are the one that's missing the point of creation – that of recognizing and thanking the Creator – and that's why you have ***dinim***, severe judgments hanging over your head all the time."

As if some bright light suddenly illuminated the darkness, the observant brother began to see a new world revealed before his eyes. He asked, "Rav Arush, please, help me understand: What about desecrating the Sabbath, failing to pray or put on tefillin, and all the other mitzvoth that are the foundation of emuna? I understand that my brother's thanks to Hashem are important, but what about the rest of the mitzvoth? How can anybody ignore the fact that he goes against Hashem's will almost all day long?"

"Hashem is patient," replied the author. "Since your brother has awakened to the inner dimension of emuna – that of thanking Hashem and accepting with love all that Hashem does – he'll undoubtedly reach the outer dimension of emuna, that of fulfilling the mitzvoth. Hashem doesn't expect a person to become a Moses in one day; He has patience, and it's worth His while to wait for your brother's return to observant Judaism. You'll soon see how your brother's emuna will lead to his joyous observance of Torah. Since his first steps toward Hashem are based on emuna and gratitude –

and not on fear of punishment or other self-serving motives – his subsequent steps toward Hashem will lead to his loving fulfillment of the mitzvoth and to his full and complete teshuva."

"But you," added the author, talking straight to the observant brother's heart, "as an observant Jew, could have easily attained a high level of emuna, since the mitzvoth illuminate one's soul with the light of emuna. **An observant person's lack of emuna shows that his or her fulfillment of the mitzvoth is mechanical, for observance with the proper intent connects a person with emuna**. It's like a person with a company car that fails to use the car for its designated purpose, and therefore doesn't arrive at his specified destination. On the other hand, your brother is like a person that has reached the specified destination without the benefit of a company car. Just as the boss would certainly chastise the first person, you've been having a rough time in life, to awaken you from your mistaken concepts. If you add emuna to your Torah learning and observance, and thank Hashem for *everything*, you'll see how your life turns from bitter to super-sweet, almost immediately!"

The above account of the two brothers should help us readjust priorities and understand that emuna is *the* objective of our tour of duty on this earth. We also learn that we can't judge a fellow human on the basis of superficial trappings.

On the other hand, some people make the tragic mistake of believing that with emuna, they don't need to observe the mitzvoth. Emuna can't possibly be complete without the fulfillment of the mitzvoth. We should consequently observe the mitzvoth and learn Torah with the intent of reinforcing emuna; as such, we use the "company car" for the right purpose.

Maintaining a clear and optimistic outlook

To attain the level of emuna that everything is for the best, we must learn that our path in life has been predetermined by Hashem.

We come to this world to perform a mission and to achieve a tikkun. The fact that every occurrence of our lives is the result of Divine Providence – Hashem's personal intervention and guidance – we can always be happy with our lot, whether things go smoothly or otherwise.

When life is rosy, we certainly have a tremendous reason to rejoice in Hashem's Divine Providence and to thank Him, because He is the source of all of our blessings. But, when life looks bleak and everything seems to go wrong, we need to remember that our difficulties are the product of the Creator's same loving Divine Providence. Life's difficulties are steppingstones that lead us to the destination that Hashem has predetermined for the ultimate benefit of each of us.

At various milestones in life, we face trials and tribulations. Sometimes, our tailor-made path in life puts us in protracted contact with certain people that cause us pain and suffering, such as a nasty employer, teacher, neighbor, commander, or in-law. Oftentimes, there's no possibility to circumvent the undesirable. Against our own will and for no apparent reason, we are periodically faced with grueling physical, emotional, interpersonal and financial challenges.

Life's trials and difficulties frequently catch us unprepared and off-guard, often delaying or totally altering our personal plans. Since people are incognizant of their individual tikkun, life's difficulties are liable to confuse and disorient them, imparting the false impression that their lives are ruined. Yet, whenever we rely on the emuna that all the events of our lives are *not* random, but the result of Hashem's Divine Providence and personal supervision of our lives, we maintain a clear and optimistic outlook no matter how hard we're being tested. With emuna, we're never confused or disoriented. We realize that Hashem is doing everything for our benefit, to enable and facilitate our developing a closer and more meaningful relationship with Him.

Nobody asked you

If we must endure the tests of unavoidable tough times, then we might as well accept them with the emuna that everything is for the best. Emuna enables us to be happy and to understand Hashem's individual message for each of us.

Even when a person doesn't succeed in grasping Hashem's message, he or she should accept their current circumstance happily, for such acceptance in itself is lofty service of Hashem. The Code of Jewish Law states (*Shulchan Oruch, O.H. 222:3*): "A person is obligated to make a blessing on the bad sincerely and willfully, in the same manner that he makes a blessing on the good, since for servants of Hashem, the "bad" is for their benefit and joy, to enable them to accept with love anything that Hashem decrees. Consequently by accepting the bad, one happily serves Hashem."

We can't hide from life's difficulties; no one asks us whether we're prepared to undergo trials and tribulations – they appear in our lives whether we want them or not. But, we do have the free choice of *how* we'll cope with difficult situations. Happy is the person that accepts life's trying times with emuna, that they are all for the best; such a positive outlook assures that the tough situation will soon reverse itself. Without emuna, a person is bitter, broken in spirit, disgruntled, and virtually defeated. Bitterness and dark moods are a magnet for additional troubles, Heaven forbid.

Genuine tranquility

The Torah praises the tribe of Issachar (*Genesis 49:14*): "He saw tranquility that it was good, and the land that it was pleasant, yet he prepared himself to suffer and became an indentured servant." The holy Rebbe Yitzchak of Varka elaborated on the above verse, and said: "He prepared himself to suffer – the term 'suffer' here has a positive connotation, such as sufferance, when one patiently endures anything that happens in life, the opposite of impatience and intolerance."

We're capable of patiently enduring any difficulty in life when we believe that everything comes from Hashem and that everything is for the best. Patient endurance, the result of emuna, paves the road to genuine tranquility. Genuine tranquility means a worry-free, peaceful, and happy existence. With emuna, we avoid untold emotional wear and tear.

Without emuna, this world becomes a purgatory worse than purgatory itself. Our sages teach us that the evil are tried for twelve months in purgatory; but, a person with no emuna dooms himself to decades of living torture worse than purgatory.

Bitterness, despair, and discontent are like acid burns on the soul; in many respects, a burn on the soul is much more acute than a burn on the body. Bodily burns heal in time, but emotional and spiritual burns lead to disputes and arguments, anger, worry, tension, stress, jealousy, sadness, revenge, despair, and depression – all because of a lack of emuna!

Happiness – the beginning of choice

We're faced with choices every moment of our lives. Most people think that choice begins by weighing the relative advantages of the options at their disposal. In actuality, choice begins with something much more basic; namely, choosing whether we'll be happy with our lot in life or not.

Choice consists of two stages: First, one chooses between being happy and not being happy. By choosing happiness, one progresses to the second stage, which is weighing the relative advantages of the options at one's disposal, what to do, how to do it, and so forth.

Choosing happiness? Yes, the choice is really up to us whether to be happy or not.

Surprised? Don't be. If we fail to make the initial choice of being happy with our lot in life, then we can't possibly weigh our options with clarity of thought and mind. Why? Sadness and depression destroy clarity of thought, and therefore rob us of our free choice. Depressed people are lethargic and ineffective; they perform the simplest tasks arduously. Hashem doesn't bestow His Divine Presence on depressed and despairing people; forfeiting Divine assistance makes good decision-making virtually impossible.

Happiness in our daily routine

When we're happy with our lot in life, we can rest assured that at least the first stage of our choices is successful. We see numerous examples of people all around us that are unhappy with their lot in life for no apparent reason. If you were to ask them why they're not happy, they'd probably lack a conclusive answer. In most cases, they're unsure about their path in life and they harbor a constant, nagging feeling that they're missing something. Simply speaking, they're not sure whether they're making the right choices.

In light of what we've said until now, when a person is dissatisfied with life, then he or she is liable to constantly make wrong choices. Proper choices are the result of a clear mind, and a clear mind is a consequence of happiness. Therefore, the prerequisite to living a directed and purposeful life free of unfortunate mistakes is the choice of being happy with our lot in life. Once this initial choice is made, we maximize the chances of success both in the spiritual and material realms of decision making.

No matter what we're doing – whether at work, in school, or in the home – by *deciding* to be happy, we subdue the evil inclination's nagging thoughts of dissatisfaction that we're missing something. By being happy with whatever we're doing right now and with our current circumstance, we repel depression and confusion. The evil inclination constantly attempts to inject thoughts of regret and dissatisfaction in our hearts, such as:

- "I wish I had a different job…"
- "I wish I had married someone else…"
- "I wish I lived in a different city…"

The examples are endless, as you well know from your own personal experience. But, by choosing to be happy with our lot in life, we avoid the pitfalls of confusion, disappointment, and depression. We maintain the clarity of mind that enables us to make the good choices that further increase our satisfaction in life.

Aspirations – the formula for success

When we truly desire a change in life, such as a new job or a new home, yet lack the ability to implement such a decision, it's a clear sign that Hashem wants us to continue in our current situation for the meanwhile. In such a scenario, we should accept Hashem's will happily, and know that the current situation is for our ultimate benefit. Nevertheless, we should express any and all of our aspirations in prayer, and devote a special timeslot to telling Hashem about our aspirations, our desires, and the course of our lives. Once we spend an hour a day pouring our hearts out to Hashem, we are able to spend the remainder of the day in happiness.

If you have the option of improving your life, by all means, go forward! But, if you see that you lack options right now, and can't implement what you'd like to, then believe that Hashem wants you to continue for the time being in your current framework; accept Hashem's loving guidance with happiness, with the complete emuna that Hashem is doing the very best for you. On the other hand, continue praying for what you want.

Even with spiritual aspirations, we need to accept our lot happily! So, when we don't make the spiritual gain as fast as we'd like to, we should ask Hashem for help, tell Him our aspirations, and in the meanwhile accept our current situation with joy. Eventually, with perseverant prayer, Hashem will grant us our wish. So, don't be discouraged when you seek to learn more but can't at the moment, or when you have difficulty in overcoming a stubborn habit, negative character trait, or bodily drive. Try your best, and ask for Hashem's Divine assistance in helping you realize your spiritual aspirations.

In summary, here's the 3-point formula for success:

1. Talk to Hashem on a daily basis, and ask Him to help you fulfill your aspirations.

2. Try your best at whatever you're doing.

3. Accept your current situation happily and with love.

You'll be amazed to see how quickly and completely – oftentimes beyond your rosiest expectations – you realize your aspirations by implementing the above 3-point formula in every aspect of your life.

Why won't Hashem let me succeed?

Many people, especially the newly observant, ask a probing question: "Why won't Hashem let me succeed? I want to get closer to Him. I want to learn more Torah, and understand what I learn. I want to get rid of a bad habit, such as overeating. I want to pray with intent, and without all types of extraneous thoughts. I'm not succeeding! Why is spiritual gain so difficult?"

Falling short of our spiritual goals is a type of tribulation, since our lives are certainly more pleasant when we taste success, understand our Torah learning, overcome our bad habits, and pray with fervor. The tribulation of interim failure in fulfilling our spiritual aspirations is also for the ultimate benefit of our souls, for the following reasons:

1. Lack of spiritual success, despite our best efforts, atones for the period in our lives when we exerted much less effort in serving Hashem.

2. Hashem delays granting us spiritual success, in other words, elevating us to a higher spiritual plateau, if our souls are not yet strong enough to receive the enhanced Divine light of the higher plateau.

3. Hashem delays spiritual success until we can properly learn to nullify our egos, so that the success won't lead to arrogance.

4. Hashem often delays success to encourage us to make a second, more concerted effort.

5. Delayed spiritual success is a test of emuna.

By accepting our interim circumstance happily and with love, and by continued teshuva, effort, prayer, and learning, we prepare ourselves as suitable spiritual vessels to receive the Divine light of spiritual success.

Teller or Talmudist?

A well-known contemporary Talmudic scholar, a pious individual of impeccable character that devoted his life to Talmudic study, suddenly found himself forced to take a job as a teller in a bank. A series of circumstances literally coerced him to trade his seat in the hallowed hall of Torah study for a swivel chair behind a teller's window.

On his first day at work, the Talmudic scholar surveyed the strange and impersonal surroundings of the bank, rubbing his eyes in astonishment: "How did I get here? What am I doing here? Why am I doing such a mundane and unsatisfying task, rather than learning my beloved Torah?" He brushed his mind's questions aside, and decided to think positively at all costs. Soon, he discovered that he could easily perform his duties while doing some soul-searching as well. “I’m not here at random,” he mused; “Hashem certainly engineered this change in my life for my own good. Either I have some soul correction to make, or some special mission to accomplish that requires me being here at the bank, or both!”

The teller-Talmudist wouldn’t allow himself sink to despair, despite the fact that he wasn’t doing what he wanted to do. He didn’t try to avoid or deny his current reality, nor was he angry at Hashem or at himself. He did what he had to do and made the best of his circumstance. During lunch break, rather than socializing with his colleagues, he’d find a quiet corner in the employee lounge to eat a sandwich from home and learn a page of Gemorra. During the concluding minutes of his break, he would send a tearful plea to Hashem to have mercy and to enable him to return to full-time Talmudic study. After outpouring his soul for a few minutes, he could then perform his tasks cheerfully for the rest of the day.

Weeks and months passed. The teller-Talmudist was steadfast in his emuna, his joyful acceptance of his current predicament, and in his prayers. Miraculously, the problems and circumstances that had forced him to take a job as a teller reversed themselves for the better, and the teller was soon able to reassume his place in his beloved hall of Torah study.

The driver of the bus

Those who live with emuna that Hashem’s Divine Providence is always for the best are happy and confident. They don’t suspect Hashem of leading them down the wrong road. Such individuals resemble those who make an intercity bus trip: They’re sure that the driver knows both how to drive the bus and how to choose the best route. With nothing else to worry about, they’re free to relax in their seats, gaze out the window, and enjoy each minute of the trip. They reach their destination happily, and go about their tasks with vigor.

Those who lack emuna are like nervous passengers on the same intercity bus. As backseat drivers, they think they can drive the bus better than the company driver. They also think they are capable of choosing a shorter and swifter route. Frustrated, they try to drive the bus from their seat in row 12. Each minute passes with bitterness and frustration, for they're sure that the driver doesn't know what he's doing or where he's going. They're worried that bus is traveling east rather than west. They think the driver's going either too fast or too slow. Those same worried passengers suffer substantial emotional stress because they lack faith in the bus driver. They reach their destinations nerve-wracked and completely worn out.

Let's pause for a moment, and ponder the profound difference between the two types of passengers in the intercity bus example: Both pay the same amount for a ticket, ride the same bus, and arrive at the same exact destination the very same time. Yet, the first type of passenger reaches the destination with happiness and complete emotional health, while the second type is a nearly-incapacitated bundle of nerves. Which type of passenger would you prefer to be?

With emuna, we arrive at our destination in life calmly, safely, and happily, prepared to energetically face any challenge that comes our way.

Without emuna, whenever a person thinks that he or she is "driving the bus" - or in other words, in charge of their own fate - then he or she is a surefire candidate for stress, anxiety, frustration, despair, and nervous breakdowns. Some people refuse to reconcile themselves to the fact that we all must undergo *tikkunim*, those soul corrections that Hashem designs for our individual benefit. Such people are constantly complaining about their unbearable suffering; they're correct, for without emuna, life is surely bitter and unbearable.

No one can escape the fact that life doesn't always proceed along the lines of our personal plans and expectations. The unexpected variables that each of us must deal with lead us down our designated path of tikkun. Why complain, cry, and rant when we can easily strengthen ourselves in emuna and live pleasant lives? All we have to do is to trust the "driver of the bus", our beloved Creator who's capably leading the universe as a whole and each of us in particular on a designated route. Like the trusting passenger, the more we strengthen our emuna that Hashem does everything for our ultimate best, the happier we arrive at any destination in life.

Patience pays off!

A person with strong emuna who experiences tremendous difficulties sounds like this: "That's the way Hashem wants things! Everything is for the best!" In the meanwhile, such an individual maintains a positive outlook and copes the best way he or she can with the tools at their disposal, while continuing to pray and express their hopes and aspirations.

Whenever we're discontented, we must make a high-priority effort to reinforce our emuna. Why? By solidifying emuna and internalizing the belief that Hashem runs the world and does everything for the best, life becomes a Heaven on earth. The opposite also holds true: Purgatory is the bitterness of discontent that corrodes a person's soul like spiritual acid, the result of one's own lack of emuna. Amazingly, one's lack of emuna becomes one's own worst punishment in life.

Rabbi Menachem Rekanati, the famed 14th Century CE Italian kabbalist, was a simple merchant until the age of 80. He dreamed of devoting his life to Torah study, but never had the opportunity. Despite his circumstance, he continued to aspire, to yearn for Torah study, and to pour his heart out to Hashem in daily personal prayer. For decades, he begged Hashem for the privilege of totally immersing himself in the sea of Torah. After his 80th birthday, a tzaddik came to him in a dream and gave him a golden goblet to drink from. When he woke up, he discovered that the wisdom of Torah had been revealed to him; during the next two years of his life, he wrote some forty texts of intricate Torah and Kabbala commentary!

If we need to mobilize a strong measure of emuna during periods of discontent when no particular major difficulties plague us, then we certainly must rely on emuna in order to cope with times of crisis. By searching for meaning in our current situation, and cementing the belief that everything is for the best, we not only turn discontent into content, but hasten the advent of happier times.

The only way to attain genuine emuna is to spend an hour a day of introspection, confessing our wrongdoings to Hashem and assessing our emuna. We must evaluate ourselves and ask, "Am I putting my emuna to practice in all phases of my daily routine?" With perseverance, we'll reach the level of emuna that everything is truly for the best, as we'll see in greater detail later in this book.

Liberty of the brain

A happy person's brain is at liberty to search for and understand the messages that Hashem instills within all the stimuli of our environment. Without the chains of negative emotions, we can more readily discern where Hashem is taking us. Even if we don't fully understand what's happening in our lives, with emuna, we can pray and ask Hashem to open our eyes and help us make the right choices.

Understanding Hashem's messages, spiritually awakening ourselves, and learning how to correct what needs correcting are products of upper-level emuna, the third stage in our quest for emuna. But, we can't proceed to the third stage until we've solidified our position in the second stage, or intermediate-level emuna.

We can't make effective choices that result from upper-level emuna until we first internalize our intermediate-level emuna, namely, that everything Hashem does is for the ultimate best. Already at this level, we should be accepting life's challenges with happiness. Once we do, we're ready to understand the message contained within each challenge.

Devoid of a good hold on intermediate-level emuna, one shouldn't attempt to understand Hashem's messages. Without believing that Hashem does everything for the best, a person can't possibly reach a truthful conclusion. Truth comes from a free and clear mind; a free and clear mind comes from the happiness in knowing that Hashem does everything for the best. We therefore need intermediate-level emuna in order to avoid erroneous conclusions in discerning Hashem's messages.

Rebbe Nachman of Breslev teaches (*Likutei Moharan II:10*) that happiness and freedom from worry lead to the liberty of the brain that facilitates true mental composure.

Summary of Section Two

With intermediate-level emuna - the faith that Hashem does everything for the best combined with constant thanks to Hashem – we enjoy a pleasant, tranquil existence.

Without using the events of our lives as opportunities for personal and spiritual growth, and without constant introspection, maintaining a hold on the emuna that Hashem does everything for the best will be tricky. Only steadfast intermediate-level emuna can assure happiness, peace of mind, and successful weathering of life's difficult times. The silver lining within any cloud of tribulation is that difficulties stimulate us to seek Hashem. Our very purpose in life is to seek Hashem and to get to know Him with all our mental and spiritual faculties.

Hopefully, learning about upper-level emuna will bring us to complete emuna, thus enabling us to accomplish our mission on this earth and to achieve our soul correction in this world and in the next.

Section Three - Upper - level Emuna:

Everything Hashem Does is for a Specific Purpose

What does Hashem want from me?

The third and upper level of emuna is the belief that Hashem does everything for a specific purpose, and that each of Hashem's actions conveys a special message aimed at helping us perform our task on earth. Moreover, upper-level emuna teaches that Hashem sends us incessant stimuli that call us to strengthen our connection with Him.

Hashem does everything for a purpose. Consequently, a person with upper-level emuna is constantly asking, "What does Hashem want from me?" Such a person's thought process is logical and straightforward, as follows:

- **Observation**: Hashem exposes me to a certain event or experience in order to convey a message or to teach me something.

- **Interpretation**: I should do my best to relate Hashem's message to something in my life that need's reinforcement or improvement.

- **Implementation**: Either I need to correct a bad habit, atone for a transgression, strengthen my service of Hashem in a particular area, or to awaken from my spiritual slumber, and so forth.

The three-stage process of observation, interpretation, and implementation can help anyone – each person in accordance with his or her own spiritual level – process Hashem's messages and adjust what needs adjusting in their lives.

The overall message that connects between all the events, experiences, and stimuli of our lives is emuna. Hashem's principle desire in His universe is to bring a person to emuna; His actions therefore induce a person to learn emuna. We must consequently search for the message - the "Divine wisdom" - within a given event or experience that's designed to bring us closer to complete emuna.

Rebbe Nachman of Breslev teaches (*Likutei Moharan II:1*) that we must all make an ongoing effort to observe the Divine wisdom in everything, and to connect ourselves to the Divine wisdom in everything. When we do, the Divine wisdom of a particular creation or event illuminates our brains and souls, drawing us closer to Hashem. But, one who neither observes nor connects oneself to the Divine wisdom of a particular creation or event resembles Esau, who scorned the birthright.

King Solomon scoffed at the fool's failure to observe the Divine wisdom in everything when he said (*Proverbs 18:2*), "A fool doesn't desire understanding." In other words, a fool fails to process any of Hashem's messages, and therefore thinks that the events of his or her life are random, with no particular significance. Failure to observe is the worst form of blindness.

In essence, this entire book is built around the principle of searching for the Divine wisdom, or message, within everything around us and everything that happens to us. As a first step toward the effective observation that's an integral part of upper-level emuna, we need to internalize the Talmudic principle (*see tractate Shabbat 55a*), "There are no tribulations without transgression."

There are no tribulations without transgression

This principle is the foundation of emuna, of Judaism, and of the entire world. The renowned 13th Century CE Kabbalist and Talmudic sage Nachmanides writes in his commentary on the Torah (*Parshat Bo*), "A person doesn't earn a share in the Torah until he believes that every thing or event in life is a miracle! Nothing is the product of nature or natural course, whether on an individual or on a collective scale. The reward of one who fulfills the mitzvoth is ultimate success, while the punishment of a transgressor is eventual doom, all by Divine edict." Simply speaking, one must first believe that everything in life is the product of the Creator's tailor-made decree in order to believe that there are no tribulations without transgression. Without such emuna, one's lacks a genuine connection to true Judaism.

Those with a general belief in Divine Providence, who fail to attribute their tribulations – even the tiniest – to a transgression, err in one of two ways:

1. They think that Hashem torments His creations for no reason, or that Hashem created the world so that His creations should suffer, Heaven forbid. King David testified (*Psalms 145: 17*), "Hashem is righteous in all His ways and magnanimous in all His deeds." He also declared (*ibid 92: 16*), "Hashem is just; my Rock in Whom there is no injustice." One who believes that Hashem torments His creations for nothing consequently has a warped notion of emuna.

2. They really don't believe in Divine Providence like they say, but think that their tribulations are the result of fate, chance, or natural course, oftentimes blaming themselves or others for their difficulties in life. Such a notion is contrary to emuna.

We therefore logically conclude that a person who truly believes in Divine Providence – in other words, that everything comes from Hashem – must consequently believe that any sorrow, trouble, difficulty, and deficiency in his or her life comes from Hashem! Knowing that Hashem does everything for a specific purpose – and that Hashem is loving, just, and compassionate – leads us to the categorical conclusion that our transgressions are the reasons of our suffering.

At this point, you probably want to ask: "If Hashem is so kind and compassionate, then why does He punish me for my transgressions?" Good question; Hashem knows how terribly transgressions blemish our souls. Blemished souls diminish our ability to receive Hashem's Divine light and prevent us from inheriting an optimal place in the world to come. Therefore, Hashem sends us the tribulations that are capable of cleansing our souls. Life's difficulties are not punishments, but soul corrections from a loving Father in Heaven, designed for our ultimate good and to stimulate spiritual gain.

The belief that there are no tribulations without transgression brings us to happiness, especially when we seize the opportunity of life's difficulties to trigger a process of soul-searching that leads to enhanced spirituality and proximity to Hashem. By viewing our difficulties in life as growth opportunities; we attain true and complete emuna.

A boss or a servant?

A devout person does daily soul-searching and confesses his or her misdeeds to Hashem. One who doesn't bother with soul-searching can't be called a servant of Hashem, since he or she lives with the feeling that they're the boss. A boss doesn't have to give an account of his actions to anyone. A boss can do whatever he wants whenever he wants; one can't be a boss and a servant at the same time.

Love and devotion motivates the most laudable servant. Fear of punishment motivates the less commendable servant. Since the "boss" thinks he can do whatever he wants whenever he wants, he doesn't feel like there's anybody around to punish him. By lacking the fear of punishment, the boss doesn't even reach the spiritual plateau of the least commendable servant.

With even minimal fear of punishment, we fear the consequences of wrongdoing and therefore make a daily accounting of our transgressions, confess to Hashem, and ask for His pardon. We also pray for Divine assistance in avoiding wrongdoing in the future.

An entrance-level servant hasn't yet developed the love and respect of his master that leads to devoted service. Yet, the entrance level servant knows that he or she will be rewarded for good conduct and punished for laziness and negligence. By the same token, entrance-level emuna begins with the belief in reward and punishment: Whatever happens in life – good or bad, success or failure, pleasure or pain – all comes from Hashem.

As entrance-level emuna begins with the belief in reward and punishment, and the belief in reward and punishment is the outcome of recognizing that there are no tribulations without transgression, then cognizance that there are no tribulations without transgression is *the* prerequisite to basic emuna.

Everyone desires success and a pleasurable life. Transgressions upset the apple cart of happiness, since they create tribulations and suffering. Therefore, daily soul-searching, confession of wrongdoing, and subsequent efforts to improve our ways spare us of untold grief. If a person remains in a state of spiritual slumber and acts like a boss rather than a servant, then life's difficulties – the result of his or her own misdeeds – become even more unbearable.

One who attributes life's difficulties to anything or anyone other than his or her own transgressions is light-years away from minimal faith in Hashem! Such a person fails to account for his or her actions, never makes teshuva, falls deeper into spiritual slumber, and is therefore far removed from Hashem.

Yir'at shamayim, the fear of Hashem, begins with the basic spiritual cognizance that tribulations result from wrongdoing. The basic fear of punishment leads to the lofty fear of disappointing our beloved and compassionate Father in Heaven by doing something against His will, Heaven forbid.

Rebbe Nachman of Breslev explains (*Likutei Moharan I:15*) that a person's fears are the result of his or her transgressions materializing themselves in various stimuli that come to frighten them, and therefore trigger soul-searching and repentance. One who fears Hashem therefore doesn't need to fear anything else.

The Causes of Suffering

Sadness

The first and most common cause of suffering is sadness. Nothing invokes such severe judgments as one's complaints and dissatisfaction with one's lot in life. The Torah emphatically cites sadness as the root cause of life's curses when it says (*Deut. 28:47*), "Because you failed to serve Hashem with happiness and goodness of heart when everything was abundant."

Sad people protest, "Abundance? What are you talking about? Look at my troubles!" They disregard the thousands of life's daily blessings. By taking their blessings for granted and focusing on their difficulties, they make their lives even more insufferable.

Hashem treats a person with compassion and mercy *always*. Dissatisfied people therefore deny that Hashem's Divine Providence is compassionate and merciful. Denial of Hashem, or lack of emuna, is a major antecedent to suffering and failure. Why?

When a person is dissatisfied with Hashem's justice, the Heavenly Court open's that person's lifetime dossier to closely inspect whether he or she really deserves their current difficulties and tribulations. Inspection of a person's actual debits and credits *always* shows that they actually deserved greater tribulations than what they have, and lesser blessings than what they have. Hashem is always "caught in the act" of excessive compassion and mercy, much more than justice requires. The person's complaints are not only overruled, but they trigger new demands of severe judgment against that person.

It turns out that our disgruntlement with our lot in life is the main cause of our own suffering. Disgruntlement goes hand in hand with ungratefulness to Hashem and lack of emuna, two notorious antecedents of severe judgment.

King David suffered from untold tribulations, yet he recognized Hashem's mercy and compassion in every stage of his life. King David therefore pleaded (*Psalms 143:2*), "Do not enter into strict judgment with Your servant, for no living creature would be vindicated before You."

Suffering should initiate soul searching, since there are no tribulations without transgressions. Yet, before soul-searching, we ask ourselves if we're happy with our lot in life.

Prolonged anguish is often a result of transgressions committed against a fellow human. One who causes pain to another person cannot be forgiven for his own sins until he begs forgiveness from the victim of his misdeeds. As long as one's injustices against a fellow human go uncorrected, severe judgments linger.

Failure to observe mitzvoth

Tribulations are frequently indications that a person is either doing actions that are forbidden by Torah, or failing to fulfill the Torah's obligatory actions.

Arrogance

Tribulations can also be indications that a person lacks the emuna that "there is none other than Hashem" (*Deut. 4:35*). Hashem often uses suffering to deflate inflated egos. Oftentimes, a person's downfall is the result or his or her own arrogance. King Solomon, the wisest of all men, said (*Proverbs 16:18*), "Pride precedes destruction, and arrogance comes before failure." We can usually find a hint of arrogance and complacency before every crisis in life.

Hashem is especially compassionate when He deflates our egos, because an arrogant person can't get close to Him. The sages of the Talmud said (*tractate Sota, 5a*), "The Holy One, blessed be He, says: The arrogant person and I cannot dwell in the same world." As a result, Hashem removes His Divine Presence from the midst of arrogance and arrogant people. Wherever Hashem removes His Divine Presence, suffering sets in.

A turn for a turn

Hashem frequently employs the policy of a turn for a turn in order to teach a person why he or she is suffering. For example, a cab driver that violated the Sabbath suffered two flat tires and a speeding ticket the following Sunday morning, causing him to lose the exact sum that he earned on the Sabbath. Also, an employer that unjustly accused an employee of stealing was soon after accused by the tax authorities of cheating on his income tax.

Hashem's policy of a turn for a turn is certainly not punishment; it's a Divine method of education.

Our sages said (*Ibid. 8b*), "A person is measured in the manner that he measures others. Samson pursued the desire of his eyes and therefore lost his eyes at the hands of the Philistines[1]; Avshalom

---

1. See Judges, Chapter 16; Samson pursued the desire of his eyes and chose Delila - an

was haughty about his hair, and was therefore hung by the hair[2]; Miriam tarried an hour for Moses, and therefore all of Israel tarried for her an entire week.[3]"

Our sages also teach (*tractate Shabbat 33a*) that diphtheria – a terrible disease that begins with gram-positive bacteria in the intestines and culminates in a fatal growth that blocks the throat – is the result of slander. Just as a person's negative "gut-feelings" against someone lead to slander and an evil tongue, diphtheria begins in the "guts" and progresses to the mouth.

Elsewhere (*tractate Berachot 5b*), the Talmud tells the story of Rav Huna, whose four hundred casks of wine soured:

> Rav Huna's colleagues told him that he should do some soul searching, and contemplate why Hashem made his wine sour into vinegar. Rav Huna reacted, "What, am I suspicious of wrongdoing in your eyes?"
>
> His colleagues answered, "What, is Hashem suspicious of punishing for no reason?"
>
> Rav Huna responded, "If anyone has heard that I've committed a wrongdoing, let him come forward and tell me!"

---

idol worshiper, the daughter of an enemy nation, and a person of treacherous character - and ultimately forfeited his eyes at the hands of her people.

2. See Samuel II, Chapter 18; Avshalom was vain about his hair, among other things. Avshalom also revolted against his father, King David. While riding his mule, his hair became entangled in the branches of an oak tree; the mule kept on going, an Avshalom was left hanging by the scalp until death.

3. See Exodus 2:4; Miriam hid by the Nile overseeing her baby brother Moses, who was placed in a wicker basket and cast on the river, until Pharaoh's daughter discovered him. Later, when Miriam contacted leprosy (see Numbers, Chapter 12), all of Israel waited seven days until she healed.

> His colleagues said, "We have heard that you haven't been just with your tenant farmer, and that you failed to give him a just share of the grapevine cuttings."
>
> Rav Huna protested, "My tenant steals me blind! I therefore leave the vine cuttings for myself."
>
> The rabbis remarked, "The folk expression says that he who steals from a thief has the taste of thievery in his mouth..."
>
> Rav Huna conceded, "I take upon myself the obligation to atone and to return the tenant's rightful portion of the grapevine cuttings."

Even though Rav Huna merely committed himself to performing teshuva, but had not yet actually rectified the injustice, Hashem performed a miracle and restored the vinegar to its original state of wine. Another opinion in the Talmud says that the vinegar did not revert to being wine, but the price of wine vinegar skyrocketed and Rav Huna made a handsome profit. Either way, we see how a person's acceptance of Divine justice reverses a situation from stern judgment to miraculous compassion.

Rav Huna transgressed with a grapevine cutting, and was subsequently punished by way of his wine. With such "turn for a turn" messages, Hashem helps us understand what we need to correct.

Rashi explains (*Gen. 37:2*) how the episode of Joseph exemplifies the policy of "a turn for a turn" in Divine justice.

Joseph carried three detrimental tales about his brothers to his father; in each case, he was punished measure for measure, as follows:

1. Joseph said that his brothers ate the meat of a live animal; in turn, the brothers soaked Joseph's cloak in the blood of a slaughtered kid goat.

2. Joseph said that the sons of Leah were calling their half-brothers, the sons of Bilha and Zilpa, slaves; in turn, he was sold into slavery.

3. Joseph said that his brothers were suspicious of illicit sex; in turn, he himself was accused of illicit relations with the wife of the Egyptian minister Potifar.

Jacob was away from home for 22 years; his absence caused anguish to Isaac and Rebecca, his parents. Jacob was punished measure for measure when his own beloved son Joseph was missing and thought dead for exactly 22 years!

Judah fooled his father Jacob by dipping his brother Joseph's cloak in the blood of a kid goat and saying that Joseph was devoured by a wild animal. Judah's daughter-in-law Tamar in turn fooled him with a kid goat (*see Genesis, Chapter 38*).

Simon advised his brothers to throw Joseph in a pit; subsequently, Simon was thrown in an incarceration pit in Egypt.

Joseph's brothers caused him extreme anguish, and they in turn suffered extreme anguish in Egypt.

Thought, speech, and deed

The Baal Shem Tov teaches that grief from one's children stems from a blemish in *neshama*, the part of the soul that corresponds to thought, since the seed originates in the brain. Therefore, when a person suffers from his children, it's a measure-for-measure message to help him realize that he must rectify something in his thoughts.

Troubles from one's wife indicate a blemish in *ruach*, the part of the soul that corresponds to speech. Therefore, when a person suffers from his wife, it's a measure-for-measure message to help him realize that he must rectify something in his speech.

Financial difficulties indicate a blemish in *nefesh*, the part of the soul that corresponds to deeds. Therefore, when a person suffers from money problems, it's a measure-for-measure message to help him realize that he must rectify his deeds.

Hashem's children

Since Hashem calls us "His children", problems from our own children are likely to be "a turn for a turn" resulting from similar grief we cause Hashem, Heaven forbid. For example, when a person's son is disobedient, then that person has probably been disobedient to Hashem. Insolent children are indications of brazen and insolent parents. In our own soul-searching, we should pay attention how our children treat us, for that's an indication of how we treat Hashem. Furthermore, we should make a concerted effort to atone for our own sins against our parents.

The old adage says, "The chickens come home to roost." Ultimately, our own children treat us in the same manner that we treat our parents.

Against or complementary?

The biblical word that describes the wife as a partner in life is *kenegdo (see Gen. 2:18)*; this word has a double meaning, "against" or "complementary".

The nation of Israel is the proverbial wife of Hashem. As such, a wife's treatment of her husband reflects her husband's treatment of Hashem. A disrespectful wife is a sign that a husband is disrespectful to Hashem. A lazy wife is a sign that the husband is lax in his duties toward Hashem, and so forth.

Our sages teach that when a husband so merits, his wife is a "complementary" helper to him. But, when he isn't worthy, his wife is "against" him – an enemy! The husband's deeds actually dictate the wife's behavior.

Jewish esoteric thought teaches that a wife is the mirror of her husband – through her, he can see himself, his character traits, his strengths and weaknesses, and the like. Furthermore, the husband is like the sun and the wife is like the moon – she reflects his light. Accordingly, when she is short-tempered, he must rectify his problem with anger. When she is amiss in her responsibilities, he is most certainly faulty in fulfilling his obligations to Hashem.

Many marital difficulties are indications of the husband's lack of faith, arrogance, or lewd behavior.

Evil's Easy Street

Hashem uses the policy of a turn for a turn as an educational tool to teach *those that He loves* what they need to correct. The Talmud teaches (*tractate Berachot 5a*) that Hashem sends suffering to those He loves, for He desires to cleanse their souls of blemishes in this world, so that they can earn a lofty place in the world to come.

Some people are so steeped in evil that Hashem doesn't even bother with them. Rather than sending them tribulations that they wouldn't heed or learn from anyway, Hashem gives them their rewards in this world so that they forfeit any reward in the next world.

The righteous undergo rigorous soul corrections in this world and are rewarded with eternal bliss and gratification in the next world. The evil people that seem to live on Easy Street frequently enjoy money, power, fame, or other cheap amenities in this world, but they pay "through the nose" in the next world. Don't be jealous of people that live carefree lives; spiritually, they're falling deeper and deeper in debt. This world is like a big restaurant – after you eat, you have to pay the bill. If you don't pay in this world, then you're charged with a much steeper price in the next world.

Tribulations of love

Tribulations of love are an additional type of suffering designed especially for the righteous and the pious. Our sages teach us that if a person suffers, then he or she should initiate some serious self-evaluation and make teshuva. If their assessment of themselves comes up clean, then they've probably been lax in their Torah study. If they've been diligent in their Torah study, then their tribulations are tribulations of love.

The Middle Path

Most people don't belong on evil's Easy Street or on the tribulation trail of the righteous. The vast majority of us "middle-of-the-roaders" should remind ourselves that there are no tribulations without transgression. We therefore should train ourselves to look for the turn for a turn in our troubles, so that we'll know what to correct. Once we realize what we've done wrong, we should begin the 4-stage process of teshuva - confession to Hashem, remorse, apology for our misdeeds, and decision to improve from this moment on. Once we understand Hashem's message and act on it, Hashem doesn't need to speak to us in the language of tribulations any more!

Nobody wants trials and tribulations. But, once they come, they're a good sign, showing that Hashem cares about us very much. Tribulations are a sign that Hashem is calling us to get closer to Him.

We all desire to correct our souls, but sometimes we don't know the specifics of what we need to do. Therefore, we should talk to Hashem and ask Him to illuminate our eyes and brains, like this: "Hashem, please help me understand what I did wrong. Have mercy on me, and explain to me why I'm suffering. I want to get close to You; I want to improve, to make You proud of me. Please help me!" Perseverant and sincere personal prayer - speaking to Hashem in our own words - seldom goes unanswered. Eventually, Hashem shows us exactly what we need to correct.

If we've tried our best to understand Hashem's messages to us, but we still don't comprehend why we're undergoing the troubles we currently have, then we must resort to emuna and remember that Hashem does everything for a purpose. Here's a suggestion of how to speak to Hashem in such a situation: "Hashem, my troubles are certainly not happenstance or unjust. I believe in You and trust You with all my heart, but unfortunately, I don't understand what I did wrong to bring this (*fill in your particular difficulty*) upon myself, and I therefore don't know how to atone or what to atone for. Hashem, beloved Father in Heaven, please help me understand why I'm suffering; please forgive me and have mercy on me. Don't cast me away from You! Please shine Your Divine Countenance on me and illuminate my aching soul. Help me do Your will and correct what needs correcting…"

If, despite our repeated personal prayers, our troubles don't go away, then we should cast our brains aside and rely exclusively on the upper-level emuna that Hashem is doing everything not only for the best, but for a specific purpose as well, whether or not we understand what's going on. The acceptance of our tribulations with love and with a subjugated heart (as opposed to a haughty, complaining heart) in itself invokes tremendous Divine compassion. Frequently, as soon as we truly reconcile ourselves to our troubles, they disappear!

Accepting our tribulations with love and with a subjugated heart is the epitome of complete emuna.

Obstacles

Two main obstacles prevent us from successfully weathering tribulations with emuna, as follows:

First, when we say, "I'm not strong enough to hold on! This is going to break me!" Such a feeling reflects a lack of belief in our own inner strength and capability to withstand stress. In order to overcome this obstacle, we must internalize the vital spiritual law that **Hashem doesn't give us trials and tribulations that we're incapable of withstanding**.

Second, when we say, "Let me live in peace!" or "I don't feel like dealing with this." This is a request to go through life with no teshuva, no soul corrections, no ups and downs, and no stormy weather.

Hashem desires that we strengthen our souls; we can't strengthen our souls without being tested from time to time. Only by way of the trials and tribulations that build our emuna, do we achieve true tranquility of the soul. Trying to run away from life's difficulties rather then coping with them makes them even more unbearable. Hashem won't give in: He knows what we have to correct. The fact that we might not "feel like" correcting doesn't mean that Hashem will forget about effecting the needed tikkun, whether in this life or in a subsequent reincarnation. Our sages warned that any difficulties in this life are preferable to an additional reincarnation.

We can't live in a stupor of imaginary calm and achieve our needed soul corrections at the same time. Our entire purpose on this earth is to attain our tikkun, or soul correction. Therefore, ups and downs, difficulties, trials, and tribulations come with the turf.

A person can't decide to sit on the sidelines in this world. Once we're born, we're on the playing field; that means we have to pick up the ball of life's challenges and begin running with it toward our goal. With emuna, we'll correct our souls and win the game.

True gratification and success, both in material and in spiritual endeavors, come from emuna.

Those who are unwilling to invest effort in correcting their soul life will ultimately suffer a worse collection of trials and tribulations. Therefore, whenever we strengthen ourselves in emuna, prayer, and the fear of Hashem, we make life so much easier.

With Hashem's help, the coming chapters will show how to apply emuna to our daily lives.

Chapter Three

Tests of Emuna

This world is a classroom of emuna. Since the entire purpose of our life on earth is to learn emuna, then literally everything that happens to us in the course of day is a test of emuna.

This chapter illustrates several of the typical and seemingly "natural" occurrences that are none other than Divinely-initiated and individually-tailored tests of emuna. With Hashem's help, we'll learn how to evaluate our performance and how to pass these tests with maximum success.

Pull over to side of the road!

We're startled by the whine of a siren. We look in our rear-view mirror and see the flashing blue and red lights of a state trooper's car. A patrolman with an iron jaw motions for us to pull over to the side of the road.

Whether or not we broke the law is now immaterial; this is a sudden test of our emuna. Now is the time to activate the lessons of emuna that we learned in the previous chapter, as follows:

1. **We should believe that our current predicament is from Hashem and exactly what Hashem wants**. Consequently, there's no need to blame ourselves (*why wasn't I more careful?*), the other driver (*he was creeping – I had to pass him!*), or our spouse (*honey, can't you go any faster? We're gonna be late...)*. Certainly, there's no need to harbor malice toward the policeman, even if we think we were unjustly pulled aside. According to state traffic laws, we might be innocent of wrongdoing. But, according to the guidelines of emuna, we deserve to be pulled aside; the policeman in this case is an enforcing officer of Hashem's absolutely just legal system.

2. **We should believe that what's happening to us now is for our own ultimate good**. Therefore, we should cast aside the nagging thoughts in our brains that what's happening to us is not good. Furthermore, we should happily thank Hashem for sending us the state trooper, as this situation is certainly for our ultimate benefit.

3. **We should believe that everything in life has a reason and a purpose, and that there are no tribulations without transgression**. The state trooper is none other than Hashem's catalyst to initiate a process of soul-searching and teshuva for something we may have inadvertently done wrong. Although we were pulled aside because of an apparent traffic violation, the "natural" circumstance is only a vehicle of Divine justice designed to arouse us.

Speak with Hashem

Before we say a word to the state trooper, we should perform some quick soul-searching, think about making teshuva, and speak to Hashem in the following manner: "Hashem, You know why You sent me this tribulation. Please forgive me for my wrongdoings; help me rectify whatever I did wrong. Please have mercy on me, and don't use this policeman to punish me. Help me identify and correct the reason that I deserve to be punished."

We should neither complain nor protest to the policeman. Anger is also completely uncalled for, and flattering is just as bad.

If we've succeeded in remembering the above three lessons of emuna while focusing on Hashem, and we've avoided the pitfalls of anger, blame, and negative emotions, then we score an A-plus in emuna. Passing the test of emuna brings the rewards of happiness and emotional health in this world, and indescribable bliss in the world to come.

With emuna, we see any outcome for the best: If the state trooper lets us off with a warning, then we're certainly jumping for joy. And, even if he does give us a ticket, we activate our emuna to remember that Hashem is doing this for our very best; the fine is probably a bargain-basement atonement for something much worse that we deserved. Either way, with emuna, we're always happy!

On the other hand, people that lack emuna think that their fate is in the hands of the state trooper. They regard their current predicament as random or natural, and not the product of Divine Providence. Such folks sometimes try to sweet-talk the law-enforcement officer, and subsequently get in worse trouble. A concrete law of spirituality teaches that whenever people trust in anyone other than Hashem, they fall into the hands of the object of their trust; that's bad news, since no human has Hashem's capacity for mercy and compassion.

Usually, whenever a person tries to flatter a policeman, the policeman becomes even more stringent. Frustrated, the flatterer often reverts to anger and epithets, and unjustly accuses the policeman (*you're just trying to fill your quota at my expense; hey, loads of people are going a lot faster than I was; why are you picking on me, etc. – the list is long*), further complicating an already sticky situation. Rather than rectifying the wrongdoing that led to this predicament, the person that lacks emuna accrues even more transgressions by insulting or falsely accusing the policeman.

Here, we touch on an important principle that underlies any test of faith. **Without emuna, people easily insult, harbor ill feelings, harm, or take revenge against those who conceivably caused them damage** – all serious sins according to the Torah. As long as the sins between man and fellow man go uncorrected, then severe judgment hovers like an ax over the neck of the transgressor, making life even more unbearable.

With emuna, we save ourselves untold grief in that we accept Hashem's judgments with happiness, and we don't go around taking our frustrations out on others. Also, those who readily harm others will have to make long and arduous efforts in begging the forgiveness of *all* their victims once a year before Yom Kippur, otherwise Hashem won't listen to their prayers. With emuna, we don't blame our troubles on others, don't harm them, don't need to beg for their forgiveness, and spare ourselves of harsh judgments. Emuna makes life so much easier.

The more we attribute power to the state trooper, the lower we score on emuna. A deficiency of emuna adds insult to injury, for the lower we score on emuna, the harder our predicament becomes. Therefore, it's extremely important that we focus our thoughts on Hashem, and not on the state trooper.

Charity prevents penalties

Many penalties and other forms of financial loss occur when a person gives insufficient charity.

The Talmud teaches (*tractate Bava Basra 10a*) that a person's income is preordained from Rosh Hashanna, just as his losses are preordained from Rosh Hashanna. If one so merits, money given to charity takes the place of financial loss. When one lacks the merit of charity, financial loss manifests itself in taxes, penalties (*such as traffic and parking tickets*), doctor bills, broken appliances, and so forth. Consequently, charity prevents penalties.

> Rebbe Yochanan Ben Zakai had a dream on the night after Yom Kippur (*ibid*), that his nephew was destined to lose seven-hundred dinars that year. Rebbe Yochanan therefore hounded his nephew all year long for donations to a number of charitable endeavors. By the year's end, Rebbe Yochanan had extracted 683 dinars in charitable donations from his nephew.

On the eve of Yom Kippur, a Roman tax collector appeared on the nephew's doorstep and demanded the sum of seventeen dinars in back taxes. The nephew and his family trembled even after the tax collector left, worried that they were now under the close inspection of Caesar's cruel occupation government. When they expressed their fears to their saintly uncle Rebbe Yochanan, he said, "Don't worry! The seventeen dinars is all that you are liable - you won't have to pay an *agora* (cent) more!"

"How do you know?" questioned the skeptical nephew. "Do you have connections with the tax authorities, or maybe you're a prophet?"

"I have no connections to the authorities, nor am I a prophet or the son of a prophet. Yet, I do have connections with the supreme ruler - Hashem! At the beginning of this year, He showed me how much you stood to lose - 700 dinars. I almost succeeded in extracting the entire sum from you for charity. But, since you still owed seventeen dinars, the tax collector served as a messenger to complete your predestined loss! If you hadn't previously donated the 683 dinars to charity, then you'd have lost the entire 700 dinars to tax collectors and other cruel messengers, receiving only grief in return. But, since you now have the merit of charity, you'll see blessings and success in everything you do!"

"Dear Uncle," cried the nephew and his family, embarrassed by all the time and effort their saintly uncle exerted in their behalf all year long, "why didn't you explain that to us in the beginning of the year? If we knew that the financial loss was preordained, and that charity is a substitute for

> penalty, we'd have gladly given the entire sum to charity!"
>
> "I wanted you to give charity with no ulterior motive," replied Rebbe Yochanan ben Zakkai, "and not just to save yourselves from a Heavenly edict." The nephew and family thanked him, and committed themselves to give as much charity as they could possibly afford, having learned the power of this lofty mitzvah.

Frequently, the financial loss that people suffer is simply the completing payment of a preordained penalty for the current year. Heavenly accounting is exacting to the penny; but, whenever we take the initiative and willfully give to charitable causes, we prevent the anguish of losing money in all kinds of negative circumstances.

Atonement for sins

The preordained annual financial losses aren't the only root causes of losing money. Transgressions can also invoke additional financial loss, for one's dearest possessions - health, money, and so forth - are atonements for sin. Preemptive charity prevents penalties in this area as well. A person who willfully gives charity not only cleanses sin, but reaps the wonderful benefits of this important mitzvah. Without charity, a person becomes a triple loser: First, he or she will have to involuntarily part with their money; second, they'll have to suffer the pain, anguish, and accompanying aggravation that are related to a specific financial loss; and third, they forfeit the benefits that they would have earned had they given charity.

To avoid becoming a three-time loser, one should become accustomed to giving charity on a regular basis. The satisfaction of donating to the worthy poor, to the sick, to those in need (both material and spiritual), and to the advancement of Torah study in the world is infinitely preferable than losing money on medical bills, broken appliances, car breakdowns, taxes and fines. Whereas the latter brings only grief, the former serves as a first-class ticket to success in this world and eternal happiness in the next world.

Let's go back to the state trooper that pulled us aside: Our quick self-evaluation should be whether or not we gave enough charity. Without thinking twice, we should pledge an additional amount to charity, and say outright, "I hereby pledge (*such-and-such amount*) to (*your favorite charity*)!"

Charity is a tremendously worthy endeavor. If the lack of charity was the reason that we were stopped by the policeman, then the pledge of charity can almost instantaneously tip the scales of harsh judgments in the opposite direction. Hashem can turn the state trooper's heart around, and turn a four-hundred dollar, four-point fine into a mere vocal warning. With charity, the entire predicament can turn itself around for the best.

The prosecutor becomes counsel for the defense

A trial or court case is a classic test of emuna. Like in any other challenging situation, remembering the three basic laws of emuna is the key to success. Whether or not a person is guilty of wrongdoing in this world, by contractual, federal, or state law is immaterial; the fact that he or she is faced with a court case is an indication from Heaven of outstanding spiritual debits that need rectification.

One should know that the outcome of a trial or hearing is actually determined in Heaven. A person that appears in the flesh before a judge and/or jury is simultaneously being judged in the Heavenly Court, which scrutinizes the individual's credits and debits. Once the Heavenly decision is reached, Hashem subsequently instills the "upstairs" verdict in the hearts of the judge and/or jury members in the "downstairs" courtroom.

Even though a person tries his or her best to succeed in court by hiring the best legal counsel, seeking the best witnesses and evidence, and carefully preparing arguments, a true believer knows that one can't fool the Heavenly Court. No fast-talking attorney can alter the truth of one's deeds or misdeeds as recorded in the Heavenly Court register. The verdict upstairs will dictate the verdict downstairs. Therefore, to win a court case, one's plea bargaining should be first and foremost with Hashem.

Sometimes, a person feels that he or she has an open and shut case, with complete success assured. Other times, a person may feel that there are no chances of success. Both feelings are false; Hashem decides the outcome of the case in every event. Therefore, the best way to prepare for any day in court is to carefully examine oneself, confess any and all wrongdoing to Hashem, express remorse for one's sins, ask for Hashem's forgiveness, rectify one's actions, and make a firm commitment to improve from this point onward.

Even when a person makes a sincere effort of teshuva – something that will undoubtedly help one's case or ease a severe verdict – he or she should be emotionally prepared to accept an unfavorable outcome. One's efforts at teshuva don't always suffice to clean the entire list of Heavenly debits.

One's emuna undergoes a special test in the face of a negative outcome or judgment, when found guilty or liable; this is the time to summon the power of emuna. The unfavorable decision is not the result of the other side's superior lawyer, our lawyer's mistakes, insufficient preparation, or untrue testimony. The judge and jury aren't to blame either. Negative judgments in a flesh-and-blood litigation are the sole results of insufficient teshuva. The task at hand is to accept the court's (*Heavenly and earthly*) decision lovingly and with emuna and to increase one's efforts of teshuva and prayer until the trouble is over.

When we make genuine heartfelt teshuva, we witness how Hashem turns a prosecutor into a counsel for the defense.

By making teshuva in preparation for our day in court, we receive a perfect score in emuna. We'll enjoy the fruits of our efforts even in this world, as follows:

1. We are spared from harsh judgments.

2. By strengthening our emuna, we merit enhanced proximity to Hashem.

3. We avoid slander, anger, frustration, bitterness, and blaspheme, and we earn the rewards of happiness and emuna.

The above fruits are immediate rewards in this world. Even more, the tremendous dividends of teshuva and emuna assure our eternal bliss in the next world. Nothing brings a person closer to Hashem than passing difficult tests of faith in this lowly and oftentimes confusing material world.

On the other hand...

People that lack emuna think that flesh-and-blood judges, juries, attorneys, and witnesses dictate the outcome of a case. Such folks harbor hundreds of trepidations and limitless complaints about the judges, their own legal counsel, and the other side. They'll readily depart from the truth to advance their case. When they put their trust in their lawyers, their lawyers frequently become the reason of their failure in court.

A concrete law of spirituality states that whenever people trust anything or anyone other than Hashem, then Hashem lets them fall into the hands of the source of their trust, which usually turns out to be miserably helpless and pitiful. Trusting in anything or anyone other than Hashem is a complete failure in the test of emuna.

Don't think that winning a day in court by way of teshuva and emuna is a fantasy. Dozens of people that implemented the author's advice discovered that even hostile judges came to their aid. Many have reported the amazing results that preparations of teshuva and prayer bring about in the courtroom.

Freeing the Imprisoned

Incarceration is an extreme test of faith. A person in jail can't blame anyone for his or her predicament – not the judge, the prosecutor, or the witnesses. Hashem puts people behind bars to atone for their sins.

Sometimes innocent people are found guilty and convicted. Usually they suffer from extreme feelings of anger, frustration, and bitterness because of the injustice that has been done to them. But, if they would earnestly search their own souls and objectively evaluate their deeds in light of the Torah's commandments, they'd find themselves guilty of serious wrongdoing. Why? The Heavenly Court doesn't decree incarceration for no reason. So, even if a person is innocent of the charges against him, he might be guilty of some other wrongdoing that led to the Heavenly verdict of imprisonment. Therefore, one should accept the predicament lovingly and use it as an opportunity for teshuva and soul correction.

A prisoner's daily routine should revolve around teshuva, prayer, and charitable deeds. He or she should talk to Hashem as much as possible in personal prayer, asking Hashem for strength, guidance, a shortened sentence, and a quick release from jail.

Confessing to Hashem is vital for an inmate's spiritual and emotional welfare, as are the other principle acts of teshuva, namely, expressing remorse for one's transgressions and deciding to improve from this point on. To merit true and complete teshuva, a person must also pray constantly for Hashem's assistance and guidance, as well as asking Hashem to lead him or her on the right path. One must also pray that Hashem protect them from negative friends and influences, and send them good messengers that will help them correct their lives. The more prayer – in one's own language – the better!

Joseph the tzaddik danced in prison

Any person that faces such a difficult and taxing test of faith can be reassured in knowing that if he or she musters the emuna and inner strength to accept the current predicament with love, then the entire situation is likely to turn around for the better.

Joseph was incarcerated on trumped-up charges (*see Genesis, chapter 39*). Even so, he accepted his plight with happiness. The Midrash tells us (*Yalkut Shimoni, Vayashev, 145*) that Joseph was a "jumping man", in other words, he was accustomed to singing and dancing all day long as an inmate. How could he act like that, as a lone Hebrew prisoner in a cruel Egyptian jail? He simply trusted in Hashem, and believed that everything was for the very best.

By virtue of Joseph's amenable, cheery disposition, the warden took a liking to him and placed him in charge of the other prisoners. Joseph literally did whatever he pleased whenever he pleased. The minute his Heavenly-decreed sentence was up, he was virtually rushed out of prison to become the second most powerful man in all of Egypt – the world's greatest superpower at that time – overnight!

Suppose that Joseph would have lacked emuna, and would have moped around his prison cell with a long and sour face, complaining about his lot in life. Hashem's Divine Presence departs from the midst of depression and complaint. Without Hashem's intervention, Joseph certain wouldn't have become the warden's favorite inmate. As a lone, dejected Hebrew prisoner, he might have suffered all kinds torment from the other prisoners – murderers, thieves, and rapists of the meanest and lowest order. He could have rotted in jail for years, not even daring to dream of freedom, much less of meteoric success as the vice-premier of Egypt! In short, without emuna, he would have suffered a living death.

A long list of tzaddikim including Rebbe Schneur Zalman of Ladi, Rebbe Yisroel of Ruzhin, Rebbe Nathan of Breslov, and Rabbi

Chaim ben Attar spent time in prison, all on false accusations. Yet, they took advantage of their predicament to devote their entire time and energies to prayer, Torah learning, and the service of Hashem. Many even composed classic works of Torah nuances and religious thought behind bars.

No matter how unbearable a situation may seem, a person can take solace in knowing that his or her life is in Hashem's hands and under His personal care. In retrospect, we always see how Hashem does everything for the very best.

If Joseph and the abovementioned tzaddikim accepted their incarceration lovingly and with happiness, despite the fact that they were all falsely accused and convicted, then a less righteous person should certainly do so as well. One should also remember that imprisonment is frequently a substitute for a much more serious tribulation or punishment. Consequently, a person should actually thank Hashem for being in jail.

Hashem reproves those that He loves

A prisoner should never forget that Hashem loves him, listens to his prayers anywhere and anytime, and wants him to make teshuva. If he's smart enough to utilize his time for prayer, teshuva, and whatever good deeds he can do behind bars, then Hashem will surely help him find favor in the eyes of the jailers, the warden, and the parole board. A person should maintain the faith that Hashem has an infinite number of ways to free him from jail.

The Heavenly Court has a serious complaint with a person that doesn't take advantage of imprisonment for Torah learning, prayer, and teshuva. In jail, a person doesn't have to worry about making a living, paying bills, or going to PTA meetings. Most inmates have plenty of time at their disposal; Hashem gives them the conditions that are conducive for introspection and teshuva.

Logically, and in accordance with emuna, an inmate should be well-disciplined and respectful to the guards and prison authorities, and kind to his fellow inmates. Noble deportment behind bars invokes everyone's admiration, as well as enhanced Divine compassion. Emuna makes a jail sentence so much more bearable.

Many former inmates have testified that their term in jail was an actual turning point in their lives for the better, having terminated their sentences as emotionally and spiritually stronger and healthier people.

"I shall heal your afflictions" *(Jeremiah 30:17)*

Sickness is a severe test of emuna. Therefore, a sick person must recognize the three principles of emuna, as follows:

1. Hashem makes a person sick; one should avoid attributing sicknesses to natural causes or to human error.

2. Hashem sends sickness for a person's ultimate benefit.

3. Hashem wants the sick person to initiate a process of self-evaluation, attempting to identify any possible wrongdoing that might have led to the sickness, and then make teshuva accordingly.

A sick person that acts according to the three principles of emuna achieves a high score in emuna, a speedy physical recovery, and substantial spiritual gain.

On the other end of the scale, those who lack emuna become disheartened, depressed, and often complicate their physical suffering with emotional ills. Such people find physicians miserably disappointing. Even worse, they fail to correct the root spiritual cause of their sickness.

A Divine License to Heal

Apparently, medicine is an applied science just like all the other applied sciences. Researchers delve into the cause of disease, experiment with various disease-inhibiting agents, and then convert successful laboratory findings into commercial medicines and modes of treatment.

Medical research appears to be straightforward and logical. The Almighty instilled us with the intelligence to observe, investigate, and solve problems for the betterment of mankind. Not only that, but it's our duty to devote our mental resources to worthwhile endeavors, particularly for the benefit of society. Electricity, computer technology, and labor-saving appliances are a few examples. Man should therefore invest his God-given power of intelligence to cure illness and relieve human suffering.

Our sages reinforce this outlook and interpret the passage (Exodus 21:19), "And he shall provide a cure," as a Divine license to heal people. In fact, a number of Judaism's greatest rabbis were extremely knowledgeable in medicine, such as Maimonides and the Baal Shem Tov.

Apparent logic therefore tells us that medicine is an applied science just like all the other applied sciences, and the more we devote to medical research, the more we'll overcome illness and suffering.

Man and Divine Providence

Medicine would be a simple, straightforward applied science if its sole challenge were healing a physical body. But, that's not the case. The body is lifeless without its spiritual life-spark, the soul. Physical treatments and medication can't cure an ailing soul. Since body and soul are connected, then their mutual health and wellbeing depends on more than nature and natural law. Human health depends on Divine Providence, Hashem's personal intervention in our lives.

Since all of creation was designed as an agent to facilitate man's free choice on earth, we can understand how man benefits from the Almighty's personal attention to the tiniest detail of his life in general and his health in particular.

Nature operates according to Divine will, even though it's not always apparent. The further away a creation is from man and the less it directly affects his life, then the less apparent the Divine Providence. Therefore, it seems that the stars and the great galaxies go their merry way in their clear and predefined celestial lanes, according to the dictates of nature and seemingly devoid of Divine intervention. This is only an illusion, since the galaxies don't appear to have anything to do with our daily lives. In truth, their orbits in space are the product of Divine decree; they simply have a static task that doesn't change.

As opposed to the stars and other faraway creations, dynamic daily change is an indication of Divine Providence. Look how our lives change so drastically from day to day: one day, we're challenged with income problems. The next day, our children act up. Then, a health crisis pops up. No day is ever the same, for Hashem is constantly sending each individual the messages that he or she needs to stimulate soul correction.

His body is dear to him

Divine Providence plays a greater role in a person's health than in any other area of a person's life. Pains and afflictions of the body and soul are Hashem's prime tools in arousing people to correct what they need to correct, for several reasons:

First, a person might remain apathetic about a variety of other trials and tribulations. He or she won't necessarily undertake serious introspection after losing a hundred dollars. Yet, few are able to ignore something that directly affects their own bodies, such as sickness or severe negative emotions. This is what happened to

Job. At first, Hashem gave the Satan license to test and torment Job, but not to strike him down with illness.

Even though Job lost his money and buried his own children, he didn't crack at the emotional seams. The Satan said to Hashem (see Job, chapter 2), "A person will give anything for his own skin. Afflict his flesh, and we'll see if he continues to bless you!" The Satan claimed that no test of faith is as difficult as a sickness or injury. Job's steadfast faith was shaken once his entire body was afflicted with infectious boils.

We therefore learn from the Book of Job that bodily afflictions are the most difficult type of tribulations for a person. The moment a person becomes ill, money and other amenities are no consolation. On the contrary, they heighten the person's feeling of misery for he can't enjoy them. What good is a big bank account, diamonds and jewels to a person with an ulcer, diabetes, and a cardiac condition whose diet is sorely limited and can't even enjoy a meal? And what good is a healthy body if a person suffers from a tormented soul? That's why "be healthy" – *tihye ba'ri* – is the most common blessing in the Hebrew language. Since one cares so much about one's health, Hashem can readily arouse a person by way of his or her health.

Health is one of Hashem's prime tools in arousing people for an additional reason: The body resembles the Torah. The body has 613 parts - 248 appendages and 365 tendons. Correspondingly, the Torah has 613 mitzvot – 248 positive ("do") mitzvoth and 365 negative ("don't do") mitzvoth. Each of a person's appendages corresponds to one of the positive mitzvoth, and each of his or her tendons corresponds to one of the negative mitzvoth. Therefore, when a person transgresses a particular mitzvah, Hashem arouses that person to teshuva by afflicting him in the particular appendage or tendon that corresponds to the blemished mitzvah. As such, a person can understand what he or she did wrong and correct it.

The holy Baal Shem Tov once visited a sick man on the verge of death. At the man's bedside, the Baal Shem discussed his condition with the attending physician. The doctor said that there is no hope for the man to live more than a few hours, for his disease has destroyed all his tendons.

The Baal Shem Tov asked the physician to wait for a moment while he approached the sick person, who lay unconscious in bed. A minute or two later, the patient opened his eyes and asked for a sip of broth. Gradually, the color returned to his face. The physician couldn't believe his own eyes. He said to the Baal Shem Tov, "I can't believe what I'm seeing! This person's entire body was finished – not a single tendon was intact. There was no way he could live. What did you do?"

The Baal Shem Tov replied, "You are correct. Not only that, you are truly an expert physician. You made no mistake – all the patient's tendons were destroyed. This person repeatedly transgressed so many negative commandments that his tendons deteriorated. Only now, I spoke to his soul, and he agreed to atone for his sins. Once he committed himself to teshuva, his tendons regained their vitality."

Divine Considerations

The Tikkunei Zohar teaches us (P'tach Eliahu, Introduction section 17) that Hashem runs the world in accordance with our actions. Hashem created the world in order to show us his magnitude, and can operate the world mercifully or in exacting stringency according to our actions. When people behave in an upright manner, then the world is a place of harmony and loving-kindness. On the other hand, injustice, immorality, and cruelty invoke stern judgments and calamity. This is Hashem's "measure for measure" mode of running the world.

Sickness is directly rooted in a person's misdeeds. Consequently, medicine and medical professionals – as advanced and as skillful as they might be – cannot possibly take into consideration such Divine considerations as the patient's spiritual debits and merits, his efforts to atone and improve, and so forth. No professional – as talented as he or she may be – can override a Divine decree. If Hashem decrees that a person should be sick for a week, then no treatment in the world will help him get well any faster. The opposite holds true as well – if Hashem decrees that a person shall recuperate – despite all medical logic – then that person will get well immediately.

Imagine two identical twins that grew up together in the same home with the same parents, ate the same food, and so on. Maybe when they were small, they appeared to be equally healthy. But, as they grew older, each had his own separate health problems. This is proof that one's health is not determined by nature, but by one's actions. If nature were the determining factor, then both twins who were born and raised in identical circumstances should have had identical health profiles.

Miracles and Wonders

The principle that nature plays no role in human healing becomes even more apparent when we see that as soon as a person corrects the spiritual cause of his or her ailment, the ailment disappears without any natural intervention at all. If nature governed healing, then the sick person should have continued to suffer despite whatever efforts at teshuva that he or she made. And, in the cases where seemingly irreversible damage had been caused, nothing should have helped!

Since nature does not dictate health, and we see with our own eyes that people who have earnestly repented have miraculously recovered even from terminal ailments, we can conclude that health and healing defy natural laws[4].

---

4. Even though health defies nature, the Torah commands us to make every effort to care for our health. This includes proper diet, exercise, and avoiding substance intake such as

I have witnessed this principle in action countless times. In hundreds of cases where I instructed sick people how to rectify the misdeeds that led to the sickness, they were blessed with dramatic improvements in their health as soon as they did teshuva and bettered their ways. Even in my own personal experience, I've seen how my own health problems were solved as soon as I realized what I was supposed to rectify.

I'll share with you one of my own personal experience. Once on Shabbat, I suffered from a massive toothache. My entire jaw was swollen and infected – the pain was excruciating. I told my family that I must do an immediate root treatment[5].

My family was astonished. "Since when is one allowed to go to the dentist on Shabbat?"

"But I must do a root treatment," I answered. "The pain is unbearable and it's no mitzvah to suffer on Shabbat. I'm going to the greatest of physicians for a root treatment – to Hashem, blessed be His Name."

I went to a nearby field and asked Hashem to enlighten me as to the spiritual root of my ailments, in other words, to show me what I did wrong to deserve the toothache, the infection, and the resulting swelling. I did some serious soul-searching until I laid a finger on something I shouldn't have done. I asked forgiveness for this misdeed and made complete teshuva the best I could. Within a few minutes, the swelling went down and the pain disappeared, with no antibiotics or any other natural explanation. I realized that the toothache was only a wake-up call, and as soon as I rectified my actions, Hashem no longer needed the wake-up call.

---

tobacco and alcohol. Jewish religious law's health statutes may be found in the Rambam, Hilchot Deot.

5. "Root treatment" is the Israeli way of saying "root canal" treatment. The author meant it as a play on words, alluding to the core solution to his problem and not to the dental treatment.

There is no nature!

Our encouragement to the sick is don't despair – there is no nature! Whoever chooses the option of teshuva and prayer will see major miracles. When The Creator decides to cure someone, He doesn't need any help.

Rebbe Nachman of teaches (Likutei Moharan I:62), "The principle misconception of those who are far away from emuna in Hashem is that they visibly see a world governed by the stars. Each person has his own misconception: some think the world is governed by nature, and that the world behaves according to natural law. Others believe that there is a Creator, but that they must worship an intermediary, such as the mistake of the golden calf.

"Many are ensnared in the trap of the intermediary, in other words, they believe in Hashem but they also believe that the intermediary determines their fate, such as their business or livelihood. They then invest their hopes and main efforts to their business dealings, since they believe that their business dealings determine their livelihood, and without their business dealings, Hashem won't be able to provide for them, G-d forbid. The same goes for medical matters, when they put their faith in the intermediary rather than in Hashem, **as if, G-d forbid, Hashem won't be able to cure them without doctors and medicines.**

This is not so! Hashem is the cause of all causes and the reason of all reasons. One must believe in Hashem only, and not in any intermediary or other cause."

Outright Miracles

As further proof of what we're saying, here are two events from the past that many people witnessed (see Rebbe Nachman's Discourses, 187):

> One of the Rebbe's followers once came to him. He had a serious ailment in his arm and was in such great pain that he could not move it at all. He had his arm in a sling and was totally unable to lower it. The Rebbe's followers told him that this cripple was very poor and could not afford the expensive salts and other remedies that he needed for his arm.
>
> The person was sitting at the Rebbe's table for the Sabbath noon meal. The Rebbe remarked that the man certainly had faith. All present agreed. The Rebbe discussed this awhile and then repeated himself, asking again if the man had faith. Again, those present answered yes.
>
> Suddenly the Rebbe commanded the cripple, 'Lower your hand!' The cripple stood there amazed and everyone else was also very surprised. What was the Rebbe saying? The man had been afflicted for a long time and it was absolutely impossible for him to move his arm. Why was the Rebbe telling him to do the impossible?
>
> However, as soon as the Rebbe gave the order, 'he decreed, spoke and it was fulfilled' (Job 22:28). One of his followers removed the man's sling and he instantly lowered his arm. He was totally healed by what was an obvious miracle. He regained full use of his arm which remained healthy for the rest of his life.

Many people sat at Rebbe Nachman's Shabbat table at the time, and witnessed the above happening, which goes to show that healing is above nature. The sick man's muscles and tendons had been badly degenerated, and nothing explains how he instantaneously regained use of his arm. Perhaps we could believe that torn and disintegrated muscle fiber could be revitalized after lengthy treatments, but instantaneously? Who can do such a thing? Only Hashem – Physician of all flesh – can perform such a miracle. The sick man merited a full and instantaneous recovery by virtue of his emuna.

The second event happened here in Israel, about thirty years ago. Rabbi Yisrael Abuchatzera from Netivot, affectionately known by all as the "Baba Sali" of saintly and blessed memory, ordered a cripple out of his wheelchair in the presence of many witnesses. This is yet another proof that there's no nature at all. How can degenerated body tissue and nerves that have been out-of-use for years suddenly come back to life? Only Hashem is capable of such an act. In this case, the tzaddik's fervent prayers and unshaken belief in Hashem were the catalysts in the cripple's ability to stand on his feet once more.

The professor from Annipoli

Hashem is the physician of all flesh and only He can cure.

> Once, a Jew visited the renowned tzaddik Rebbe Mordechai of Neschiz, and complained of a severe illness. The tzaddik asked, "Have you visited the famed professor from Annipoli?" The sick Jew replied that he never heard of such a person. "In that case," added the tzaddik, "go see him - he can surely help to cure you!"
>
> The sick Jew heeded Rebbe Mordechai's advice, and made a difficult, backbreaking wagon trip to Annipoli. When he arrived at the township, he asked the first Jew he encountered where the famed professor lives. The local Jew shrugged his shoulders, and said that there's no such thing as a doctor or medic in all of Annipoli, much less a famous professor. The sick Jew's heart broke - had he made this entire excruciating journey for nothing?

> "What do you people do when you get sick, with no doctor or medic in town?" asked the sick Jew.
>
> The local answered, "Whenever people here are ill, they make teshuva, pray to Hashem, ask Hashem to cure them, and then they get better."
>
> The sick Jew, brokenhearted, turned his horse and wagon in the opposite direction, and made the long, hard, bumpy trip back to Neschiz. He had a serious complaint to lodge with Rebbe Mordechai the tzaddik: "You know how sick and weak I am, Rebbe! Why did you send me all the way to Annipoli for nothing? There's not even a country doctor in that one-horse town!"
>
> Rebbe Mordechai smiled patiently. "Didn't anyone there explain to you what they do in case of sickness if they don't have a doctor?"
>
> The sick Jew replied, "Yes, they did; somebody gave me a perfunctory answer that they pray and make teshuva, then they get better."
>
> "That's the professor of Annipoli," answered the tzaddik. "It's Hashem! Whenever people turn to Him, He cures them. He's the professor that the people of Annipoli turn to. He's available 24 hours a day, and doesn't charge for house calls. He can even turn bread and water into miraculous medicine, for it is written (*Exodus 23: 25*), ***'He shall bless your bread and your water, and remove sickness from your midst.'***"

The son of the famed "Chofetz Chaim" of saintly memory related that his mother seldom sought the services of a physician during the years that she raised her children. Whenever someone in the family became sick, the Chofetz Chaim instructed her to distribute forty pounds of bread to the poor, and he himself would pray for several hours in the attic. Shortly thereafter, the sick child would recover.

Only Hashem knows

The Gemorra teaches (*tractate Avoda Zara 55a*), that "immediately before disease and suffering are cast upon a person, they are sworn to leave on a certain day, at a certain hour, by a certain person and by a certain medicinal agent." Rebbe Nachman of teaches (Likutei Moharan II:3) that all the above conditions must be met for a sick person to be cured. If so, how can a physician cure anyone? A doctor cannot possibly cure a person unless he or she is the designated Heavenly messenger with the proper cure at the proper time. Even more so, how does a sick person seek a doctor's help if he or she doesn't know if that particular doctor happens to be the designated messenger? As such, going to doctors is lighting betting on horses – maybe you'll win and maybe you won't.

Pidyon Nefesh: Redemption of the Soul

Nevertheless, a person can do something about the Heavenly edict that limits curing to "a certain day, at a certain hour, by a certain person and by a certain medicinal agent." Once the edict is rescinded, then any doctor with any standard treatment can affect a cure.

There are three steps to rescinding a Heavenly edict – teshuva, asking tzaddikim to pray for the sick person, and a *pidyon nefesh*[6], as Rebbe Nachman of writes (ibid.):

---

6. Pidyon nefesh literally means "redemption of the soul." In effect it is a sum of money equivalent to the numerical value of a person's name that serves to mitigate severe judgments against that person. For example, if the sick person's name is "Ari", spelled in Hebrew aleph-resh-yud, then the numerical equivalent would be 211 (aleph=1+resh=200+yud=10). Spiritually, $211 would be the proper "pidyon" or redemption for Ari. He would give this money to a tzaddik that knows how to do a pidyon properly, and the tzaddik would use this money for charity.

"When a person makes a *pidyon* severe judgments are mitigated, and the Heavenly edict is rescinded. Then, a doctor can cure by way of his medicines, for there are no longer stern judgments and a person no longer needs the specified doctor at the specified time with the specified medicine. As such, no doctor can really cure unless a person does a *pidyon*, for a *pidyon* is necessary to mitigate harsh judgments, and then the doctor receives license to cure."

Consequently, when a person gives money to tzaddikim for a *pidyon nefesh*, then his efforts in seeking a doctor's assistance will be worthwhile. Preferably, one should give the *pidyon* to an upright rabbi who knows the proper text of the *pidyon nefesh*, such as the Breslever rabbis. One should not be stingy, as Rebbe Natan writes in Likutei Tefillot, 123: "Please have mercy so the person bringing the pidyon won't be stingy, and will give what's required to mitigate the severe judgments."

Pidyon nefesh is extremely effective. We have witnessed first-hand dozens of outright miracles, when a *pidyon nefesh* had virtually redeemed the giver's soul, having been saved from grave danger or from severe sickness.

A sick person asked me if he should go to the doctor. I asked him why he's running to the doctor so quickly. "Did the doctor make you sick? Hashem made you sick, so first you must ask Hashem why you're sick, do proper soul-searching, and make teshuva accordingly."

Medicine and medical procedures can be effective only after a person makes the proper effort to mitigate severe judgments against him or her, and to appeal to Hashem, the physician of all flesh, for a cure. Going to the doctor without prior spiritual effort shows a lack of emuna.

A doctor cannot add to or detract from a person's allotment of longevity. Therefore, one is best advised to invest one's efforts in seeking good health from He who grants life – Hashem!

Thank Hashem and be cured

Emuna, more than anything else, is conducive to healing. Therefore, the first thing a sick person should do is to thank Hashem for the sickness. This of course sounds extremely odd to Western ears, but in fact, nothing could be more logical. Here's why:

Hashem made the ailing person sick for his own benefit and ultimate welfare. Awareness of this basic fact of emuna enables the sick person to thank Hashem. The person's positive attitude makes recovery much faster and easier. Thanking Hashem for an apparent calamity such as sickness is the highest expression of emuna, since the person recognizes that even his tribulations are from Hashem and part of Hashem's personal and magnificent Divine Providence that's all for the best.

One of the new students in our Yeshiva suffered for years from a severe chronic illness. No doctors or treatments helped, and not even his own prayers and efforts to rectify his sins, until he heard an emuna lesson that everything is for the best and that a person should thank Hashem even for his deficiencies and hardships in life.

The same student decided to devote his entire daily hour of personal prayer to thanking Hashem. For days on end, he'd thank Hashem for making him sick and for all the accompanying pain and suffering. He pondered how Hashem certainly does everything for the best and consoled himself that his pain from the illness was atonement for his sins. He realized that Hashem, like a loving father, was personally cleansing his soul. With tears in his eyes – tears of joy – the student thanked Hashem profusely and sincerely for his poor health. He didn't even ask for a cure. Within two weeks, the illness had disappeared entirely, without the aid of treatment or medications. The chronic illness that plagued him for years was now a thing of the past, all because of thanking Hashem. Gratitude to Hashem is the apex of emuna and conducive to good health. The opposite is also true, for a lack of emuna is often a root cause of disease. The strengthening of emuna therefore contributes to good health.

In reality, a person does not suffer unless his or her emuna is taken away. As long as a person clings to the belief that everything Hashem does is for the very best, he or she doesn't feel any tribulations. Therefore, by reinforcing our emuna that everything Hashem does is for our ultimate good and we thank Him for it, we mitigate severe judgments. A sick person should consequently pray to Hashem for emuna that everything is for the best and that he'll be able to sincerely thank Hashem for everything. Once he starts thanking Hashem, life makes a dramatic turn for the better.

The main thing is emuna

Rebbe Nachman of teaches (Likutei Moharan II:5) that there are certain illnesses that result from a lack of emuna. Such illnesses can't be cured by physical means, only by intense prayer, teshuva, and strengthening emuna.

People of Compassion

Anyone in the medical field must know that he or she performs a lofty task in the world. Usually, those who choose a career in medicine ate people of compassion. The characteristics of mercy and compassion combined with the desire to aid humanity are wonderful incentives for learning medicine.

Nevertheless, physicians must avoid the pitfall of arrogance and remember that they are only messengers of healing, for Hashem alone decides who will live and who will die. Hashem also decides how much a person will suffer and whether he or she will be cured or not.

A physician must pray daily before he begins his day's work that Hashem will help him be a worthy emissary. His prayers should also include a special request that he merit being an agent of healing, and not an agent of death, Heaven forbid, for a doctor's slightest mistake or misjudgment can have tragic or even fatal results. Therefore, medical professionals should always plead to Hashem for Divine assistance in everything they do. They should also ask for patience, understanding, and a sensitivity of their patients.

There is no despair!

Our sages said that physicians are granted a Divine license to heal. That doesn't give him license to discourage or dishearten patients. In many cases, doctors give patients and the family members of patients a pessimistic outlook and a feeling of hopelessness. Telling a patient that he only has so much time to live is a terrible mistake.

Medical research shows that optimism and a happy attitude play an important role in healing, recovery, and resistance to disease. Such nuances as laughter therapy have reportedly helped cure a number of ailments. No wonder that Rebbe Nachman of stressed the importance of maintaining happiness and avoiding sadness and depression at all costs. Rebbe Nachman emphasizes that sickness and disease are the result of a breakdown in happiness (see Likutei Moharan II:24). Since emuna leads to happiness, emuna facilitates recovery from sickness and ailments.

Therefore, a doctor must avoid saddening or discouraging a patient. Indeed, one of his most important tasks is encouraging a patient. A doctor's word of encouragement carries far more weight than a layman's word. A doctor should also use his good influence to help reinforce his patient's emuna. Such spiritual and emotional support is inestimably beneficial to every patient.

The prognosis

The claim that a doctor must give patients truthful assessments of their situation is a fallacy. A patient shouldn't be robbed of his hopes to recover. And, even if the sick person is destined to die, he should still be surrounded with optimism and encouragement.

Those doctors who frighten and discourage patients, especially those doctors who forecast how long an apparent terminally-ill patient has to live, are actually robbing them of any chance for recovery.

Hashem doesn't reveal the day of one's death, for such knowledge could have a detrimental effect on a person. If Hashem hides the day of death, how can a mortal be presumptuous enough to think he knows it? Negative prognoses are sometimes completely inaccurate.

Even in apparently terminal cases, a gloomy prognosis robs the patient of his right to die with a feeling of optimism and faith in his heart. The doom prognosis leads to a bitter death accompanied by feelings of despair, bewilderment, and even anger at Hashem, Heaven forbid. When doctors say that the end is near, they deny patients their lone lifeline – emuna – by sealing their fate.

Stop and think for a moment: who says that the patient's condition won't make a sudden or dramatic change for the better? We've all heard of clinically-dead people that have come back to life! Are the doctors G-d, that they know what has been decreed on each patient? Hashem can change anything in the world from one moment to the next. Therefore, a sick person can recover in spite of all the doctors' negative predictions.

A patient's tiniest commitment to teshuva, to self-improvement, or to a mitzvah such as giving money to charity can lead to recovery where natural methods have failed.

In all fairness to the doctors, sometimes the patient's family members put tremendous pressure on them, demanding to be told the "truth". In such situations, a doctor should be cautious and say that according to natural circumstances, the situation seems critical, but experience has proven that Hashem's intervention can alter the picture from one moment to the next and override any natural laws.

The best advice

A physician with emuna knows that a patient's condition can change from one moment to the next. It's enough that the family gives the patient's name to a tzaddik, and the tzaddik starts praying for the patient or performs a *pidyon nefesh* for the patient. The opposite is also true: a patient can feel better and then renege on a commitment or fall from emuna and then suddenly relapse.

Either way, a physician should avoid giving gloomy forecasts: if Hashem decides to revive the patient, then the physician will lose face. On the other hand, if the physician is accurate, what does anyone gain? By scaring the patient – even truthfully - the physician is guilty of *Onaat devarim*, the Torah transgression of causing anguish to another human being. The "truth" could have made the patient suffer even more by losing hope and falling into despair.

The best advice for physicians is therefore to avoid saying anything of a committal nature, even if the patient's family applies tons of pressure. There are plenty of verbal escape routes, such as "it's too early to tell" or "we don't have enough information to make an accurate prognosis."

There are situations when a doctor wants to force his opinion on the patient in regards to a certain treatment, medicine, or operation. This is also a mistake. Even if the doctor is convinced that his recommendations are accurate, the patient must not be deprived of his free choice. Even though the doctor undoubtedly wants to help the patient, he shouldn't dramatize his own opinions by pressuring the patient.

In summary, only Hashem decides the fate of each patient. The doctor's task is to be a worthy emissary of Divine Will and Providence, and pray that he'll be fortunate enugh to be an agent of healing and not of death.

A physician should therefore tell a patient, "I'll do my best, but you should know that your health doesn't depend on me; that's why you should do your part - strengthen your emuna in trust in Hashem! No matter what the outcomes of tests are, there are many surprises in medicine and Hashem can override any natural circumstance, as difficult as it may seem. I pray that Hashem should give me the best advice in regards to your case, but you can contribute so much to your own recovery with prayer, charity, teshuva, and emuna. If we work together, hopefully Hashem will grant you a full and speedy recovery."

The main thing – don't be afraid

A patient shouldn't be afraid of doctors or their forecasts, because everything depends on Hashem anyway.

A blind trust in doctors and medicine is itself a form of idolatry. Many people are afraid to sever their dependence on doctors and medicines, as if their lives were dependant on the man with the stethoscope around his neck. Therefore, one should fear Hashem only and not the doctors or their admonitions.

Psalms

Psalms have enormous power, tantamount to an intravenous infusion of trust in Hashem. Trust in Hashem is very conducive to a person's full and speedy recovery. There are dozens of stories about people who merited miraculous recoveries from reciting Psalms.

A little boy's best friend became very ill and the doctors appeared to have given up hope. He picked up his book of Psalms, and with poignant innocence said Psalms for an entire hour in his friend's behalf. He closed the book, ran to his friend's house, and asked if there was any improvement. His friend's mother tearfully shook her head in the negative. The little boy ran home and said Psalms for another hour. Once again, he ran to his friend's house and asked if there was any change in the situation. Once again, the answer was no. The little boy ran back and forth for most of the night, when his friend's parents finally informed him that their son's fever had broken and that he was sleeping peacefully now…

Names of the Tzaddikim

Rebbe Nachman of writes in Sefer HaMiddot that reciting the names of the tzaddikim can bring about a change in nature.

A woman came to me after a growth was detected on her uterus, and said that the doctors were demanding to perform an immediate operation that would render her unable to give birth to any more children. She took my advice and recited the names of the tzaddikim. A short while later, the growth disappeared and the woman received a clean bill of health. Since then, she has given birth to more children as well.

Likutei Tefillot

A man suffered from severe back pains to the extent that he couldn't lift the slightest weight. He asked one of this generation's tzaddikim what to do. The tzaddik told him to recite all the prayers for healing in Rebbe Nathan of Breslev's classic collection of prayers, "Likutei Tefillot." He implemented the tzaddik's advice to the letter. Within a relatively short period, his back was completely cured.

Everything will turn around for the best

Never forget that Hashem is G-d. Any Divine decree can be overturned with prayer, teshuva, and charity. Our sages teach us that even if a sharp sword rests on a person's neck, the person shouldn't give up hope. "Hope" means prayer, and the most cogent prayer is the sick person's prayer for himself (see Rashi's elaboration of Genesis 21:17).

Even though doing a *Pidyon Nefesh* and reciting the names of the tzaddikim are important, nothing so invokes Divine compassion for a sick person as his own personal prayer – speaking to Hashem in his own words. A person should ask for all his needs from Hashem, and especially for healing and good health. King David said (Psalm 30:3), "I cried out to You Hashem, my G-d, and You healed me."

One of my students was in a near-fatal automobile accident that left a gaping hole in his back that exposed his spine. The gap almost reached his kidneys. The wound became infected and the doctors had given up hope. My student was conscious and well aware of his critical situation. There was no rational procedure or cure. Up until the accident, my student would devote a few casual minutes to personal prayer, but nothing more. Now, I asked him to commit to speaking to Hashem for two hours a day – he agreed.

Every night when most everyone else was sleeping, he'd wheel himself out in a wheelchair to the hospital terrace. For hours on end, he'd beg Hashem to stimulate new tissue growth around his kidneys and spine. Little by little, to the amazement of all the doctors, new tissue began to grow until the gap was completely healed.

Rebbe Noach of Lachovitch used to say that when the doctors tell a patient that there's no cure, and the patient reinforces himself with complete trust in Hashem, then all the gates of salvation and healing are opened…

A sick person shouldn't wait for the doctors or sickness to turn to Hashem. Putting one's complete trust in Hashem not only facilitates healing, but helps to keep healthy people healthy.

Don't waste a moment!

As with incarceration, a sick person should utilize available time for self-evaluation and for soul searching. Many patients lie idle in hospital beds for hours; freed from the demands of a normally busy routine, the bedridden should take advantage of the time at their disposal. Oftentimes, a sick person's bodily urges diminish dramatically, enabling one to look at the world objectively. At such times, the soul's delicate voice gets a fair hearing. Many healthy people let their bellowing bodies drown out the soul's voice.

How tragic when "loved ones" arrange for a television to be planted in front of a sick person's face! Instead of utilizing their available time for the type of soul-searching that would lead to a full recovery, they waste it on folly.

Hashem receives tremendous gratification when a person passes the test of faith that accompanies affliction. Reinforcement of faith is a wonderful way to insure good health and a complete recovery of body, mind, and soul.

Mental and emotional health

Rebbe Nachman of writes (Likutei Moharan I:173) that the soul and emuna are one aspect. Consequently, one's emotional health is directly related to the level of one's emuna. We therefore conclude that emotional disturbances result from a breakdown of emuna. Emotional confusion results from confused emuna. Emotional weakness is the outcome of weak emuna. This is a rule of thumb for all mental illness.

Allow me to clarify: I'm not referring to such mental handicaps from birth such as autism and Down's syndrome. These are the result of

Divine considerations and soul reincarnations, neither of which we are capable of understanding. Yet, when we see that a person is born healthy, but at a later age succumbs to fear, anxiety, depression, and even schizophrenia, or any other mental or emotional difficulties, the root of the problem is a blemished emuna. But here's the good news: if an emotionally-disturbed individual learns all about emuna and prays for emuna, he or she will recover from the ailment. The more a person corrects and strengthens emuna, the more he or she will enjoy mental and emotional health.

Every person – even the so-called "normal" person – suffers from emotional problems to a certain degree. In addition to fear, anxiety, and depression, people are plagued with boredom, lack of satisfaction, anger, worries, nervousness, and extreme mood fluctuations, just to name a few. Emuna cures all these ills.

What are you afraid of?

People are frozen with fear. They fear other people, their bosses, the IRS, terrorists, other motorists – the list is long. Any time they get a muscle spasm, they envision some imminent crippling or terminal disease. All these fears are expressions of a lack of emuna, particularly the lack of emuna that everything Hashem does is for our very best. A person with emuna doesn't fear anything, for he knows that he's in Hashem's care and that everything Hashem does is for the very best. This saves tons of emotional wear and tear; since Hashem does everything for the best, then there's nothing to worry about.

A person than devotes an hour a day to self-evaluation, teshuva, and personal prayer especially has nothing to worry about. If a person is making his best effort at self-improvement, then why should Hashem punish him? Such a person doesn't need wake-up calls, because he's daily arousing himself to teshuva and to self-improvement. The result of an hour a day in personal prayer is increased happiness and decreased stress and worry.

Be happy!

Stringencies in religious observance are madness; therefore, no one should be too exacting with himself. Don't worry about whether your performance of a mitzvah is perfect or not, just do what you can with innocence and with simplicity of thought and intent. Remember that the Torah wasn't given to angels, but to human beings with human limitations. Those who demand angelic deportment from themselves are therefore candidates for frustration, gloom, and disappointment that results from the arrogant feeling that they should be doing everything perfectly. A person connected to the truth is happy serving Hashem the best way he or she can, without going into hair-splitting stringencies.

Belief in our wise men

Rebbe Nachman of teaches (See Rebbe Nachman's Discourses, 67) that, "Ignoring the wise can cause insanity. A person acts insane only because he ignores the advice of others. If he would take rational advice, he could act normal. His mental state might rationalize his need to do such things as tearing his clothing and rolling in the garbage. But a wiser man than he tells him not to do these things. If he would only subjugate his will to the wise, his actions would become completely rational. Insane behavior therefore results only from ignoring the wise. Understand this well."

The above teaching obligates any rational personal to heed the words of the wise, especially of our renowned spiritual leaders. Belief in their words together with emuna in Hashem is the key to mental health. The Torah praises the children of Israel during their flight from bondage in Egypt when it says (Exodus 14:31), "And they believed in Hashem and in His servant Moses."

Torah study

Rebbe Nachman of Breslev, probably the greatest doctor of the soul that ever lived, also teaches (see Abridged Likutei Moharan, I:1) that "by learning Torah, one is saved from madness."

The Yetzer Hara, the evil inclination, wants to drive a person crazy. Our sages teach us that a person doesn't sin unless the spirit of insanity enters his brain. As the evil inclination (EI) wants a person to sin, he injects that person with a dose of insanity. The EI has all kinds of ploys to trap a person, and uses a number of different temptations and confusions to twist one's better judgment. The only way to guard against these pitfalls is by strengthening Torah learning and strengthening emuna.

Thoughts

"Evil thoughts and contemplations of lust make people crazy" (Likutei Moharan I:60). There is a very strong correlation between personal holiness and mental health. The opposite is also sad and true, that the more a person succumbs to lust and lewd thoughts, the less sane he becomes. People notoriously do insane things to fulfill their lusts, whether it be squandering hard-earned money, risking the wrath of the irate husband of the woman they covet, or breaking up their own home and ruining their own lives as well as the lives of their wives and children. Pornography adds to this insanity. Therefore, guarding one's eyes and mind from lewd and forbidden input is just as important as guarding one's mouth from swallowing poison. In fact, it's easier to poison the mind that it is to poison the body.

Torah learning, learning about emuna, sincere teshuva in the area of personal holiness, extensive personal prayer, and guarding one's eyes especially from impure books, movies, magazines, and websites are conducive to escaping the pitfalls of the type of evil thoughts and contemplations of lust that make a normal person insane.

A person should pray for happiness. Happiness and good mental health go hand in hand. True happiness comes from enhanced emuna.

Livelihood

The quality of a person's livelihood depends on his or her trust in Hashem. By way of emuna, one attains trust in Hashem. Consequently, concentrated efforts to reinforce emuna and trust in Hashem are capable of improving one's livelihood.

Emuna teaches us that Hashem sustains all His creations, from the one-celled amoeba to magnificent galaxies. Our sages say that He who gives life also gives livelihood. In other words, if one believes that Hashem is the live-giving Creator, one should also believe that the Creator sustains His creations.

Complete trust in Hashem includes the trust that livelihood is part of Hashem's Divine Providence over every creation. Livelihood is the worry of the Creator, not of the individual creation; therefore, one who trusts in Hashem is relieved of worry about livelihood and free to concentrate on his or her specific task on earth with a clear mind. Such people know that Hashem will fulfill His tasks faithfully.

The distinct sign of trust in Hashem is when a person's thoughts don't focus on money. Those who trust Hashem don't worry about where their next meal is coming from. Even when money is tight, they know that their financial problems come from Hashem. Therefore, they don't blame themselves or anyone else for their difficulties.

When experiencing a financial loss, whether in the form of a theft, a lost possession, or a breakdown, one should revert to the three principles of emuna, as follows:

1. Everything comes from Hashem, as does this particular loss. Not only does everything come from Hashem, but this is exactly what Hashem wants.

2. This particular loss is for the best, as everything else Hashem does.

3. The loss is a message from Hashem to stimulate self-evaluation and soul-searching for something that needs to be corrected, because there are no tribulations without transgression.

People with emuna know that Hashem is The Provider; therefore, when they encounter financial difficulties, they react by putting their emuna to work, as in the above three-stage thought process based on the principles of emuna.

The best way in the world to compensate for deficiency is teshuva, namely, rectifying the misdeeds that caused the deficiency in the first place. With teshuva and prayer for Hashem's compassion, a person can literally glide through financial difficulties.

By the sweat of your brow

On the other hand, those who lack trust in Hashem, Heaven forbid, attribute their financial difficulties to a long list of "villains": Either they blame themselves or others, curse their bad fortune or bad luck, or go on witch-hunts after bad omens, evil eyes, and other nonsense. Sometimes, they lament that Hashem doesn't love them or care about them, and harbor resentment toward Hashem. They think of a hundred different ploys to make money or to obtain what they want, including illegal means such as cheating on taxes or outright stealing. They do everything instead of what they should be doing – turning to Hashem and praying. They wrack their brains deciding whether to beg, borrow, or steal; they work overtime at the expense of health and family. They lack inner peace both in this world and in the next.

Without emuna, a person amplifies the curse of living by the sweat of his own brow (*see Genesis 3:19*). Emuna is the blessing that overrides the curse.

Thou shalt not steal

The more a person lacks emuna, the more he or she is liable to contemplate illegal means of making money. Dishonesty and lack of emuna are notorious partners. But, with emuna, one understands that Hashem provides a livelihood within the framework of the Torah's commandments. Any money that's destined to reach a person does so permissibly and by honest means.

Remember this important spiritual rule: **Money that one obtains by transgressing the Torah's laws (lying, cheating, withholding a worker's salary, fraud, and stealing, just to name a few) is not only cursed, but it also damages one's "kosher" money, just like a rotten apple damages the good apples in the same basket. Dishonest money invokes a torrent of troubles and tribulations.**

Trust

The best advice for solving income problems is to strengthen one's trust in Hashem. A superb method to strengthen trust in Hashem is to learn the chapter entitled "The Gate of Trust" from the classic ethics book "Duties of the Heart" by Rabbenu Bahiya. The best way to learn is as follows:

1. Learn a small segment every day, no more than fifteen lines. Review this segment three additional times.

2. The following day, learn the next fifteen-line segment, and review it three additional times.

3. Once you finish the chapter in the above manner, repeat the entire process until you internalize the principles of trust in Hashem.

People who've taken advantage of the above advice have seen wondrous improvements in their livelihood. Prayer coupled with learning "The Gate of Trust" is a remarkable income enhancer.

Those who desire to solve their financial problems once and for all should perform a spiritual "root treatment" and not ask for money at all in their prayers; instead, they should ask Hashem for emuna and trust. Why?

When we pray for money, the prayer serves as a temporary solution, like a patch on a torn pair of jeans. Prayers for money won't solve core financial difficulties. Unless we reinforce our trust in Hashem, one financial crisis will lead to another. But, by strengthening emuna and trust in Hashem, our income problems will be over! Hashem wants us to learn to trust Him; once we do, He doesn't need to prod us with financial tribulations.

With emuna and trust, we merit a pleasant and sufficient livelihood for life.

Those who are buried in debt should spend at least an hour a day in personal prayer, seek Hashem's help, make teshuva, and try to correct the misdeeds that generated the debt. They should pray to Hashem for emuna and trust, thus creating a strong spiritual vessel of trust that's a worthy recipient for Divine blessings of abundance.

Worry and trust are mutually exclusive

> A young man complained to his rabbi about financial difficulties. The rabbi told him to pray to Hashem and request emuna. The young man protested, claiming that there's nothing faulty with his emuna. "I have emuna!" he exclaimed, "but I'm worried about my old debts, my new bills, feeding and educating the children..."

The rabbi smiled, "Let your ears listen to the utterance of your mouth! You claim to have emuna, and in the same breath you say you're worried - that's mutually exclusive! The two don't go together! A person that truly believes in Hashem doesn't worry. He knows that Hashem will always feed and cloth him and his family. Here's proof..."

The rabbi showed the young man a picture of his grandson, a smiling plump toddler with rosy cheeks playing to his delight in a sandbox. "Have you ever seen a worried three-year old? No! A toddler doesn't have to worry - mommy and daddy are responsible for bringing home the bread! He continues playing in the sandbox - his task at this stage of life - and doesn't worry. He hasn't missed a meal up to now, and trusts that he won't miss a meal in the future. By the same token, you should trust your Father in Heaven while concentrating on your own task in life, without worrying either. Hashem won't let you miss a meal!"

The young man took a deep breath, letting the rabbi's words penetrate.

"Your task in life," continued the rabbi, "is to serve Hashem. Let Hashem take care of your financial situation and income worries. Speak to Hashem in this manner: 'Master of the World, there's no one else I can turn to but You, for the universe and all its contents are Yours, and You sustain all Your creations as You see fit. My livelihood is in Your hands alone and not up to me. Please, beloved Father in Heaven, send me my livelihood as You deem befitting, and teach me how to strengthen my faith, to serve You in

> happiness, and to have absolute trust in You and in whatever way You do things. Help me cling to You always."
>
> The young man adopted the rabbi's advice. The more he prayed, the more he strengthened his emuna. The more he strengthened his emuna, the more his financial difficulties disappeared.

Once we believe with complete faith that Hashem is the only address for solving income problems, our heart fills with joy and trust, knowing deep down that Hashem doesn't cast a loving son or daughter away. Just as Hashem always sent a means of sustenance in the past, He shall continue to do so in the future.

He who trusts in Hashem is encompassed in lovingkindness (Psalms 32:10)

Hashem gives a person a livelihood with no connection to that person's abilities or righteousness. Think about the example of a small child: When the child misbehaves, does the parent withhold food, clothing, shelter, or medical attention? Of course, not! If such is the case with humans – and Hashem is infinitely more merciful and compassionate than a human – it's surely the case with Hashem! Hashem provides for His creations regardless of their righteousness.

In the *Amida* prayer that we recite three times daily, we say that Hashem "sustains all life with lovingkindness" – we don't say that Hashem sustains all life according to justice. In other words, Hashem provides a livelihood for everyone – as a result of His amazing lovingkindness – and not according to whether they deserve it or not. He who grants life also grants sustenance.

Financial difficulties are frequently a message from Hashem for a person to start soul-searching. Our sages point to certain transgressions that are directly detrimental to making a living. They include fraud, theft, dishonesty, infidelity, anger, sadness, worry, spilling of one's seed, birth control without a rabbinical sanction, and a breach of family purity. These transgressions are serious breaches of emuna; if a person suffers from financial troubles and is guilty of one or more of these transgressions, then confessing to Hashem and teshuva will most certainly be conducive to a better livelihood.

If a person is not guilty of one or more of the aforementioned transgressions, then his or her financial difficulties are messages from Heaven that they need to strengthen their emuna and trust. Therefore, to relieve financial difficulties, one should concentrate one's spiritual efforts in reinforcing every aspect of faith in Hashem – learning about emuna, praying for emuna, performing a daily personal evaluation of one's own emuna, and making teshuva for any breach of emuna.

Livelihood is the prime proving ground for emuna. Here, one can't "fake it," because the results of emuna are reflected in one's inner peace, or lack of it. Either you believe that Hashem provides for you, or you run around in a frenzy thinking that you provide for yourself.

Rebbe Yitschak Breiter, of blessed and saintly memory: A lesson in trust

Rebbe Yitschak Breiter was a pious martyr whom the Nazis murdered in the Holocaust. Before World War II, he had a well-paying position as the accountant of a large Warsaw factory that enabled him to devote ample time to Torah study and to the service of Hashem.

When the prewar economic depression hit Poland, Rebbe Yitschak lost his job. The news of his layoff struck his family like lightning on a clear day, but Rebbe Yitschak maintained his composure. Once he saw that there were literally no jobs available, he sat down in the House of Study and immersed himself in Torah and prayer. The more the national economy worsened, the more Rebbe Yitschak remained glued to his Gemorra. His trust in Hashem never wavered in the slightest.

Other people roamed the streets in search of a little bit of work or a loaf of bread. Yet, the Breiter family always had enough to eat. Miraculously, they received their livelihood from all sorts of unexpected sources.

> One day, Rebbe Yitschak sat in the House of Study absorbed in a complicated question of Talmudic law. A total stranger approached him and handed him a sizable donation. Rebbe Yitschak showed no surprise or excitement, politely thanked the man, blessed him, and returned to his learning. The donor began to leave, but made an about-face when he reached the doorway.
>
> "Excuse me, rabbi, but a certain question sticks in my mind and bothers me," said the donor. "King David said (*Psalms 37:25*), *I have been a youth and also aged, but I have not seen a righteous man forsaken nor his offspring begging for bread*. If so, how is it that a righteous man like you - who learns Torah and serves Hashem day and night - has to appeal to others for his livelihood?"
>
> Rebbe Yitschak pondered the question for a moment, and replied, "Go to the market place, to so-and-so the rich man's store, and see how his son stands on the sidewalk in front of the store hawking for customers; the boy is hoarse by the time he succeeds in convincing someone to come inside and buy something from his father. So, isn't so-and-so's offspring begging for bread? Yet, I sit here learning Torah and praying to Hashem; did you see me call out to anyone? Did I appeal to

> you for a cent? You approached me on your own initiative and gave me just what I needed for my family's sustenance."

Our sages teach that as soon as people believe that Hashem provides for them, they earn a portion in the world to come. The Gemorra explains (*tractate Berachot 4b*) that anyone who says Psalm 145 three times a day merits a portion in the world to come, since this particular Psalm is conducive to emuna and trust in Hashem, as it states in verse 16, "You open Your hands and provide for every living thing." While emuna and trust enhance one's income, worry destroys it.

Rebbe Nachman of Breslev cites several Talmudic concepts that link one's livelihood to emuna (*see Sefer HaMidot, emuna*). For example, anyone with emuna is destined to be wealthy; emuna invokes enhanced income; the happiness that comes from emuna invokes success; one who includes Hashem's name (i.e. prayer) merits a doubled income; emuna is conducive to livelihood and more…

Consequently, one's main efforts in making a living should be the constant strengthening of emuna and trust in Hashem. With emuna, one's entire needs are fulfilled.

Business

A businessperson without emuna is miserable.

> A depressed and harried merchant once came to his rabbi. The rabbi's immediate spiritual prognosis was, "Your business and money problems result from the fact that you think you're the boss, and therefore all the worries are on your shoulders. You depend on your brains, your business acumen, and your talent, and therefore suffer bitter disappointments when

things don't go the way you want them to. Even worse, you put your trust in people - customers, suppliers, banks, and the like - and they let you down, lie to you, and cheat you."

The rabbi let his bombshell penetrate for a moment, and continued: "If you only realized that Hashem runs your business, and you're only a mere clerk, then your job would become much simpler; you wouldn't need to worry, you wouldn't need to suffer, and you wouldn't need to lose your temper. As a clerk, you could concentrate on doing your job and let the Big Boss - Hashem - worry about the rest. Tons of pressure would fall off your shoulders."

"How do I make Hashem the boss?" asked the businessman.

"Simple," answered the rabbi. "You tell Hashem, 'Master of the World, I want You to handle my affairs. I have no way of knowing whether the banks and the suppliers are giving me a square deal, or whether my customers intend to pay their bills and the like. You see everything, even the deepest thoughts of a person's heart. You know whether a prospective transaction will be profitable or not. I want You to make the decisions. Please, Father in Heaven, help me trust in You only. If a deal is no good, don't let it be completed; but, if a transaction is worthwhile, please, make it happen!"

The businessman opened his eyes wide in amazement. "Rabbi, are you telling me that Hashem intervenes every time a housewife walks into my store?"

"You better believe it!" answered the rabbi. "Hashem puts the desire in her heart to purchase the exact product that's now on display in your storefront window. Hashem can also screen a prospective employee for you, or give you the wisdom to expand or limit the business in a profitable manner. If you consult Hashem before every transaction, put all your trust in Him and ask for His guidance, you're bound to succeed!"

A businessperson that prays for enhanced emuna learns to manage affairs without stress and anxiety. When he puts his trust in Hashem, nothing upsets or frightens him.

Basically, we can choose one of two paths in commercial life (or any other phase of life): Either we appoint Hashem as the Chief Executive Officer of our company/business/affairs – consequently enjoying a smooth and worry-free life – or we shoulder the problems on our own, with the accompanying stress, worries, nerves, and health problems.

Juggling money

"Financing" is a disease. Hashem decides how much money we have. Hashem also gives each of us the necessary funds for whatever He deems that we need. Let's suppose that we want a new car, but can't afford it; this is a clear sign that Hashem doesn't deem the new car necessary at this point in time.

Many of those who lack money think they can outsmart Hashem by financing, or "plastic purchasing". They often juggle funds by borrowing from one source to pay off another. Finance and credit card debts mushroom because of their tremendous interest rates. So, by trying to circumvent Hashem and purchasing things on credit or on loans, people dig deep financial pits that they eventually fall into.

Most loans, credit purchases, and "buying on time" indicate a lack of emuna. With emuna, we're satisfied with whatever Hashem gives us. If there's no money for the new car, then Hashem wants us to continue driving the old car in the meanwhile. Believers don't fall into the traps of "a dollar down and a dollar a week". Hashem doesn't lack funds; if He wants us to have the new car, He gives us the wherewithal.

Suppose that we want to open a business, and have $50,000 to our disposal. In such a case, we should look for a small business – a candy store or newspaper stand, for example – and get to work! Hashem doesn't want us to borrow an additional $500,000 for something larger; who says that we'll be able to repay such a loan?

People that lack emuna are prone to inflated egos; "What, I should sell candy or ballpoint pens?" They think that they should be big businesspeople, and can only succeed by juggling large sums of money. When we lack a large sum, it's a clear sign that Hashem doesn't want us juggling large sums.

Some people think that they're making big money by juggling money that's not really their own. If they'd check carefully, they'd see that the cost of financing eats up all their profits. Moreover, "jugglers" are dependant on the mercy of cruel institutions like banks and finance companies. As soon as a bank or finance company closes the loan faucet for a juggler, he or she falls on their face. Stories of juggler bankruptcy are all too common.

Most jugglers entertain fantasies of grandeur. If they had emuna, they'd realize that Hashem decides how much money they make, on a daily, weekly, monthly and yearly basis. Suppose that Hashem gives the juggler $100,000 a year, but the juggler wants double that sum. He or she ends up *wasting* money by hiring more workers that they don't need, spending needless funds on advertising, or by disproportionate spending trying to increase their business.

With emuna, a person stops juggling, and makes the best out of his or her resources at hand. Emuna people aren't jugglers; they're frugal, run their business or spend money on an uninflated scale, and are satisfied with what they have.

King Solomon said so brilliantly (*Proverbs 28:20*), "A man of faith will increase blessings, but the impatient to be rich will not be exonerated." In other words, the people of faith are satisfied with Hashem's blessing, and by virtue of their satisfaction, they get even bigger blessings. They're careful with their money, don't spend needlessly and consequently don't fall into debt.

Even though they seek advice from experts such as investment brokers, accountants, or other financial advisors, people with emuna ask Hashem for success, in this manner: "Hashem, thank You for providing my daily needs. Guide my investments and/ or business in such a way that I make a profit, so that I'll be able to give substantial amounts to charity and to perform Your commandments. Please help me accept any outcome – whether profit or loss – with complete faith."

The prophet said (*Jeremiah 17:7*), "Blessed is the man who trusts in Hashem, and Hashem will be his security." King David promised that those who trust in Hashem will always be encompassed by Divine compassion (*see Psalm 32*). On the other hand, those who lack emuna and put blind trust in financial advisors or other flesh-and-blood, as if the mortal they depend on gives them their sustenance, are almost always disappointed. The prophet also said (*Jeremiah 17:5*), "Cursed is the man who trusts in people and makes flesh-and-blood his strength." Trusting in anyone or anything other than in Hashem is a formula for failure.

Rebbe Menachem Mendel of Kotsk interprets the Midrash (*Mechilta, Beshalach 17*) that says, "The Torah was granted to those who eat the manna." The manna was the sweet Heaven-sent bread that Hashem provided for the Children of Israel during their forty years of wandering in the desert. The manna would descend from Heaven daily, enough for each family's daily needs. In other words, a person who trusts in Hashem is like one who eats Heaven-sent bread. Since he has the confidence that Hashem will send him an income without working around the clock, he has the time to devote to Torah learning. As such, the Torah becomes the inheritance of those who trust in Hashem, the ones who resemble those that ate the manna.

With emuna, a person understands that Hashem continues to provide our daily needs to this day. Emuna frees energy wasted on running after money for prayer and Torah learning!

The Successful Businessperson

A fundamental principle in emuna that underlies one's effort to earn money - whether by commerce, negotiations, trading, finance, or any other exchange of funds or goods - is that a person's livelihood is predetermined from Rosh Hashanah.

Our level of trust in Hashem is the practical manifestation of emuna in our lives. Trust includes the awareness that Hashem sustains all His creations, and that He does His job dependably. When we trust Hashem, we're not worried where our next meal is coming from; we know that He who has fed us in the past will continue to do so in the future. We also know that our livelihood doesn't depend on our craftiness or cunning – it depends on Hashem only.

No one can detract from the income that Hashem designates for a person. The Talmud states emphatically (*tractate Yoma 38b*) that one human is incapable of touching a fellow human's intended portion. Equipped with this basic fact, we never need to worry or fear anyone or anything.

Trust in Hashem – internalizing the fundamental principle of emuna that our livelihood is predetermined and exclusively from Hashem

– enables us to conduct our business affairs with confidence, a clear mind, and a healthy outlook. Stress, anxiety, and worry fall by the wayside. With trust in Hashem, we go through life with inner peace, avoiding the pitfalls of crazy wheeling, dealing, and chasing money at the expense of our physical, emotional, and spiritual health. Sound exaggerated? Here's what futile chases after money do to a person:

- Emotional damages – worry, anger, stress, and anxiety that also result in depression and severe changes of mood;
- Physical damages – the above emotional strains increase chances of heart disease, digestion disorders, strokes, and cardiovascular problems, Heaven forbid. Also, they are springboards for substance use and addiction, namely, alcohol, tobacco, and drugs.
- Spiritual damages – money chasers forget the Torah's laws, and often resort to dishonesty, fraud, thievery, and other transgressions, all of which severely blemish a person's soul.

With trust in Hashem, a person doesn't think about money all day long. Peace of mind is only two words away – **Hashem provides**.

Business is one continuous test of faith. Businesspeople are tested every single second: If they believe that their livelihood comes from Hashem, then they're calm and composed, conducting their affairs on an honest basis. If they believe otherwise - that their income depends on their own efforts and aptitude - then they're most likely working much too hard and wasting energy looking for all types of ploys to make money.

One's entire life depends on the emuna that Hashem provides for every creation. Emuna creates a clear, clean, and shining spiritual pipe that abundance flows through, directly from Heaven to a person's bank account or dinner table. Drinking from the pipe of emuna is like drinking from a silver goblet. Without emuna, one drinks from the spiritual equivalent of a sewer pipe, where one's income is contaminated with negative emotions, bad health, and damage to the soul.

Decide which option in life you'd prefer, because basically, there are only two:

First, you can believe that Hashem predetermines your income, and that every last cent designated for you will reach you at an exact time and in its entirety, if not from one source, then from a different source, if not today, then tomorrow. As a result, you are calm and composed, and avoid the troubles of illegal and dishonest business procedures, hypertension, ulcers, and cardiac arrests.

Or second, you don't believe in Hashem or in His ability to support you, and you bang your head against the wall trying to make a living, angry and irritable most of the time because life is a living death. You sink into debt, you're confused, and you can't think clearly with the tensions and stress that weigh on your brain. Oftentimes, you catch yourself cutting the corners of honesty and wholesome business practices in trying to make an additional buck.

Remember! A person receives his or her Heavenly stipend to the cent. By cheating, lying, or dealing dishonestly, a person won't earn a cent more.

Here's an example: Joe and Harry are both store owners; each is destined to earn one hundred thousand dollars this year. Joe earns his money honestly and in good faith, and therefore enjoys it. Harry wants a lot more money than what Hashem gives him, so he wheels, deals, lies, and steals, bringing in a gross income of an additional fifteen thousand dollars. Harry will now suffer sicknesses, accidents, home damages, income tax investigations, law suits, and any number of other aggravations. As a result, he'll lose the fifteen thousand that *wasn't* destined for him, and he won't enjoy the hundred thousand that *was* destined for him, since he'll be busy running to doctors, lawyers, repairmen, and the like.

The story of Yossele

The Baal Shem Tov had a disciple named Yossele. Yossele's evil inclination tempted him to steal. Unable to overcome his urge, Yossele decided to try and steal at night, when the entire township was fast asleep. He set his first sights on Lady Sara's mansion, the vast three story residence on the outskirts of the township where the rich spinster lived.

Sara was the only daughter of a wealthy merchant who died and left her all his wealth.

Yossele sneaked up to the mansion, and to his delight, found the gatekeeper snoring away in a deep slumber. Two overfed dogs sat by the gatekeeper wagging their tails. Yossele couldn't believe his good fortune - even the front door to the mansion was unlocked! Not a single servant was in sight.

Quietly, as if walking on eggs, Yossele entered the mansion. He never saw so much abundance in his life - rich carpets from Persia, crystal chandeliers from Vienna, paintings from the leading galleries of Paris and Amsterdam. He tiptoed through the parlor to the drawing room; once, Yossele had come here to receive a donation from Sara's father, who made no effort to conceal the whereabouts of the safe.

He moved aside the painting of the waterfall in the drawing room, and lo and behold, there was the safe. Yossele barely turned its dial, and the unlocked door simply popped open! Diamonds, gold, and stacks of paper currency stared him in the face.

Yossele was astonished at how everything proceeded so smoothly: The guard slept, the dogs didn't bark, the front door was open, all the servants had disappeared, and even the safe was unlocked. As strange as it seemed, Yossele felt like he was receiving Divine corroboration!

"Why's Hashem making this so easy for me?" Yossele asked himself. "Strange, it looks like all these riches are just waiting for me to take them." The more he stared at the wealth before his eyes, the more his heart pounded with guilt. He remembered his Gemorra that said a person's livelihood is predetermined. "If so," he argued with himself, "why should I be touching anything that doesn't belong to me?"

Yet, the diamonds and the stacks of money seemed to be calling his name – *"Yossele, take us..."*

Yossele's Torah background, his conscience, and his good inclination were gaining the upper hand in his inner struggle; a spark of emuna kindled a fire of faith in his heart. "If all these riches are really mine, then they'll come to me by honest means; certainly – there's no need for me to transgress Hashem's commandments and steal!"

Suddenly, Yossele felt an awesome fear of Hashem, as he stood on the verge of a terrible felony. "Hashem, save me!" he yelled, turning abruptly and running out of the house without taking a thing.

The following day – in the evening hours – after having spilled a river of tears and a flood of remorse while begging for Hashem's forgiveness, Yossele received a summons from the Baal Shem

Tov. Obediently, he proceeded to his master with no delay.

"Sit down, Yossele," said the Baal Shem Tov cordially, offering him a chair. "How are you feeling?"

"F-fine, b-baruch Hashem," stuttered Yossele, expecting the worst chastisement imaginable.

"Yossele," said the Baal Shem Tov, "I received a message from Lady Sara – do you know who I'm referring to?"

A tremendous lump parked itself in Yossele's throat; he could barely breathe, let alone speak. He cleared his throat several times, while his face alternately changed colors from a bright crimson to a pale yellow to an ash white. He was sure that Lady Sara reported the attempted theft to the Baal Shem Tov. Even if she didn't, nothing escaped the limitless spiritual vision of the tzaddik. Yossele wanted to jump in a hole and then have the ground devour him. He was so ashamed…

"Yossele," the Baal Shem Tov continued, "Lady Sara, as an orphan and as an only child, has asked me to be her guardian and to advise and assist her in conducting her affairs…". The Baal Shem Tov paused, and his probing, Heavenly, ice-blue eyes seemed to penetrate the fibers of Yossele's soul.

"…Lady Sara asked me to find her a suitable *chattan;* she wants to get married. She desires a pious husband, who'll spend every waking hour in the study of Torah and in the service of Hashem. She doesn't want a businessman who'll manage her commercial affairs, for she can do that herself; her father trained her well, and she's most adept in the business world. She wants a husband that will be isolated from the outside world, whose entire energies and aspirations will be channeled toward Torah."

Yossele nearly fell off his chair; he was expecting to be consumed by a bolt of lightning at any second, but instead…

The Baal Shem Tov smiled warmly. "You know, Yossele, when Lady Sara first approached me several weeks ago, I couldn't think of a suitable candidate. Later, Hashem gave me the idea that the time has come for you to take a wife, and that you and Sara would make a splendid match. I want you to prepare yourself for the wedding; the High Holidays are drawing near, so I think that you and Sara should be married with no further delay."

Any bombshell - even a sweet one - requires time to digest. Yossele stepped out of the tzaddik's house, his head spinning, into the warm midsummer Ukrainian sunshine. He sat down by the river, and contemplated the vastness of Hashem's Divine Providence to the tiniest detail, His mercy, and His phenomenal lovingkindness. "What if I hadn't withstood the test?" he asked himself, and almost fainted when he contemplated the hypothetical consequences. If he'd have stolen, he'd have stolen money that would ultimately have come to him by permissible means! Instead of being Lady Sara's bridegroom and a pious Torah scholar with all his needs taken care of, he would've been a lonely, common thief out on the street with nothing!

> Yossele saw life as a tightrope - the thinnest line separated between good and evil, happiness and despair, magnificent success and utter failure. He thanked Hashem for giving him the strength to withstand temptation and to pass the test of faith. He also realized that good fortune and abundance readily come to a person without forcing the issue. Hashem has His timetable.

For money – or anything else – to carry a blessing, it must reach a person by permissible means. When someone prematurely or illegally takes what is not theirs, they endanger losing what's currently theirs *and* what's destined for them.

Understandably, not everyone receives such a clear preview of the abundance that's in store for him like Yossele did. Also, few realize that their future needs are already taken care of. Our efforts in making money are merely tests as to *how* we'll make our money – in honest, straightforward means, or by shady deals, bickering, fraud, swindling, and the like. In essence, we are all like Yossele – with emuna and patience, we'll receive all our needs.

Maybe you're thinking about Yossele's good fortune in marrying a rich woman. Know full well that even if Yossele didn't marry Lady Sara, if her money was earmarked for him, he would have received it anyway, by any number of means. Hashem is not limited in the number of ways He sends people their livelihood.

Everything has its hour

A merchant with emuna needs to know that every article in his or her inventory is under the influence of absolute Divine Providence. Hashem decides when a certain object – whether a twenty-room mansion or tube of toothpaste – is sold, to whom, and at what price. According to Kabbalistic thought, each object has spiritual sparks of holiness that belong or gravitate to a certain soul; that soul will ultimately acquire the object, as a soul correction both for the object and for itself. Elaborating on this concept, Rebbe Nachman of Breslev writes (*Likutei Moharan I:52*) that everything has its hour, when it ultimately returns to its spiritual root.

For example, if the sparks of holiness in a particular carrot are rooted in the soul of a tzaddik, the tzaddik's wife will eventually go to a certain vegetable stand on a certain day and pay a certain price for a certain pound of carrots. She'll then come home and feed her husband the certain carrot whose spiritual sparks are rooted in his soul. Once the tzaddik makes a blessing over the carrot and eats it, the carrot attains a lofty spiritual correction. In the case of a carrot or other foodstuff, it physically becomes a part of the tzaddik!

In light of the above example (which is none other than a drop of water from a vast sea, for the subject of soul corrections necessitates an entire volume in itself), any business deal – barter, trade, purchase, or sale – occurs **only** when and where Hashem decides. When the time is ripe for a certain commodity or piece of merchandise to reach the domain of a particular soul, the transaction is completed – not before and not after.

If a purchaser and an object don't have a spiritual common denominator, they won't come together at any price or under any circumstance. Therefore, it's senseless for a pushy salesman or overpowering merchant to try and force something on a customer that he or she doesn't want.

Many businesspeople have related stories about seemingly useless merchandise that they sold at a tremendous profit, or about products that they thought would be best sellers that ended up collecting dust on the shelves. Realtors have all experienced prospective buyers that turn their noses up at a certain house or piece of property, and three months later end up purchasing the very same piece of real estate. Every field has its own examples of Divine Providence. Everything has its hour.

Negotiating in faith

The Talmud teaches (*tractate Shabbat 31a*) that the very first question the Heavenly Court asks a person when he or she leaves this world is, "Did you negotiate in faith?" Those who incorporate emuna in all of their dealings will be able to answer a proud "Yes!"

Emuna in business means that a person is fair, honest, and sticks to his or her word. With emuna that livelihood comes from Hashem, a person doesn't resort to criminal or immoral means in acquiring money.

A merchant with emuna doesn't make untrue claims about his goods, for he knows that the right buyer will come along and pay the right price at the right time for a particular item. He neither pressures nor flatters a prospective customer, for he knows that livelihood comes from Hashem, and not from the customer. Nevertheless, he is polite and respectful to the customer, for that is also Hashem's will. He doesn't try to force a sale, for he knows the customer will ultimately regret, complain, or return the purchase, or even give the merchant and his business a bad name and reputation. A merchant or businessperson without emuna – when forcing a deal – always becomes a loser in the long term.

Nothing frightens a businessperson with emuna. He or she isn't disappointed when a prospective customer walks away. With emuna, one knows that if profit doesn't materialize from transaction A, then it'll materialize from transaction B. People frequently attain money by means that have nothing to do with their field of endeavor; we've all heard stories such as the not-so-successful dentist that made a lot of money in the stock market or the all-too-plain housewife that turned a good idea into a thriving on-line business.

A businessperson with emuna is not only guaranteed a pleasant, worry-free life in this world; his or her integrity and emuna earn a lofty place in the world to come. People with emuna don't go around lying, cheating, and damaging other people, and are therefore spared from untold anguish in both worlds.

On the other side of the coin, businesspeople that lack emuna think that their livelihood depends on the customer. Such folks believe that money and success depend on their own acumen, and therefore will readily stretch the truth or compromise their principles in their exaggerated efforts to make a living. They often make promises they can't keep or slander their competitors, violating the Torah's ordnance of wholesome speech. Inadvertently, they accumulate a long list of spiritual debits that leads to suffering in both worlds.

Businesspeople or other professionals that lack emuna are almost always plagued by arrogance and an inflated ego. When Hashem grants them success, they pat themselves telling themselves how clever, wonderful, and talented they are. When they attain more money than they deserve by deviating from the realm of integrity and fairness, they pride themselves in their ability to "make" money. But, money made in such a matter will ultimately sour. Dishonest money is poison, both spiritually and materially.

Have you ever seen an arrogant person fail to complete the transaction that he or she wanted to complete? Some vent their frustrations in temper tantrums, curses and complaints; others eat themselves up inside. Heaven only knows the amount of strokes, heart attacks, ulcers, and emotional instability that stem from a simple lack of emuna.

The choice

Apparently, there's room for confusion; we frequently see successful businesspeople that couldn't care less about emuna. Furthermore, many of them are hard-hitting wheelers and dealers that you wouldn't want to buy a used car from. Yet, they succeed in selling ice to the Eskimos or pulling off any number of legendary deals by virtue of their powers of persuasion or fast talking. Where's the Divine Providence? We all know that so-and-so made millions from crime, graft, or corruption, laughs all the way to the bank, and basks in the Bermuda sunshine this very minute. What's going on here? Where's Hashem?

Our sages provide the answer: Hashem gives free choice to a person to do good or evil. Suppose that Hashem would send a bolt of lighting from Heaven to strike down a person every time he or she lied, or sent a ten-thousand dollar check to a person every time he or she told the truth. Soon, no one would lie and everyone would tell the truth, but that's not free choice – it's coercion! A system of rewards and punishments makes no sense outside the context of free choice. Therefore, Hashem conceals His Divine Providence in order to leave people the free choice to do good or evil.

When people choose the path of emuna, their livelihood reaches them effortlessly, honestly, and without knocking their brains out or flattering others. But, if they choose the path of arrogance and lack of faith, then Hashem will allow them to believe that they are controlling their own destiny. In actuality, they receive exactly what Hashem intends for them to receive. Often, a dishonest businessperson is the mere "stick" in Hashem's hands that steals from or cheats a person that has been destined to suffer a loss. Hashem enables people with severe spiritual debits to serve as the executors of a bad decree; nevertheless, such executors will be ultimately punished.

Wait until the time is ripe

Everyone knows that unripe fruit is not only bitter, it causes stomach aches. When people try to forcibly seal a deal or make money before the time and circumstances are ripe, they also suffer.

Suppose that a merchant forcibly sells an item to a customer that doesn't want it. Since the item is not intended for that particular customer, the customer won't derive satisfaction or benefit from the item. For example, either it won't function properly, or it will be ruined in the customer's domain. The customer may file a complaint or lawsuit against the merchant, causing substantial grief and financial loss. As such, many losses can be traced to a lack of emuna.

Forcing the issue, or acquiring money by dishonest means, can sometimes lead to disastrous results for generations to come. Imagine that a person fraudulently acquires a lot of money; this money – in honest means – would have reached his hands and the hands of his descendants over the next three generations. But, since he has greedily swindled to acquire funds that are not yet "ripe" for picking, he has stripped the financial tree whose fruits were intended for the use of the swindler's children, grandchildren, and great grandchildren. Three subsequent tragedies occur:

1. The swindler's unripe funds will turn sour in his hands – either he will be taken from his money or his money will be taken from him.

2. The swindler's children, grandchildren, and great grandchildren will likely suffer dire poverty or extreme financial problems.

3. The swindler will have to undergo excruciating soul corrections in the next world.

Remember the following golden rule: **What is yours will reach you in good time. You don't have to forcibly grab that which is intended for you anyway.** When you believe that Hashem will provide for you, then your life will be calm, pleasurable, and productive. If you think that your fate and livelihood is in your own hands, then life will be a hell on earth of strain, pressure, and disappointment strewn with untold obstacles, including the temptation to attain money by dishonest means. The choice is yours.

Gambling

Gambling is a terrible sickness, even more addictive than alcohol, tobacco, or drugs. It literally buries people, and reduces them to subhuman level. Gambling and emuna just don't mix.

The lust for money is the root cause of the gambling affliction, which not only drives a person insane, but makes him or her forget Hashem, truth, and emuna in Hashem's Divine Providence, Heaven forbid.

Gambling looks like a road to easy money; but, the glitter of "easy street" is none other than a deceptive avenue to a living death of bitterness, broken families, debt, loan sharks, and utter despair.

Gambling makes a person's head spin. The *Yetzer Hara* (Evil Inclination) has a standard template for trapping people in this death trap: He shows a person someone that made a windfall in the casino; that person now thinks that he's the next in line for the pot of gold. With a fantasy of fantastic wealth that tickles his imagination, the gambler wastes all his money chasing the rainbow of riches. A gambler will sell his business, home, and car to keep the dice rolling; he forgets about his wife and his children; if he could, he'd sell them too.

Profit that's nothing but a loss

According to Jewish law, money won in gambling is considered an illegal acquisition; the gambler is deemed an unreliable individual whose testimony is unacceptable in a religious court (*see Shulchan Oruch, Choshen Mishpat 34:16*). Money won in gambling has no blessing; the gambler won't see any benefit from such gains, for gambling money is spiritually putrid.

The gambler always loses

On Rosh Hashanah, a Heavenly decree determines how much each person will profit or lose in the coming year. For example, let's suppose that John Doe is destined to earn $150,000 this year, but he'll also lose $30,000.

If John Doe does all the tricks in the world, and hires an army of statisticians and computer analysts to advise him how to bet on the dice, he still won't make any more than his annual allotment from Heaven. But, if he perseveres in prayer, gives liberal amounts to charity, and goes out of his way to help those in need and to educate his children in Torah, he can receive *more* that the original allotment.

But – pay close attention – by gambling, he is liable to lose *more* than his predetermined loss, even his entire assets. John Doe the gambler not only endangers his house, his possessions, and all his money, but is likely to fall into a deep pit of debt that enslaves him for the rest of his life.

Either way, the gambler is a loser; his winnings are money with a curse, and he won't earn a cent more than what's destined for him without gambling. Yet, his losses are liable to be limitless. Is it worth it?

Cruel as a crow

Crows are known to be cruel; they worry about themselves, and they don't feed their young. Hashem's amazing care for crow nestlings is one of the creation's miraculous phenomena (*see Job 38:41, Psalms 147:9, Midrash Tanchuma, Ekev, b*), otherwise they'd die of starvation.

Hashem doesn't give a person money for his own exclusive use; a person's allotment includes the stipend for his wife's and children's needs. As such, most of a person's money is earmarked for the sustenance of his dependants; if he were single, he'd probably earn a lot less.

The gambler has no right to gamble the food from his children's mouths or the shirt off his wife's back. When he does, he's worse than a crow; a crow doesn't provide, but doesn't take food out its nestlings' mouths either.

On a spiritual level, the gambler will be punished for the pain and anguish he causes to his loved ones. Again, he's a double loser – in this world and in the next.

The gambler thrives on the suffering of others

Gambling is more than problematic on the level of morality. In most cases, one person's winnings are another person's losses. There can be no blessing to funds earned from the sorrow of another human. Even if a gambler wins, how can he enjoy monies that were destined to be the food and clothes of the loser's family?

A person that believes in The Almighty avoids even the slightest contact with gambling.

The lust for gambling is rooted in denial of Hashem; therefore, a gambler that desires to kick the habit must pray to Hashem for emuna. He must beg Hashem to help him trust that all his livelihood and all his needs come from Hashem by way of magnificent Divine Providence. Gambling, like other morally-questionable ways of attaining money, rusts the crystal-clear shining pipes of abundance. Hashem doesn't need the gambler's help in providing his preordained annual income.

Lottery tickets

According to the letter of Jewish law, lottery winnings are permissible, because they're not the losses of another person. Nevertheless, purchasing lottery tickets isn't 100% congruent with the spirit of emuna.

If a person does desire to purchase a lottery ticket, he or she should purchase a single ticket only; if Hashem wants them to win the lottery prize, He'll arrange that their ticket bears the winning number.

One who purchases multiple lottery tickets shows that he or she trusts statistics or enhanced chances, and not in Hashem. He or she also wastes money that was intended for their basic needs.

Lottery tickets are therefore a test of faith: Folks that believe in Hashem's Divine Providence won't purchase more than a single ticket. If they win, congratulations! If they lose, they know that Hashem didn't want them to win, and that the money would have been detrimental to them. Accepting the outcome of a losing lottery ticket without disappointment earns a mark of "excellent" in emuna.

Without emuna, people buy multiple tickets to increase their chances. By putting their faith in probability or luck, they not only waste money but fail the test of faith.

A difficult test

A sudden windfall, such as an inheritance or a winning lottery ticket, is a serious and difficult test of faith. Experience shows that many people that acquired sudden wealth ultimately suffered severe emotional and spiritual maladies. Why?

Most people lack the emotional and spiritual gear that's required to successfully deal with more than they're accustomed to. As a result, they become disoriented and arrogant; suddenly, the nouveau-riche husband no longer wants his wife, and vice versa. They entertain fantasies of glamour and grandeur, as if their money entitles them to more. Oftentimes, they use their money imprudently, squander it, or make senseless investments. They fall prey to con artists, greedy relatives, newly-found "friends," or white-collar swindlers such as unethical lawyers, accountants, or investment brokers. Frequently, their new riches are one continuous migraine headache.

Emuna is a proper and capable spiritual vessel for handling wealth. A wealthy individual with emuna knows that money belongs to Hashem, and is none other that a temporary deposit in his or her hands in order to implement Hashem's commandments. As such, he or she doesn't slip into arrogance; they know that Hashem can take their money away at any instant, so why boast about it? They give a minimum of 10% to charity; the wealthy on the highest level of emuna give 20% of their earnings to charity. They are forever grateful to Hashem and display their gratitude by supporting Torah institutions and worthwhile charitable endeavors. With emuna, a person passes the test of wealth with flying colors.

The opposite is true where there's no emuna. The wealthy, especially the newly wealthy, are consumed by the fear of losing their money. They become arrogant and disoriented. Their dream of money turns into a nightmare, for they have no one to trust. They fail the test of emuna.

Happiness or wealth

The desire for quick money shows a lack of emuna. Those who believe in Hashem know that the quality of their lives doesn't depend on the amount of money they have, but on they extent they acquire emuna and succeed in performing Hashem's will.

Prayer, charity, and teshuva are the only solutions to financial difficulties. If Hashem gives a person the tribulations of financial straits, then money won't solve that person's problems; he or she will only get a different and possibly worse set of tribulations.

Teshuva is the only way to end tribulations, since there are no tribulations without transgression. As long as a person refrains from making teshuva – even with all the money in the world –

he or she will suffer because of their outstanding and uncorrected transgressions. But, with teshuva and a clean spiritual slate, people can live a sweet and pleasant life even if they don't have a cent in their pockets.

Rebbe Aaron of Kiblitsh was direly poor, yet phenomenally happy all the time. Once, a wealthy friend told him that he envies him. The rich man said that he's always buying gifts for his wife and children, yet they're never satisfied and they're constantly bickering. But, since Rebbe Aaron's smiling disposition is always so pleasant, his family is happy despite their material deficiency.

Consequently, a person should be satisfied with his or her lot in life and not strive for riches. Our sages said that the more one has, the more one worries. In any event, the best and only way to acquire one's needs is prayer, appealing to our merciful Father in Heaven for His Divine blessing and compassion.

"Shalom Bayit" – Peace in the Home

The main test

The main tests of a person's faith are in the home, with his wife and children, who unwittingly test his faith from morning 'til night. They make demands on his time, his money, and his nerves. Sometimes they frustrate and humiliate him, and never seem to be satisfied. Emuna is the only way to pass these tests.

The challenges of a marital relationship require a higher level of emuna than difficulties outside the home do. While a person can often avoid friction and confrontation on the outside, it's difficult to escape trying situations at home. Furthermore, a person can change his friends and associates a lot easier than he can change his spouse, for a marital relationship is much more obligating.

The true *tikkun*, or soul correction of a person, begins only once that person marries. Unmarried people normally manage in life without having to invest concerted effort in acquiring emuna. But, the demands of a wife and children make life virtually unbearable without emuna.

For example, unmarried people can normally avoid anyone they don't get along with, for in most cases, they're not forced to maintain contact. When a person is able to walk away from a challenging predicament, his or her emuna isn't taxed at all. Where there's no need to cope, there's no test!

On the other hand, a responsible married person simply can't walk away from a family. His wife and children are his diagnostic test of emuna. In the framework of a family environment, he can know whether he truly has emuna or not.

Here's an example: Robert is a bachelor that works as a marketing representative of a big company. If one of his colleagues insults him or bothers him in any way, Robert has a quick tongue and even quicker temper; he's more than ready to heap a double dose of venom on anyone that steps on his toes. Sometimes, Robert will roll with a verbal punch in order to preserve an image that he wants to create for his customers. It serves his best interests to appear on the outside as a distinguished individual of impeccable character, especially if it helps him seal a deal.

In reality, Robert is short-tempered and ego-centric. In a marital situation, he'd either destroy his wife and children, or end up divorced. To avoid either of these two dismal fates, he must learn emuna; otherwise he'd never pass the tests of a family environment.

A married person should be a giver, not a taker. Incessantly, he must provide for the needs of his dependants, listen to their troubles, and grant them time, attention, and understanding. To perform the task of a giver, a person needs to be calm and composed – without emuna, inner peace and composure are utterly impossible.

An unmarried person can wear an artificial smile and convince the world that he or she is happy and fulfilled. But, after marriage, the true measure of a person's happiness is revealed, especially when he has to brighten up his household with joy and confidence. A husband can't possibly make his wife and children happy when he himself is miserable. True happiness is impossible without emuna, and marital life is a key testing ground of emuna.

Relationships outside the home, especially in the norms of modern society, are based on mutual advantage. "Scratch my back and I'll scratch yours" is the type of thinking that indicates costumed, self-serving relationships that are designed to attain money, fame, dignity, social standing, advancement, and recognition. But, at home, a person removes the mask of self-serving diplomacy and acts naturally. If he lacks emuna, he'll hate giving without getting – such a person will surely have tension at home, to say the least. If he desires "shalom bayit" – peace in the home – he'll have to learn emuna.

Emuna and shalom bayit are directly proportionate

Here's an important rule of thumb: **A person's shalom bayit is directly proportionate to his measure of emuna; the higher the emuna, the more peaceful the home**. Once a person marries, he or she can *really* attain lasting emuna.

A husband and wife must learn from the outset of their relationship to look at everything that happens in the home from the standpoint of emuna. Almost every daily occurrence between them, their children, their family members, or their respective colleagues at work is a test of emuna. Therefore, they need the constant support system of the three levels of emuna. Emuna, teshuva, and submission to Hashem's will are not only the best problem-solving tools in the home; they're the **only** problem-solving tools in the home.

Happy with their lot in life

The Gemorra *(tractate Taanit 23b)* tells a delightful and pointed story:

> Rabbi Manni came before Rebbe Yitschak ben Elyashiv and complained, "I can't stand my wife – she's not at all pretty."
>
> Rebbe Yitschak ben Elyashiv asked, "What's her name?" Rabbi Manni said that his wife's name is Hanna. "Then let Hanna be beautiful!" declared Rebbe Yitschak ben Elyashiv, a tzaddik whose every utterance was a surefire blessing.
>
> Hanna became gorgeous. Shortly thereafter, Rabbi Manni returned to Rebbe Yitschak ben Elyashiv with a new complaint: "Ever since you blessed my wife, she gets more and more beautiful. The more beautiful she is, the haughtier she gets!"
>
> "If that's the case," said Rebbe Yitschak ben Elyashiv, "then let Hanna return to her prior status." Rabbi Manni came home, and was greeted by a smiling, pleasant, but quite ugly Hanna.

Rabbi Manni loved his newly "uglified" wife because she was so modest and pleasant, and completely his! This Talmudic anecdote exemplifies how Hashem knows what's best for each one of us.

Emuna in Divine Providence is the faith that everything Hashem does is for the best and for our ultimate individual benefit. With this level of emuna, we're always happy with our lot in life, knowing unequivocally that even life's deficiencies are the product of Hashem's personal intervention in our lives for our ultimate good.

Hashem gives each of us what we need to attain our soul correction and to accomplish our mission on this earth.

Contrastingly, a person without emuna has endless complaints. The wife blames her husband for all of her troubles. The husband has nothing but complaints and criticism about his wife, and is positive that she's the root of his suffering. Understandingly, their household is a pressure cooker; their children undoubtedly harbor an assortment of emotional maladies. Such a couple flunks the test of emuna.

Consequently, one's entire livelihood, happiness, personal welfare and the welfare of one's spouse and children all depend on emuna.

Divorce

This section is a must for those who desire true peace in the home as well as for those who are contemplating divorce or are about to be divorced. If you're divorced already, then this section will be help you plan and manage your life from now onwards.

One of this generation's eldest and wisest spiritual leaders said that the alarmingly high contemporary divorce rate is the result of a pampered generation that doesn't realize that marital success requires hard work. "We also had our share of difficulties, misunderstandings, and quarrels, but we never considered the option of breaking up the marriage," he said. "Our goal was to build a successful relationship; we were therefore prepared to invest the needed efforts to reach our goal. Had we lacked the patience and perseverance required in marriage, we wouldn't have reaped the fruits of sons and daughters, grandchildren, and great grandchildren that fill our lives with joy."

This section is aimed to correct the misconception that a good marriage is automatic. Couples with problems look at happy couples as if the latter simply enjoy good fortune; that's far from the truth. Even a marriage between two righteous people of impeccable character is plagued with its share of tension and disagreements. Any human being must learn to compromise and sacrifice in order to make peace with a second human being.

Many marital counselors teach that marriage is give-and-take. According to Chassidic and Jewish esoteric thought, it's only giving.

The eye of emuna

Since the purpose of creation is emuna, and the Creator wants each of us to fulfill our purpose, He therefore presents us with opportunities to learn and to develop emuna. Marriage is the prime proving ground of emuna. Therefore, by learning the principles of emuna, one maximizes the chances of success in marriage.

Conversely, the lack of emuna is the root cause of divorce. A person with emuna can overcome marital strife by way of teshuva and prayer; those who lack training in emuna often resort to divorce as a solution to their problems.

Usually, divorce doesn't clean a person's slate of problems. The old set of problems (tension in the home, quarreling, and the like) are simply replaced by a new set of problems (lawyers, nasty hearings, alimony, child support, property and financial battles, and so on). More often than not, the divorce-related problems are worse than the marital problems were.

Without emuna, unhappily married people blame their troubles on a long list of culprits from a lying matchmaker to nasty in-laws and bad luck. But, with emuna in Hashem's Divine Providence, a person realizes that his or her own transgressions are the cause of their suffering, for there are no tribulations without transgression. So, with teshuva and with basic coaching on how the Torah expects a person to act in a marital relationship, anyone is capable of marital success.

As long as a person fails to make teshuva and rectify past misdeeds, marital suffering is perpetuated. The best marital counseling won't help a person that fails to make teshuva; it's like pouring fine wine into a filthy glass. Without teshuva, divorce won't bring relief to a person either.

No one can escape from Hashem. Consequently, divorce without teshuva only makes a person's life more unbearable. Rebbe Nachman of Breslev once remarked that if a person isn't prepared to suffer a bit, then he or she will suffer a lot.

Marital problems are a test of faith. A couple should know that once they reach the *chuppa* together, they are soulmates with a mutual soul correction. With proper efforts, they can attain perfection. But, the road to marital bliss is bumpy at times. Without emuna, many married people want to get off the train as soon as the ride isn't 100% smooth – nothing could be a bigger mistake!

Proper marital instruction

As long as two people are still married, almost any problem can be solved. Once they're divorced, nothing is solved.

Proper marital instruction has saved thousands of couples. The author's tapes and CDs on marital coaching have even saved hundreds of couples, even those that had already started divorce proceedings. These lessons are so cogent that the author refuses to listen to people's marital complaints until after they've first listened to his lessons on the subject. Without proper marital instruction, problems simply recur.

With instruction on emuna, teshuva, and the Jewish marriage, couples cast away thoughts of divorce. The standard reaction to our method of marital instruction is, "What a pity that I didn't learn these things before! I'd have saved myself so much suffering..."

End of the war, or the beginning?

People idealize divorce as a magical solution to their problems. Let's see if that's really true:

Divorce is not the end of the war, like many think; it's only the beginning of strife that lasts for a lifetime. New problems and new tensions continually sprout, especially in the areas of educating their mutual children. Family affairs, such as weddings and Bar Mitzvas, become nightmares. Former spouses are placed in embarrassing situations where they have to encounter former and frequently hostile in-laws. Second wives and husbands are forced to mingle with ex-wives and husbands. As such, divorcees usually dread affairs that married people eagerly anticipate their entire lives.

Every time a divorced couple has to meet again, such as on the occasion of a child's graduation or family affair, old wounds are torn open. Long-forgotten memories return to haunt them. When they see their "ex" with a new spouse, jealousy and bitterness eat away at their hearts. Mixed feelings of anger and revenge rob them of their happiness.

Conflicting interests in the divorced couple's relationship with their mutual children is a minefield of problems. Even with contractual agreement and court orders, visitation always presents practical problems and becomes a bone of contention. Money and child support are even worse; new problems always arise that weren't defined in the divorce agreement, such as who will pay for the child's summer camp or swimming lessons. No one is ever happy. Divorcees are known to manipulate children as weapons. Everyone in the family suffers.

Those people who come in contact with divorcees – such as rabbinical advisors – know how terribly divorcees suffer.

Divorced couples have extreme difficulty in coping with routine problems - such as a child's health or learning impairment – that married couples take in stride. Such challenges also trigger arguments and accusations, where one side accuses the other of neglecting the children, not loving them, and so forth.

In short, as long as a person is married – no matter how difficult the situation – things can be corrected. Once there's no more home, there's no love, unity, or base to build upon; problems fester and become worse.

The wounded heart

Divorcees frequently wake up after the fact. Once the divorce is completed, many divorcees feel a gaping wound in their heart. They have difficulty adjusting to their new situation, for the pangs of longing and loneliness give them no rest. When the smoke of the divorce battle clears, they find themselves more miserable without their mate than they were while still married.

The Torah calls a writ of divorce *gett kritot*, literally translated, "a writ of severance." This is most appropriate, since according to Jewish spiritual thought, the souls of two married people are actually two halves of a whole. So, when the two split up, their souls are severed from one another; this is tantamount to undergoing heart surgery with no anesthetic – it's torture!

Loneliness lingers. Before the divorce, people tend to entertain all types of fantasies about the rosy future and the dream second-marriage that awaits them. Once the divorce is over, they discover that their personal value on the mate market is a lot lower than they previously thought. Men aren't standing in line for divorced women, especially those with children. Conversely, women are wary of divorced men. Divorce is a serious stigma that complicates finding a new mate.

Divorcees won't admit it, but many of them regret their divorces and would turn the clocks back in time if they only could.

Remove anger from your heart

The emotional wounds of numerous divorcees manifest themselves in rage, insult, and compulsive feelings of revenge. The hatred and anger that they harbor toward their ex-mates act like emotional acid that corrodes the walls of their hearts.

As long as one side harbors hatred, both sides will suffer. Hatred and anger invoke stern judgments both on the person who hates and on the hated. Therefore, from a spiritual standpoint, a divorce solves nothing when hate and resentment linger on afterwards.

While still married, it's much easier to make peace. After a divorce, forgiving and forgetting – a must for both sides in order to rebuild their broken lives – is virtually impossible.

The real solution

Before taking the irreversible step of divorce, stop and think: With some basic instruction and good will, a person can save his or her own life as well as the lives of their children. They'll also save tens, even hundreds of thousands of dollars. All they need is to swallow a bit of pride and to express the willingness to start anew.

The author's recorded CDs on marriage counseling that have saved hundreds of marriages in Israel are now available in English worldwide. These recordings should be heard over and over until the principles of a happy marriage become second nature.

Ignorance

Most divorces are caused by the husband's ignorance of the principles of peace in the home. For example, a husband that isn't guilty of extreme behavior – he's not a wife beater or a criminal, makes a living, and is faithful – can still fall on his face in marriage if he criticizes and is constantly finding fault with his wife. He turns her life into a living death.

With even minimal instruction on marital success, a husband will learn that the **first rule of peace in the home is to refrain from criticizing his wife, even when the situation is perfectly justified**. A woman wants to feel loved and respected; criticism – even the slightest – does the opposite. Even worse, it makes a woman nervous and destroys her self confidence. By criticism and finding fault, a husband destroys both his wife and his marriage with his own two hands. The author has saved untold marriages by coaching husbands on this point alone.

After criticism, the second culprit behind unhappy marriage is the **husband's unwillingness and/or impatience to listen to his wife**. With no mate to talk to or to share the burdens that weigh heavy on her heart, a wife is doomed to frustration and unhappiness. When she sees how her husband animatedly listens to other people, she becomes sorely insulted. Her entire aspirations in marriage were to find a soul-mate that would make her happy and illuminate her soul. With a husband that doesn't respect or cherish her enough to give her minimal attention, she loses all will to stay married.

Children are not even a consolation for a woman that feels unloved, neglected, and disrespected. Even though she has a deep dread of divorce, she'll demand it at all costs when she sees a hopeless future. A woman prefers loneliness to a purgatory of constant criticism and humiliation.

After the powder keg has blown, the amazed but ignorant husband shrugs his shoulders in innocence and asks, "What did I do wrong?"

He can't possibly know how he broke the rules of *shalom bayit* if he never learned them.

Here's good news: It's never too late to learn. Now is the time to add emuna in our lives.

This chapter hasn't presumed to cover all of life's test situations, but by applying the principles of emuna that we've practiced in this chapter, we're certainly better prepared to meet any and all of life's challenges.

The many tests

Until now, we've elaborated on a few of the main types of emuna challenges. The lessons we learned can be applied to every area of our lives. For example:

Buying or selling a house or apartment – even when the purchase or sale of your home goes smoothly, this is no easy process. One needs considerable patience and emuna, for many problems are liable to arise on the way. Sometimes the contract signing is delayed or cancelled altogether. Meanwhile, one may have bought, sold, or rented a new house or apartment. Maybe the other side is late with a payment, causing you to be delinquent on your new payment schedule. The numbers of things that can go wrong defy description.

One must believe that all the difficulties are exactly what Hashem wants, and therefore refrain from getting angry, nervous, or depressed. Hashem sends difficulties as an indication that we have something to correct, so we should utilize our energy in trying to understand Hashem's messages by devoting time to personal prayer and introspection. Strengthening emuna will also save us from bickering and falling into needless legal battles that will only deplete our time and money. As soon as a person realizes that difficulties are from Hashem and react with prayer and teshuva, the difficulties amazingly work themselves out.

Feuds with neighbors – relations with neighbors are catastrophic when based on power and not on emuna. Some feuds last for years. But, with emuna, neighbors readily compromise and bridge gaps, so everything turns out for the best.

Disagreements - Rebbe Nachman of Breslev teaches (see Likutei Moharan I:258) that when people gang up against someone, they can make him fall from his spiritual level and ruin his emuna, Heaven forbid. We can therefore understand what King David said in Psalm 119, "Many have persecuted, but I have not wavered from Your laws." Despite King David's many opponents and enemies, he never veered in the slightest from his service of Hashem.

Having people against you is a difficult test of faith. A person with weak emuna will succumb to feelings of hatred, vengeance, and a burning desire to retaliate. Such negative emotions will only distance him further from Hashem. But, with emuna, a person will pray to Hashem and let Hashem fight his battles. Eventually, the enemies fall by the wayside.

Job hunting – this is a challenge that's often accompanied with frustration, disappointment, insult, and bitterness. But, when a person looks for a job and applies emuna to his search, the process becomes simple and pleasant. He knows that any rejection is from Hashem because that particular place of employment would be detrimental in some way.

In general – life throws many tests of emuna in our path. In fact, every single difficulty in our lives is a test of emuna. One needn't feel blame or feelings of inadequacy. Therefore, there's no need to persecute yourself. Accept that your difficulties are all from Hashem to facilitate and to stimulate your spiritual growth, and all for the best. Every time a person successfully passes a test of emuna, he or she moves up another rung in the spiritual ladder, assuring a better life in this world and in the next.

The four sons – substitute for suffering

There's a way to mitigate or to altogether neutralize our suffering and tribulations in this world, as we'll see in the following example:

A father punishes his son. If the son is stupid, he bears malice in his heart toward his father and hates him.

If this son has some sense, he understands that he was punished for a reason, even though he doesn't like the punishment. When he realizes what he did wrong, he admits his wrongdoing, expresses his remorse, apologizes, and promises to improve his ways. Even if he doesn't understand exactly what he did wrong, he asks his father's forgiveness in a general manner and says, "I'm sorry for upsetting you, Dad – help me to avoid making the same mistakes in the future."

A truly intelligent son realizes that his father loves him and that the punishment was for his ultimate benefit. He therefore willfully accepts the punishment, turns to his father and says: "Dad, I know that your intent was to wake me up and to bring me closer to you. Thanks so much for paying such close attention to me – that really means a lot to me. Dad, please explain to me what I did wrong and help me improve…" Once the father shows the son his mistake, the son expresses remorse, admits the mistake, asks his father's forgiveness, and makes a firm resolution to do better in the future.

The third son is on a lofty level of spiritual awareness. He appreciates tribulations since he recognizes that he has deficiencies that need correcting.

Then again, there's a fourth son who surpasses all of his three brothers. He doesn't wait to be punished in order to improve his ways. Every day, he does a thorough process of self-evaluation where he weighs everything he did that day and asks himself if his deeds are really upright in light of his father's requests and standards. He then speaks to his father every single day and says, "Dad, by virtue of the wonderful education you gave me, I was fortunate in doing such-and-such good deeds. Thanks so much. On the other hand, I don't think my speech or behavior in a certain situation today was the way you would have wanted. I'm really sorry and I'll try my best to strengthen this weakness…"

The father of such a son glows with satisfaction and gratification. "What a beautiful human being! What a sensitive, considerate, and humble son! He doesn't wait for me to punish him – he's always trying to improve. Even if he were to do something seriously wrong, how could I punish him? He's constantly evaluating himself; he's always striving to fulfill my wishes. So, even if he does make a mistake, I'll just give him a gentle hint. With his sensitivity, he'll surely understand." The father will want nothing more than to fulfill this wonderful son's wishes.

Continuing to ponder his sons, the father says, "I wish my other three boys would come and speak to me on their own initiative every day. If they only realized how much I loved them, they'd ask for whatever they want and I'd be happy to give it to them. Even my son that bears malice toward me would realize how much I love him if he would only speak with me every day."

The loving son

Imagine a loving son or daughter that thanks a parent profusely every single day for every little amenity that he or she received. Imagine that the same son or daughter always confesses wrongdoing without having to be reprimanded. If that's not enough, the son or daughter always seeks more and more of the parent's love. If this were your child, how in the world could you ever punish him?

We can now understand how to be Hashem's beloved sons and daughters. All we have to do is to set aside an hour a day for prayer in solitude, whether out in the field, in the office or in the kitchen at home, and speak to Hashem – our beloved Father in Heaven – in our own words. We take stock of everything we did in the previous twenty-four hours since our last session of *hitbodedut*, or personal prayer in solitude. We judge ourselves on three levels – thoughts, speech, and deeds. We rectify our wrongdoings and resolve to improve. We ask Hashem to bring us closer to Him. Such a process of personal prayer frees a person from stress, worry, sadness, and all other negative emotions. Even better, when we judge ourselves, Hashem doesn't let the Heavenly court judge us, and we save ourselves untold anguish and severe judgments.

Pay attention

One who devotes an hour a day to personal prayer is on an even higher spiritual level than a person who accepts his tribulations with joy, for the former doesn't wait to be aroused by tribulations; he seeks to serve Hashem more and more on his own accord.

The Gemara says (tractate Berachot 7), that one measure of self-discipline is more effective than a hundred lashes. As such, the self-disciplined person saves himself limitless troubles in life.

Dear reader, stop and think about the wonderful gift that Hashem has given us by enabling us to speak to Him whenever we want to, any time day or night. We can now begin to understand what Rebbe Nachman of Breslev meant when he said that *hitbodedut* is more virtuous than literally anything else!

The power of simple prayer

An hour of *hitbodedut* and soul-searching is so cogent that it can protect the entire world. Rebbe Nachman of Breslev once said (Sichot HaRan, 70), "How do we allow Hashem to bring harsh decrees to the world? We must call Hashem away from all His other tasks. We must draw Him away from decreeing harsh decrees to the world. We must tell Him to put everything else aside and listen to us, for we want to ask Him to draw us close. For when a person wishes to speak to Hashem, He casts aside everything else. Evil decrees are even set aside at this time. Hashem puts aside everything and only listens to the person seeking His presence."

The amazing meaning of the above discourse is that any person – man, woman, or child, regardless of their current spiritual status, even the lowest and most contemptible person on earth – has the basic right to approach G-d and to speak to Him! Not only that, but Hashem listens! And who knows – maybe this very minute, some terrorist's or tyrant's evil designs are being foiled because the local street cleaner is talking to Hashem. If people would be speaking to Hashem round-the-clock, there could be no harsh decrees in the world.

A group of students in the Lubliner Yeshiva in Poland had a twenty-four hour personal prayer vigil. One of the young men would always be engaged in *hitbodedut*. For some reason, the police detained one of the boys and the chain of continuous personal prayer was broken. On that day, the holocaust began.

Dear reader, *hitbodedut* is both pleasant and gratifying. It's not difficult, either. Could there be anything more ideal than speaking to the all-powerful King who can give you anything you want?

Imagine that the leading and most prestigious matchmaker in the vicinity calls a single young man for an hour's conversation. Who would refuse such a meeting? Imagine getting an hour's audience with a Bronfman or a Rothschild, or some other multi-millionaire that might be in a position to help you financially. Who would be too lazy to meet such a person? Imagine giving a sick person the opportunity to seek the advice of the world's leading doctor. What daft person wouldn't take advantage of such a chance? Our hour of solitary personal prayer is an hour with the all-powerful King and Master of the World, Physician of all flesh, in whose loving hands are life, livelihood, our soul-mate, or anything else we need!

Speaking to Hashem is one-stop shopping for all our aspirations, needs, and all our heart's wishes.

For those of our readers that have not yet experienced the joy of personal solitary prayer, we'd like to emphasize that it's tailor made – that's why it's called **personal** prayer. You can speak to Hashem anywhere, anytime, and in any language. Use your local slang even, and speak in any way that makes you comfortable. You can stand or sit, or even lie in your bed under the covers. Make yourself comfortable, and speak your heart out. You can tell Hashem anything you like.

Drop everything else

If that's the story, then why isn't everyone talking to Hashem? Why are there so many obstacles to something so beautiful and natural?

The answer is that the *Yetzer Hara*, the Evil Inclination knows the value of personal prayer. He knows that it's the ultimate expression of emuna and the fulfillment of our very purpose on earth! He knows that a person who does daily *hitbodedut* will attain a full soul correction and overcome the obstacles and difficulties of life in this world. For that reason, the Evil Inclination does his utmost to weaken a person and discourage him from doing any solitary personal prayer. He tells you, "What, are you crazy? What do you think you'll accomplish by wasting an hour and talking to the trees. Besides, since when do you have a spare hour?" The Evil Inclination gives you one-hundred eight different reasons for not talking to Hashem in personal prayer.

Our wise readers will surely conclude that no matter what, we have to drop everything else and designate an hour for personal prayer. Daily personal prayer is a new lease on life, a special sweetness! As in the previous example of the four sons, Hashem's greatest gratification is when His beloved sons and daughters approach

Him daily with personal prayer, self-evaluation, and requests for everything they need. Even if they don't succeed in rectifying everything they need to, Hashem waits patiently and doesn't punish them.

One of the most important items on our daily personal prayer agenda is asking Hashem to help us strengthen our emuna, as in the following sample personal prayer:

Please Hashem, give me complete emuna. Help me believe that there's no evil in the world, that everything is in Your hands and that everything is for the best. Give me the emuna that You love me just the way I am, and that You derive gratification from me.

Give me the complete emuna that there is no one but You, in other words, anything that distresses me is simply a rod in Your hand in order to arouse me to seek Your proximity. Give me the complete emuna that there's no one to blame for my troubles – not my wife, nor my in-laws, nor my boss – my moments of displeasure in life are all wake-up calls from You, beloved Father.

Give me the complete emuna that there's no need to torture myself and to tear myself down. Help me direct my energies into the positive endeavor of prayer, and help me believe in the power of my prayers. Beloved Father, help me feel that You are with me – there is no greater gift or feeling. Help me scrap my bad habits and to do Your will. Give me the desire to pray, and help me realize that all my spiritual and material deficiencies are merely the result of insufficient prayer.

Give me the emuna that everything is in Your hands, Hashem. Let my principle efforts be channeled in the direction of prayer, and let me depend on Your magnificent loving kindness and not on my sorely limited ability and aptitude. Let the prayers flow forth from my heart, soul, and lips always...

Rabbi Levi Yitzchak Binder of blessed and saintly memory told me that when a person ascends to the Heavenly Court after his one-hundred-twenty-year go-round on this earth, the Heavenly Judges will open a big book – the story of that person's life, where every thought, utterance, and deed is recorded. Each page represents a day in that person's life. On every page where it's written that the person did an hour of personal prayer, the page is turned and that person is not judged for anything he may have done wrong on that day. But, on a day with no *hitbodedut*, the person is meticulously judged for every thought, utterance, and deed of that particular day.

Now we know why the Evil Inclination puts up such a fight against personal prayer. Every day is a new war for our hour of *hitbodedut*. For that reason, we have to be courageous and not give in. *Hitbodedut* is the gate to connecting with Hashem!

Chapter Four

The Virtues of Emuna

The virtues of emuna are so vast that they defy description. Emuna is the root and foundation of a person's task in this world. As such, every one of us needs to reinforce his or her emuna. By strengthening emuna, we perfect our character. Rebbe Nachman of Breslev teaches that emuna is the leg that the entire world stands upon.

Emuna is the spiritual vessel for Divine abundance, invoking the best blessings of health, personal welfare, and livelihood.

Emuna is a mighty spiritual force. With simple and pure emuna, one longs for a greater connection to Hashem, and rises to higher spiritual heights.

Emuna is the foundation of holiness. One who attains emuna achieves a purification of the soul.

Emuna brings a person to the level of true patience, composure, and inner peace; in the context of such an emotional climate, a person maximizes his or her intellectual and functional potential to the hilt.

Rebbe Nachman of Breslev teaches (*Sefer HaMidot, emuna*) that emuna brings blessings into a person's life. Emuna gives a person an enhanced spiritual insight and awareness, enabling one to more readily understand the rationale behind the events in their environment.

By virtue of emuna, not only is one forgiven for all transgressions, but harsh edicts are overturned.

Rebbe Nachman of Breslev writes (*Likutei Moharan I:7*) that a lack of emuna perpetuates the Diaspora and exile. Conversely, enhanced emuna hastens the full redemption of our people.

The descent of the soul to this world

The soul is a tiny spark of Hashem within each and every one of us. In the non-tangible upper worlds of pure spirituality, the soul is able to bask in the sublime delight of Divine illumination, an unfathomable pleasure that makes any physical pleasure seem like darkness and disgust.

Superficially, the soul in its original non-corporal state seems close to Hashem; in truth, though, the soul is distant from Hashem because it has not yet acquired the knowledge of Hashem. The soul – before its descent to the lowly material world - simply knows of the existence of this wonderful, indescribably pleasurable spiritual illumination, but nothing of the illumination's source or nature.

Imagine that you meet a wonderful person that reflects goodness, wisdom, calm, and compassion. Even though you don't know anything about this particular individual, you'd be interested to know more.

In the spiritual realm, there is no evil inclination, no difficulties, no trials and no tribulations. The soul basks in magnificently gratifying Divine light – it needs nothing else. The soul in such a state doesn't ask for mercy, for Divine compassion, for assistance, or for forgiveness. It has no needs and therefore doesn't have the opportunity to become acquainted with Hashem's attributes.

The entire purpose behind Hashem's creation of the world is to reveal His Divine compassion to His creations. Rebbe Nachman of Breslevwrites (*Likutei Moharan I:64)*, "Hashem created the world by virtue of His compassion, for He desired to reveal His compassion, for with no creation, to whom could He show His infinite compassion? For this reason, He created the universe – from the loftiest spiritual realm to the lowest order of materialism – in order to reveal His compassion."

Since the purpose of creation is to reveal Hashem's compassion, we can only get to know Hashem by descending to this world.

Here, we need His Divine compassion every single second, seek it, recognize it, and thereby fulfill the purpose of creation.

A pleasure to meet you!

Let's clarify the above concept with the following anecdote:

> The Rabbi of Tulchin once complained to his teacher and spiritual guide, Rebbe Nathan of Breslov: "I'm sorry that I didn't have the privilege of knowing Rebbe Nachman of Breslev personally."
>
> Rebbe Nathan answered sternly, "And who has the audacity to think that they 'know' their Rebbe? Yosef Frunick?"
>
> Yosef Frunick was a simpleton that operated a ferry on the river. All day long, he'd transfer people from one side of the river to the other. Rebbe Nachman of Breslev used Yosef Frunick's services frequently. Yosef therefore enjoyed boasting, "O-ho, I used to spend a lot of time with Rebbe Nachman - I knew him well!"

Rebbe Nathan desired to stress that a physical knowledge of someone or something is meaningless. Yosef Frunick knew what Rebbe Nachman looked like, but he hadn't the slightest idea about Rebbe Nachman's enormous spiritual stature. To begin to know Rebbe Nachman, explained Rebbe Nathan, one must learn and practice his teachings. Therefore, a disciple in a latter generation can know a *tzaddik* better than a contemporary acquaintance that saw him in the flesh.

Yosef Frunick not only saw Rebbe Nachman; he actually touched him several times while assisting him on and off the ferry. Yet, physical proximity has nothing to do with spiritual awareness. In effect, the simple and crass ferryman was as far removed from the *tzaddik* as east is to west. He had no idea of Rebbe Nachman's holiness, his wisdom, his teachings, his spiritual prowess, his capabilities, and the breadth of his holy soul. He simply helped him cross the river.

The same principle applies to the knowledge of Hashem: The soul in the upper worlds takes pleasure in the light of Hashem without knowing anything about Hashem. It therefore resembles the ferryman who boasted that he knew Rebbe Nachman, when in reality, he knew nothing more than the color of Rebbe Nachman's beard.

Rebbe Nachman himself defines proximity as spiritual awareness *(see Likutei Moharan I: 21)*, when he writes, "By virtue of spiritual awareness – the knowledge of Hashem – one achieves a oneness with Hashem." Therefore, by seeking a connection with Hashem in the physical world, one can actually get to know Hashem better than the mere proximity to Hashem in the spiritual world. It may not be apparent, but Hashem's presence is everywhere; the advantage of the material world is that it enables spiritual gain, whereas the spiritual world does not. This is an apparent contradiction, but a cardinal principle of spirituality.

In the material world, we need Hashem constant assistance, especially to successfully weather the trials and tribulations of this world. This is the environment where our souls can really tell Hashem, "A pleasure to meet you!"

By the sweat of your brow

No one likes to feel like a beggar. We receive gratification by knowing that we earned what we have. For that reason, the soul actually desires to descend to the "war zone" of the material world in order to rightfully earn a lofty place in the proximity of Hashem where it can bask in Divine light. As long as the untried and unproven soul derives unearned pleasure in the spiritual world, it is sorely embarrassed in front of those souls who have rightfully earned their places. Since Hashem wants the soul to have complete pleasure, He gives it the opportunity to achieve the status it desires.

Concealment

When the soul descends to this world, it falls into an abyss of spiritual darkness, where Divine light is hidden within layer after layer of concealment. A thinking person asks, "How can the soul possibly find Hashem and get close to Him in an environment where everything seems to hide or deny Hashem's very existence?" We see with our own eyes that few people – even so-called "religious" people – succeed in cutting through the layers of darkness and concealment to reveal Hashem's splendid illumination.

Let's look for an answer by examining the various layers of concealment, as follows:

First concealment - nature: The laws of nature appear absolute, and therefore conceal Hashem's individual Divine Providence over each creation. We would think that if Hashem wanted to make His presence apparent through the material world, He'd perform many more miracles so that everyone would make no mistake about His existence and reign.

Second concealment - humans: Human beings obstruct Hashem's illumination and emuna; since they have free choice, they are able to do what they want when they want. When they lie or steal, a bolt of lightning doesn't appear from the sky to kill them. When they help a blind or crippled person cross the street, an angel doesn't dive down to earth in order to put a $100,000 check in their pocket. On the surface of things, Hashem doesn't react to their good or evil, so where's Hashem? Even worse, since most people have no idea what emuna is, their speech and outlook reflects heresy and agnosticism. Why doesn't Hashem make it easier to believe in Him?

Third concealment – the body: The physical body that hosts the soul is the coarsest form of material matter, with needs, drives, and lusts that pull in the exact opposite direction of spirituality and Godliness. The body strongly gravitates toward physical amenities and further conceals Hashem's Divine light from the soul. Why must the body be so crass? Couldn't Hashem have created a more spiritually-refined and receptive body, so that it would be easier to recognize Hashem?

Fourth concealment – trials and tribulations: Life in this world conceals the presence of Hashem in many ways. The Hebrew word for world, *olam,* is a derivative from the world *he'elem*, or concealment. The trials and tribulations of daily life – financial difficulties, sickness, crime, international strife, emotional pressures, and many more – all conceal Hashem's lovingkindness. Terror, fatal accidents, crippled children, and other apparent injustices and human suffering render emuna nearly impossible. Where is Hashem?

Couldn't Hashem have made life easier on us, without holocausts, tsunamis, and terrorist bombing?

Fifth concealment – Torah and mitzvoth: The Torah and mitzvoth are themselves the most difficult concealments of Hashem's light, for on the surface of things, many commandments hamper a person from living in this world. For example, even if we sorely need the money, we're not allowed to work on the Sabbath. We're required to fast on certain days, even when the weather's hot and dry. During the early morning hours – the best and most productive work time – we have to put on tallit and tefillin and pray. Even though we have urgent business to attend to, we're required to devote time to learning Torah.

It seems that the Torah and the mitzvoth are totally incongruous with life in this world. From a mundane standpoint, they simply hamper and limit a person, making a hard life even more difficult. Why didn't Hashem adapt the Torah more to life in this world?

From the standpoint of emuna, the Torah and mitzvoth facilitate a person's success and happiness in the world. Yet, most people are incapable of looking at the world from the standpoint of emuna. Why does Hashem give them room for confusion and error?

The biggest concealment lies in the lack of clarity as to what exactly constitutes Hashem's will and a Torah lifestyle. Even rabbis disagree as to what Hashem wants from us. Even worse, from those who choose a Torah lifestyle, few truly succeed in getting close to Hashem.

Do you feel like screaming? Doesn't all this sound unfair? Everything seems to work against us in our search for Hashem and for emuna. Doors of difficulties shut in our faces and the entire world seems to be pitched against us to prevent us from feeling Hashem's presence in our lives. We're bombarded with agnostic and atheistic stimuli from morning until night. We turn to Hashem's Torah for consolation, and even it seems to push us away. Why does the Torah have to be so unclear, and open to such a wide range of argument and interpretation? What's a person supposed to do?

If the purpose of the soul's descent to the material world is to get to know Hashem, then why is it such a difficult task? Couldn't life be made easier? It looks like the soul is fighting a losing battle. Why?

Discovery

The constant struggle of life in this material world is exactly what drives a person to seek Hashem.

As soon as we realize our futility against all the forces in the world that work against us, we become modest. Modesty is an important prerequisite for emuna, since a modest person knows that one is incapable of navigating the troubled waters of this world without Hashem's help. Consequently, we turn to Hashem, and develop a strong desire to feel Hashem's comforting influence in our lives.

Modesty, emuna, and desire are basically one entity. The recognition of our limitations leads to modesty, modesty leads to emuna, and emuna invokes a strong desire and longing for Hashem. Once our emuna is developed to the point where we actively seek Hashem, life becomes sweet and gratifying, despite the tribulations.

Why wait for times of trouble? The more we truly seek Hashem, the more we improve the quality of our lives. Even if we don't suffer from any earth-shaking difficulties, we should nevertheless turn to Hashem on a regular basis. Our Talmudic sages teach that we should constantly thank Hashem for the past and cry out for the future (*tractate Brachot, 54a*). By regularly speaking to Hashem – thanking for the past and requesting for the future, even in good times when things are going our way – we begin to feel Hashem's Divine Providence and His magnificent compassion in every breath we take.

Now, imagine that you're 100% healthy, you have all the money you want, you're successful in everything you do, people look up to you, and you do and buy whatever you want whenever you want. Sound like a blessing? It's not – on the contrary, it's a curse. Many famous, rich, and successful people succumbed to despair, emptiness, substance abuse, and even suicide, for they failed to seek Hashem. The loneliest existence on earth is a life without Hashem, G-d forbid.

So, when Hashem sends us troubles as a reminder to seek Him, He's doing us a tremendous service. Yet, if we're wise enough to seek Hashem when our lives are progressing on a positive mode, then Hashem doesn't have to resort to trials and tribulations in order to awaken us from spiritual slumber.

As soon we contemplate the purpose of life and realize that the chase after material gratification leads to nowhere, we are ready to channel our desires and energies into satisfying the needs of the soul and seeking the proximity of Hashem. With spiritual eyes that gaze toward the ultimate objective of life, apparent troubles in this world suddenly become valuable opportunities for spiritual growth that enable us to incorporate Hashem into our lives.

When we discover that our life's purpose is to get to know Hashem, life becomes sweet, gratifying, and meaningful. Attributing everything to Hashem smoothes out life's bumpiness – we thank Hashem for our successes and don't despair about our failures. We take advantage of life's trying times to strengthen our relationship with Hashem. Suddenly, we discover that every stimulus in our environment is a tiny message from Hashem calling us to come closer. Nothing is sweeter than receiving a personal message from our glorious and compassionate Father in Heaven.

Once we develop the awareness that our environment is Hashem's way of talking to us, we sharpen our perception to the events in our lives. A person that's receptive to Hashem's messages is constantly reacting to whatever Hashem is relaying. For example, they construe one event as a message to correct a certain flaw, or another occurrence as a wake-up call to make teshuva. Their lives become one harmonious story of constant spiritual gain.

Difficult situations require reinforcement of emuna. When we remember that trials and tribulations are designed to bring us closer to Hashem, and not to cast us away, we weather them much more easily and successfully.

Hashem created the world in order to reveal His limitless compassion. By getting closer to Hashem, we gain a better understanding and insight into His vast goodness. So, when we remember that our struggles and suffering are designed to bring us closer to Hashem, we avoid falling into the traps of anger, anxiety, and despair. On the contrary, we run even faster to Hashem.

Slowly but surely

People ask a basic question: If Hashem wants me to get closer to Him, why doesn't He simply reveal Himself to me?

Imagine that the electric company wanted to save money, so they closed down their transformers and relay stations, and sent a direct cable from their main generator to your house. When you'd turn on the switch to your 100-watt bulb in the living room, 50,000 watts of power would come through the cable. The bulb would burst to smithereens in a split second. Even worse, the cables in your walls would explode, and the whole house could catch fire. For that reason, the electricity can't reach your home without a series of transformers, circuit breakers, and relays that reduce the core power of the generated electricity to a measure that you can safely use.

By the same token, Hashem's Divine light is infinite and unlimited. For our own benefit, Hashem doesn't give us an illumination that is too strong for our souls to handle, otherwise we'd "burn out" - die, become insane, or lose our faith altogether, Heaven forbid. Consequently, Hashem – like a good coach – gives us opportunities to strengthen our spiritual selves so that we'll be sturdy enough vessels to receive an increased portion of Divine light.

Every time a person undergoes a test of faith, overcomes an obstacle in his or her performance of a mitzvah, or fights against temptation and bodily urges, he or she strengthens their soul and becomes a proper vessel for increased Divine light. The greater the illumination, the closer one gets to Hashem and vice versa. As we come closer to Hashem, life becomes ever so sweeter.

The Talmud tells the story (*see tractate Chagiga 14b*) of four sages that entered the "citrus grove", allegoric of the upper spiritual worlds. One died, one went insane, and one lost his faith altogether. Only Rabbi Akiva entered safely and returned safely. The first three lacked the spiritual vessels that were required for such a high-level exposure of Divine light. Rabbi Akiva, on the other hand, had reinforced his spiritual self to the extent that the illumination not only did not damage him; it was gratifying to him, since he was a proper vessel for such a level of Divine light.

Rabbi Akiva was the son of poor converts. He exerted tremendous effort in refining himself during his transformation from common peasant to monumental Torah scholar with tens of thousands of disciples. Rabbi Akiva couldn't rely on a blue-blooded pedigree or a father that was a great rabbi. Spiritually, he was a self-made man. At forty, he began the long road of Torah and teshuva, hampered by indescribable difficulties, poverty, and limited natural learning capabilities. The Gemorra teaches us that he spilled rivers of tears in begging Hashem to enable him to learn and comprehend the Torah. He was so poor that he slept in a barn. But, the disadvantages of his life fueled his burning desire to get close to Hashem. Through years of effort, deprivation, suffering at the hands of the Romans, and being cast away by his father in law, Rabbi Akiva continued slowly but surely in his tenacious and relentless efforts to learn Torah and to refine his soul. As such, he became an exquisite vessel of spirituality that far exceeded his better-advantaged contemporaries.

Rabbi Akiva's three colleagues had easier lives than he did; each of them came from families of high social standing and each was a great scholar in his own right. But, they lacked Rabbi Akiva's depth of spiritual strength and were therefore damaged by an excess of Divine light.

Knowing that our difficulties in life are the vehicles that actually strengthen our souls and bring us closer to Hashem, we become girded with the strength to handle any situation. What could be a bigger encouragement than knowing that Hashem wants to bring us closer to Him? So, when we look at our lives through eyes of emuna, we instantly become both stronger and happier.

Don't be jealous of someone that has an easy life – that's not a prize. Any champion athlete knows that without pain, there's no gain. People that haven't been tested are very limited in their capability to understand faith or to get close to Hashem.

Now that we realize that benefits of life's difficulties, we can clearly understand why Hashem sent our souls to this lowly material world.

Your path

Life's difficulties serve another important purpose – they help lead each of us on the path of our individual mission on earth. If we don't understand the underlying message within the trying situations we encounter, then all we have to do is ask Hashem to guide us and help us understand. With relentless personal prayer, we are assured of finding our individual path in the world.

Looking for the light

Every time we use the power of prayer to overcome a difficult situation, we enhance our awareness of Hashem's magnitude. Stress and anxiety result from a lack of spiritual awareness that's tantamount to darkness. Recognition of Hashem is the light that illuminates the darkness. Consequently, when we "look for the light," in other words, when we search for the Divine message within tribulations and realize that Hashem is using them to stimulate our personal and spiritual growth, despair becomes hope. Life's overwhelming situations become challenges that we're ready to meet when we look for the light within the darkness.

My soul thirsts

We live in a world that conceals and diminishes Hashem's light. Our bodies block and subdue the Divine illumination of our souls.

Yet, life's trying times are what cause the soul to yearn for its Creator. Since the soul is spiritual, it thirsts for Godliness. Nothing can satiate it other than Hashem's Divine light, as King David wrote (*Psalms 42:3*), "My soul thirsts for Hashem, for the living God."

The soul derives virtually no gratification from material amenities. A long list of celebrities who had everything a person could dream of – money, vacation homes, swimming pools and tennis courts in their back yards, fame, and literally anything that money could buy – yet many of them became insane or committed suicide. They had everything but they had nothing.

When the soul feels darkness, it becomes restless. The feeling of unrest, emptiness, and a squirming sensation in the abdomen indicates the soul's longing for Hashem. By searching for Hashem's light, the soul attains proximity to Hashem. Hashem illuminates the soul's darkness, thus helping the soul to overcome its difficulties. As a result, the soul gets to know, love, and appreciate Hashem more and more.

An ongoing saga of difficulties

The more a person has problems, the more he or she is likely to seek Hashem, just as a person in darkness seeks the light. Even if a person seeks Hashem just for the sake of relief, and not for the loftier motive of adding Godliness to his or her life, they still discover Hashem's infinite mercy and compassion.

The Talmud says (*tractate Nedarim 81a*), "Beware of the sons of the poor, for they shall become the scholars of Torah." The struggles of lads from impoverished families stimulate them from a young age to seek Hashem; they subsequently develop a strong measure of emuna and thirst for Torah.

King David suffered untold difficulties from a tender age and thereby sought Hashem constantly, ultimately reaching the level of a prophet and Hashem's anointed. He composed The Book of Psalms, the world's foremost collection of personal prayers. Our sages teach us that our ancestral mothers Sarah, Rebecca, and Rachel were barren because Hashem wanted to extract their prayers. If they would have had children with no difficulty, they'd certainly have prayed much less, both in quantity and in intensity. If we examine the lives of the great tzaddikim, we find almost always that their lives were an ongoing saga of one difficulty after another.

Life's difficulties are a clear sign that Hashem wants to bring us closer to Him.

Obstacles enhance desire

Rebbe Nachman of Breslev writes (*Likutei Moharan I:66*), "The degree of longing is enhanced by the obstacles that stand in the way of the goal, for when a person is prevented from attaining his wish, then his desire is greatly enhanced."

With the above principle in mind, we can view the difficulties, troubles, trials, and tribulations of life in a positive light. As soon as we encounter difficulty, we should arouse our desire and longing for Hashem, for the very purpose of trying situations is to bring us closer to Hashem.

Jeremiah the prophet says (*Jeremiah 30:7*), "It will be a time of trouble for Jacob, but from ***it*** shall he be saved." In other words, the same dire situation that Hashem saves Israel from is the catalyst that drives the Jewish people closer to Hashem. The serious trouble stimulates them to pray from the depths of their souls and to seek Hashem. As such, the trouble is ultimately a gem of untold value. Hashem says (*Ezekiel 33:11*), "I do not desire the death of the wicked, but that he should return from his evil ways and live."

Hashem doesn't want us to suffer; He wants us to live upright lives and to be happy. Life's difficulties are wake-up calls to initiate soul-searching on two levels, namely, to prod us to seek Hashem and to stimulate teshuva and character development. If we were always successful, we would most certainly become smug and arrogant, never seeking Hashem, and never correcting a single character flaw. So, if we had everything, we'd really have nothing.

Joy of living

Life is joy and happiness. Only a happy person can be called "alive". Practically speaking, "life" and "happiness" are synonymous, since life indicates a joyful state (just as conversely, death indicates a forlorn state). Many people have beating hearts and functioning lungs, but they lack the joy of living, for they lack emuna. Rebbe Nachman of Breslev teaches that without emuna, life isn't worth living; the smallest difficulties in life sink the non-believer into sadness, depression, and despair. Without emuna, a person suffers from worry, stress, confusion, and self-persecution.

Rebbe Nachman explains that the non-believers are incapable of understanding or effectively coping with situations that don't go according to their plans or wishes. They feel helpless at the hands of "fate" and "nature" that torture them with no rhyme or reason. On the other hand, people with emuna seldom lose composure, since they realize how life's trying times are for their ultimate best. Consequently, they live joyful and sweet lives, in this world and in the next.

Agnostics and atheists have no life in this world or in the next. If you check closely, you'll find that beneath the veneer of an artificial smile, you'll find them to be anxious, worried, and stress-ridden. Their lives are full of inexplicable difficulties, day-to-day struggles of survival or a never-ending chase for material amenities that almost always elude them. The believer, in contrast, understands what he or she is doing in the world and how life's challenges are milestones for personal and spiritual growth designed to accomplish a clearly defined goal.

To taste the joy of life, one needs emuna. Knowing that everything in our lives is an eternal gift from our loving Father in Heaven for the very best provides the joy of life that fuels inner strength. With emuna, a person is also able to put the difficulties of this life in proper proportion, especially when looking at the ultimate goal of eternal bliss in the next life.

The war against Amalek

Amalek is the symbol of evil and a nickname for the *Yetzer Hara*, or evil inclination. His main weapon is the venom of doubt; he injects doubts of emuna within a person's mind and heart. As soon as a person begins to doubt Hashem, he or she encounters immediate difficulties that are designed to make them cry out and seek Hashem again.

The Torah relates (*Exodus, chapter 17*) that the Children of Israel defeated the Amalekites only by virtue of emuna. When Moses' hands were extended to the Heavens in prayer, Israel held the upper hand. When Moses' hands fell, Amalek gained the upper hand. The Mishna in tractate Rosh Hashanah asks hypothetically, "Do the hands of Moses win or lose a war?" The Mishna answers its own question and says, "As long as Israel cast their eyes skyward and subjugated their hearts to their Father in Heaven, they overcame their enemy – if not, they fell." We therefore conclude that Amalek wins when a person forgets Hashem, Heaven forbid.

Looking skyward

Consequently, Amalek – the evil inclination – strives to destroy a person's emuna, so that he or she won't look skyward. With emuna, a person is protected against the evil inclination. When the wall of emuna crumbles - Heaven forbid - a person is exposed and defenseless. By looking skyward and remembering Hashem, Amalek is disarmed.

Whenever a person suffers, he or she simply can look skyward, call out to Hashem in personal prayer, and ask for help. No prayer goes unanswered, for Hashem is near to those who call Him in earnest.

Emuna, whose practical manifestation is prayer, is the only surefire weapon against the evil inclination. For this reason, we should all strive to constantly enhance our emuna and powers of prayer.

The purpose of Torah and mitzvoth

The purpose of Torah learning is to bring a person to emuna. Enhanced emuna leads to stronger illumination of the soul. The more a soul is illuminated, the more the soul is capable of recognizing its Creator. As such, learning Torah and performing mitzvoth – with the goal of getting to know Hashem as opposed to ulterior motives of personal gain, prestige, and so forth – is the express purpose of a person's existence in this world.

One's spiritual level

The Gemorra (*tractate Pesachim 50a*) tells about Rav Yosef the son of Rabbi Yehoshua ben Levi who became so sick the he reached the state of clinical death. By Hashem's grace, Rav Yosef recuperated after his soul had entered the threshold of the world to come. His father asked him, "What did you see in the spiritual world?"

Rav Yosef answered, "I saw an upside-down world; the high were low and the low were high."

Rabbi Yehoshua ben Levi commented, "You saw a clear world," in other words, an accurate picture.

Let's elaborate on the above simple but very profound thought: Many people in this world enjoy wealth and prestige, and are considered "high society." But, in the spiritual world, they're on the bottom rung. The opposite also holds true; certain people in this world are humiliated, ridiculed, or persecuted, yet in the next world they enjoy a high level of status. A person's spiritual level is determined by the extent to which he or she developed their emuna and successfully passed life's many tests of faith during their term in the material world.

Emuna is the root and foundation of life. The prophet (*Habbakuk 2:4*) said, "And the righteous will live by emuna." With emuna, a person is assured a good, gratifying and meaningful life in this world and in the next. As emuna increases, so does one's spiritual status.

Greatness and insignificance

The prophet says (*Samuel I, 16:7*), "For a person sees the eyes and Hashem sees the heart." In other words, we lack the tools to judge the true status of another person. People tend to evaluate the worth of others according to money, wisdom, beauty, or pedigree; such yardsticks are both deceiving and inaccurate. They often show a great person as insignificant, or an insignificant person as great.

An illiterate person could feasibly be a greater individual than a doctor or university professor, especially if the former has strong cognizance of his mission in the world and the latter does not. One who possesses a strong cognizance of Hashem far surpasses the person that has no idea who created the world and for what purpose, even if the former is a street cleaner and the latter is a nuclear physicist. Isaiah the prophet teaches (*Isaiah 1:3*) that a person who has no awareness of Hashem is on a lower spiritual level than an ox, when he chastises Israel for forsaking emuna: "An ox knows its Creator and a donkey its Master's trough; Israel knew not, for they failed to observe." In other words, the ox and the donkey are aware that Hashem sustains them, but he who blindly seeks a life of physical amenities never finds Hashem.

Emuna – the best merchandise

In light of everything we've discussed in this chapter, a person would be smart to invest the bulk of his or her efforts in attaining and developing emuna. Emuna is the world's most important commodity.

The Gemorra teaches (*tractate Shabbat 31a*) that the first question a person is asked when he or she leaves the material world is, "Did you negotiate in faith?" The basic interpretation of this question is whether a person dealt fairly and honestly in commerce. But, on the allusive level, the person is being asked whether he or she negotiated to acquire the commodity of faith – **emuna** – by learning emuna, talking emuna, practicing emuna, and striving for emuna.

The Zohar teaches that Hashem manipulates entire worlds so that two people will come together and discuss emuna.

Emuna is the key to true happiness and success in this world, as well as the only guarantee of success in the next world. This chapter has briefly touched on the benefits of emuna, but essentially, there're no limits to its virtues. Happy is the person that obtains true and lasting emuna.

Chapter Five

Emuna and Emotions

Emuna is the foundation of emotional health. This chapter delves into the connection between emuna and emotions to illustrate the critical role that emuna plays in our everyday lives and in our general well-being.

Part 1: Sadness

Sadness is an emotion that directly results from the lack of emuna.

An important principle of emuna teaches that Hashem bestows His personal Divine Providence on each creation. Hashem provides each human – His most sophisticated creation – with a unique set of conditions that enable the individual to develop faith and to get to know Him. Hashem tailors each set of conditions to each person; usually, a problem or deficiency is the catalyst designed to stimulate a person's spiritual development. Some people are afflicted with physical ailments while others suffer financial problems. Some people have grief from their children while others encounter marital difficulties. These tribulations motivate a person to seek Hashem; without them, he or she might never raise their voice in prayer.

With emuna, we never succumb to sadness or despair, for emuna teaches that Hashem does everything for our ultimate benefit. We learn that our difficulties in life are all for the best, to bring us closer to Hashem. But, without emuna, life presents plenty of reasons to be sad and depressed. Since a state of deficiency and imperfection are ingrained in creation, life is never exactly how we want it to be. Without emuna, we would be disappointed and saddened dozens of times every day, as soon as things don't go our way.

A soldier in an elite unit or a champion athlete uses the rigors of arduous training as a growth opportunity to attain excellence in his or her respective endeavor. A candidate for the Olympic boxing team doesn't cry when he gets punched in a workout; on the contrary, he uses his pain as a learning opportunity to better his performance. In like manner, the person with emuna isn't saddened by life's difficulties; he or she uses them as springboards for spiritual growth.

As soon as individuals without emuna don't get their own way, they start blaming themselves or those in their proximity. They fall into sadness. Even if they have a general belief in Hashem, they accuse Him of torturing or persecuting them for no reason.

With the spiritual awareness that life's difficulties are Hashem's way of bringing us closer to Him, we never sink into a state of sadness or despair. We utilize our situation for prayer and teshuva, ultimately getting closer to Hashem and rising above our difficulties.

Trials and tribulations make ideal spiritual vessels for getting close to Hashem. They resemble fire – when properly contained and harnessed, fire is a marvelous source of energy that does wonders such as cooking, heating, and healing. Likewise, trials and tribulations provide the spiritual energy that can propel a person closer to Hashem.

There's no comparison between the emotional and spiritual strength of a person that has achieved proximity to Hashem by way of trials and tribulations and a person who's been accustomed to an easy life. Whereas the former enjoys strong spiritual and emotional inoculation and can successfully weather the most trying situations, the latter succumbs to stress and anxiety at the slightest hardship. That's why the drug companies are doing billions of dollars of business in the environment of a spoiled generation that lacks emuna.

No deficiency

Let's take our train of thought one step further: Sometimes, a person suffers from a bad habit or a lustful drive that's a direct hindrance in serving Hashem and getting close to Him. In such a case, one has an apparent "right" to be sad. He or she asks, "How can I be happy when I have this craving for certain things that are directly against Hashem's will?" One person feels compelled to smoke a cigarette on Shabbat while another craves cheeseburgers. They feel sad and guilty that they can't overcome their lusts and bodily urges.

Here's news: Hashem made them crave cheeseburgers, cigarettes on Shabbat, or whatever else their bodily drive is. Emuna teaches that physical appetites – like everything else in life – come from Hashem. Hashem instills a particular lust or bodily drive in a person to direct that person to his or her needed soul correction. For example, if in a previous life, a person failed to observe the commandment to refrain from cooking, eating, or enjoying milk and meat in any way, then in this reincarnation, he or she might be instilled with a strong drive to eat cheeseburgers. Why? Overcoming the drive to eat cheeseburgers – or any other combination of milk and meat – is the very mission of their soul on earth. With emuna, they're happy for the opportunity to correct!

Hashem gives us our faults, drives, and bad habits for our own good, to facilitate the correction of our souls. This is ample reason for rejoicing, not sadness!

If a person maintains composure, prays, and performs regular soul-searching, he or she will discover that their apparent deficiencies are not deficiencies at all, but catalysts for personal growth and correction. Without emuna, life's difficulties and personal flaws are reasons for disorientation and despair. When we're sad, we don't accomplish anything, especially not a soul correction. Only emuna can save us from sadness and despair.

The disadvantage is really an advantage

When we look at the Torah and the glorious annals of the Jewish people, we see how our history's leading personalities suffered from seemingly insurmountable disadvantages.

Moses stuttered and grew up in the house of a non-Jew – Pharaoh, king of Egypt. Moses never received a formal Jewish education, yet he became the holiest of prophets of all time and Hashem's chosen messenger to lead the Jewish people out of Egypt.

Samson was lame, yet he became one of history's mightiest men who cast fear in the hearts of his enemies, even after his death!

David was an outcast; his own father and brothers thought that he was an illegitimate child. He was also short. Yet, he overcame the giant Goliath. He was also chosen to replace Saul – a man of perfect attributes – as the king of Israel and Hashem's anointed.

A weak and insignificant woman – Yael, the wife of Hever the Kinnite – saved Israel from the hand of the mighty Sisera.

The Maggid of Mezeritch was lame in both legs, yet he became the tzaddik of his generation and the successor of the holy Baal Shem Tov.

Abaye – the Talmudic sage whose name is written on almost every page of the Gemorra – was an orphan. His father died before he was born and his mother died in childbirth. Such dire disadvantage didn't prevent him from becoming one of Israel's leading wise men of all time.

The continuation of the above list is long and exhaustive. Few are the silver-spoon success stories in Jewish history.

The above examples teach us that personal disadvantages do not hamper a person's level of achievement; on the contrary, those who have coped with difficulties have developed a stronger capability to realize more of their potential. This concept is clearly understood when we look at a weightlifter – his muscles are the product of extensive exposure to stress and exertion.

On a spiritual plane, a people with disadvantages are humble. They must appeal to Hashem for assistance in overcoming their relative disadvantages. By including Hashem in their lives, they make much greater progress than the non-disadvantaged who don't include Hashem in their lives. Consequently, the disadvantage is actually an advantage, because it serves as a catalyst to bring us closer to Hashem.

I called out from the depths

A person in trouble, suffering, or downtrodden and persecuted, must fall back on his or her emuna to keep on going. In physics, every action causes an equal and opposite reaction. Spirituality is the same. The greater one's difficulties on life, the more one must cling to Hashem. The more one clings to Hashem, the higher the spiritual gain. Suffering and tribulations are therefore portals to spiritual gain.

If a person were constantly successful in everything that he or she did, with no troubles in life whatsoever, then it's doubtful that they'd ever seek Hashem. Such people easily become arrogant, and arrogance is an iron barrier totally separates a person from Hashem's light. Conversely, the more one nullifies one's own ego, the more one becomes a befitting vessel for Divine illumination.

Emuna manifests itself in courage; the more a person feels the presence of Hashem, the less he or she fears anything or anyone. King David expresses this concept so beautifully in Psalm 23 when he says, "Though I walk through the valley of death, I fear no evil, for You (Hashem) are with me."

Trying situations are torture without emuna. Those with nothing to fall back on easily succumb to sadness, despair, and depression.

They are frequently angry and embittered. In extreme cases, they lose their will to live.

Positive thinking

The primary choice of a person under pressure is whether he or she will succumb to negative thoughts and believe in them, or strengthen themselves with emuna, replace feelings of sadness with optimism and happiness, and cling to Hashem. In the latter case, problems always turn themselves around.

Positive thinking means thoughts of emuna, that Hashem can rescue any of us from any situation in the universe. With emuna, there's no such thing as despair in the world. Hashem can turn any predicament around for the best. A person with emuna is aware that difficult times are growth opportunities that enable a person to strengthen his or her relationship with Hashem.

Let's take the example of a person who's been unsuccessful over a long period of time in finding his or her soulmate. This is no easy trial; the *Yetzer Hara* pounces on opportunities like this to infuse despair and depression into a person's heart and to destroy their emuna altogether. But, with emuna, a person turns to Hashem in prayer, as follows: "Hashem, please forgive me for whatever misdeeds I might have done that have hampered finding my soulmate. Please help me correct what needs correcting; You Yourself know that a person can't truly correct his or her soul without being married. For that reason, please help me find my partner in life."

Positive thinking comes from the *Yetzer Tov*, the good or holy inclination. Negative thinking and emotions are all products of the *Yetzer Hara*, the evil dark side.

Emuna vs. heresy

Let's see the difference between emuna and heresy in a personal crisis: The emuna train of thought is reflected by the *Yetzer Tov*, and the heretical train of thought is reflected by the *Yetzer Hara*. The following chart shows the contrasting way each speaks inside a person's head and heart:

Yetzer Hara and Heresy say:	Yetzer Tov and Emuna say:
I'll never solve my problem.	If Hashem wants, He can solve my problem this very minute!
Hashem forgot all about me.	Hashem forgets no one. He loves each of His creations, including me. His Divine Providence is for the very best.
Hashem doesn't want to help me.	Hashem created me as an act of Divine compassion; within this particular predicament is the spark of salvation.
I don't know how to pray. I've got no will to pray. I find prayer belabored and difficult.	I'll ask Hashem to help me pray, to teach me how to pray, to open my mouth in prayer
I'm a loser. I never succeed.	Success is from Hashem. If I turn to Hashem sincerely, He'll certainly help me succeed.
Nothing ever goes my way.	Everything goes my way; my setbacks are from Hashem, so that I'll realize my nothingness and turn to Him for help.

Somebody gave me an evil eye.	There is no one but Hashem; no one can do me harm against Hashem's will. From this moment on, I'll try harder to look at others favorably, so that they'll look at me favorably.
Everything is dependant on my own efforts.	My efforts mean nothing; as soon as the right time comes, my soulmate will find me! All I have to do is pray…
I'm lazy.	I'm lazy because I don't believe in myself. I tortured myself and fell into depression. I'll ask Hashem to help me believe in myself so that I'll be happy and energetic. Hashem will surely have pity on me and help me.
I blew it; the solution to my problem slipped through my fingers.	Even if I missed the train, Hashem will send me another train. Whatever happened, that's what Hashem wanted!
There's no correction for my soul.	Hashem can remedy any situation and correct my soul as well.

Notice that in the above table, the Yetzer Hara speaks all the time about "I" and "me" and the Yetzer Tov speaks about Hashem. The Yetzer Hara inflates a person with egotism, despair, and heresy, while the Yetzer Tov gives the person emuna, encouragement, and optimism.

Use the above table to insert your own thoughts on whatever challenge you're facing at the moment, and see which the dominant force in your life is right now.

Sadness – your enemy

Whenever we meet the challenge of a problem with emuna and optimism – knowing that everything is from Hashem and everything is for the best – we easily overcome the sadness, depression, and worry that only make matters worse.

Take for example a husband and wife: A husband is commanded to make his wife happy. If he sees that she's down in the dumps, and because of that he becomes gloomy too, then their problem becomes all the more acute. As soon as the husband becomes melancholy, the Divine Presence departs from him and he therefore forfeits Hashem's help. The household then becomes a disaster area.

But, when a husband looks at a delicate situation as a test of faith from Hashem to stimulate and enhance teshuva and emuna, he won't allow himself to fall in the trap of despair. He'll destroy sadness – his enemy – by asking for Hashem's help, strengthening his emuna, and smiling at his wife in optimism. His smile is not only encouraging, it's contagious.

Grievances or emuna

Rebbe Nachman of Breslev describes sadness as the statement of complaint when a person is angry with Hashem for not giving him what he wants.

Anger expresses a lack of emuna, when a person fails to acknowledge that Hashem's Divine Providence is for the very best. An individual with emuna has no complaints and harbors no grievances against Hashem, Heaven forbid, and is positive that everything Hashem does is for their ultimate benefit.

When a person forgets about Hashem, he or she falls into a fear of natural forces – whether human or otherwise – which they perceive as obstacles or barriers to what they want. The more a person forgets about Hashem, the more he or she fears those forces and succumbs to anger, anxiety, and impatience. Even worse, when people attribute their problems to themselves, they fall into depression and despair. When they don't accept their lot in life with happiness – in other words, when they lack emuna - they're expressing their grievances with Hashem!

Big gains vs. tiny losses

One of the *Yetzer Hara's* prime ploys is to magnify a person's faults while concealing their good points. In this way, the Yetzer robs many of their joy in life. There's not a person on earth that isn't full of good points; if a person were to realize his or her good points, they'd be happy all day long.

Imagine that a person is an investment broker that on a given day has made a net profit of one hundred million dollars on the commodities market. Yet, on one small transaction, he incurred a loss of five thousand dollars. Along comes someone and yells, "You loser! Don't you know anything about investments? Your future is finished! When the whole world finds out about the five grand you lost, you won't have a single client. You're down the drain!" That someone is the Yetzer Hara – the epitome of all evil, destroying a person from within.

If the broker has emuna, he'll throw the Yetzer Hara right out of the 24th story window; if he lacks emuna, he'll be running to his psychiatrist.

To be happy, it's important to focus on your good points – your million-dollar gains. Don't let the minor losses bring you down.

Self persecution

Self persecution is a prime cause of sadness and depression. Self persecution is another expression of deficient emuna, when one blames himself for his failures.

One may ask, "How can I be happy when I fail?" The answer is simple: With emuna, a person addresses a setback by saying that **this is what Hashem wants and it's all for the best!**

Let's take an example: A women is married for eight years already and she hasn't yet been blessed with children. Without emuna, she starts persecuting herself in all sorts of ways, such as: "I'm not normal; I'm not deserving of children; Hashem doesn't want anything to do with me; I was born with bad fortune…" and so on. These thoughts are the sole result of insufficient emuna, for she thinks that childbearing is dependant on **her**, when in actuality, she has little say in the matter. Children, like everything else in life, come from **Hashem**.

So what should the childless woman do? She'd best be advised to pray to Hashem, as follows: "Hashem, You can help me. Show me why I don't have children and what's lacking in me. If I lack emuna, give me emuna! If I haven't prayed enough, help me pray more! Teach me how to ask for what I need; I know that everything You do is for the best and that You want our prayers just like You wanted the prayers of our forefathers. Ultimately, I believe that You'll make me a mother too."

Here's an important rule: **Most people are sad and depressed because they feel they're failures and they lack hope. This is the product of negative thoughts about themselves, the result of self persecution. Self persecution results from a lack of emuna.**

Emuna says, "Hashem can help me this very minute; and, even if Hashem decides not to help me, it's still for the best." Emuna and sadness are mutually exclusive.

To break the cycle of sadness, one must stop persecuting oneself. In order to put an end to self persecution, one needs emuna. In order to obtain emuna, one must talk to Hashem in extensive personal prayer, and ask for emuna. As such, talking to Hashem in personal prayer can literally uplift a person from the depths of sadness and depression.

Self persecution begins as soon as a person says, “I didn’t succeed.” This is a faulty way to think. The right way is to say, “Hashem doesn’t want me to succeed right now, and this is surely for the best, because He wants me to learn something or to strengthen something. He probably wants me to strengthen my emuna; I’ll do just that and ask Him to help me!”

By focusing on Hashem rather than on oneself, a person breaks the cycle of self persecution. The awareness that every occurrence in life is from Hashem and for the ultimate good is the basis of emuna and the key to a happy mood, no matter what.

Growth power

In essence, emuna is growth power. It’s the moving force that helps a person achieve personal gain more than anything else in the universe. Emuna gives a person the will to live and the power not only to withstand tough times, but to gain by them. Emuna resembles the deep roots of a tree that enable it to withstand wind, storm, and drought.

The power of emuna is vast. One with emuna fears nothing. He or she retains composure under stress and meets challenges with a smile. With emuna, one is confident that Hashem listens to every prayer and never forsakes us. Knowing that there’s Hashem to turn to always, in any circumstance, a person is always happy.

Part 2: Anger

Anger destroys lives. Anger ranges from the quiet fuming embers in the heart to outward rage and expressions of violence. Anger can be unfounded, based on an imagined reason, or apparently justified. Since our sages condemn the anger of the apparently justified type, all other forms of anger should certainly be avoided.

Everyone desires to break away from the chains of anger, but few really succeed. The key to removing anger from our lives is emuna.

Living our emuna

Anger management and such partial solutions as self-control exercises fail to uproot anger. Only emuna can completely dislodge anger from a person's heart. People with high levels of emuna are not affected by anger.

Since a person comes to this earth for the purpose of soul correction, it's virtually impossible to avoid situations that stimulate feelings of anger. Hashem pits us against all types of people and events that are not to our liking; with emuna, we realize that everything is from Hashem and for the best. Without emuna, we're dangerously susceptible to anger.

By living our emuna, we avoid anger. Even when others treat us unfairly, insult us, or cause us extreme injustice, by focusing on Hashem and remembering that everything He does is for our ultimate benefit, we don't succumb to anger.

Even when things don't go the way we'd like them too, or when we're disappointed in ourselves or in our shortcomings, with emuna, we're not upset; we realize that overcoming life's difficulties and our own shortcomings are the very reason we're alive on this earth, so we don't get angry. Instead, we simply roll up our sleeves, and get to work!

When we observe life's difficulties as personal messages from Hashem, not only do we avoid anger, but we achieve a high level of gratification. Nothing is more satisfying than receiving a message from Hashem, understanding it, and taking necessary action on it.

Spiritual awareness

With emuna, we uproot anger; with spiritual awareness, we acquire emuna. Therefore, in order to uproot anger from our lives, we have to beg Hashem to help us achieve spiritual awareness. Spiritual awareness is the cognizance that Hashem runs the world and does everything for a specific purpose. Consequently, nothing in the world is random or coincidental.

King Solomon said (*Ecclesiastes 7:10*), "Anger rests in the bosom of fools." Foolishness is ignorance, and ignorance is the opposite of awareness. As such, the more a person is spiritually cognizant of Hashem, the less he or she is subject to anger. Children, for example, easily become upset when they don't get their way, because they haven't yet developed spiritual awareness. Maturity therefore is not so much a function of chronological age as it is of spiritual awareness.

A person with highly developed spiritual awareness and strong emuna won't be upset even when subjected to extreme insult or humiliation, for he or she realizes that their trial or tribulation is coming from Hashem to facilitate their own soul correction. On the contrary, they're happy!

A false god

Anger has more of a negative effect on the body and the soul than all the transgressions of the Torah. The Zohar teaches that even if a person has learned Torah extensively and performed good deeds, he or she loses all merit by succumbing to anger. Anger resembles a spiritual acid that literally corrodes a soul. The Zohar calls anger a "false god" that chases away a soul's holiness.

Angry people consequently lose all connection with Hashem. When a person gets angry, his or her soul departs; dark-side forces of evil instantly fill the void created by the soul's exit and gain control of the angry person. One must work very hard to escape such a spiritual abyss. Teshuva can only be effective when accompanied by learning emuna and overcoming anger. One must uproot anger to regain the holiness of the soul.

The key to life's riddles

We often hear inexplicable and unexpected phenomena such as:

- The couple that had a great marriage, and now all of a sudden, the wife is demanding a divorce;
- The two partners that built a thriving business, and now one is demanding that the other buy out or sell out;
- A person was making a nice living, and suddenly he or she can't make ends meet for no apparent reason;
- A formerly level-headed person suddenly begins acting like a wild man.

The list is long. One master key unlocks all of the above riddles – anger. By becoming angry and losing his or her holy soul, the person's life took a sudden turn for the worst. The wife no longer wants to live with a husband whose actions are governed by the dark side. Abundance eludes such a person, as do sanity and reason as well.

Nothing in the world is worth losing the holy soul. Anger is worse than the allegorical person that sells his soul for some amenity, for with anger, one gets nothing in return. On the contrary, even this world becomes a purgatory.

Purity of the heart

The only way to purify a heart of anger is to learn and relearn the principles of emuna. Once we learn about emuna, we must pray to Hashem and ask that emuna become second nature, like breathing or seeing. The more we attain emuna, the more we drive away anger and purify the heart.

Angry at Hashem

The following principles may sound harsh, but the more you think about them, the more you'll realize how true they are:

- **The angry person is actually angry at Hashem!**
- **The angry person is angry with Hashem's way of doing things!**

It's no picnic

Difficulties – like everything else in life - come from Hashem to stimulate teshuva, to encourage correction of a detrimental trait or bad habit, or to cause a person to seek Hashem.

Many individuals seek a life of leisure and are therefore angered by life's difficulties. They have no idea what they're mission is on this earth, namely, to correct their souls. Correcting the soul – like any other worthwhile accomplishment – requires dedication and hard work, whereas a picnic requires neither. Life is no picnic, but a picnic can't correct a soul.

In light of the above, anger is frequently the result of moral and spiritual laziness, when a person isn't willing to rise to the challenges that Hashem presents for the person's own benefit.

Part 3 – Jealousy

With emuna, a person knows that he or she has a unique soul with its own special task and soul correction on earth. Hashem, by way of His compassionate individual Divine Providence, gives each soul the qualities and conditions it requires to achieve its objectives. With this in mind, the strong believer never falls into the pit of jealousy.

Imagine that your soul correction and mission in life is to be a jet pilot. Hashem gives you a special set of talents and aptitudes that help you earn your wings. Your tailor-made path in life leads you to the cockpit of an F16, where you achieve greatness and your objective in life, flying at Mach 1 high above the clouds. Would you be jealous of a person with a yacht? Most certainly not!

Living a purposeful life

Jealousy is an indication that one hasn't yet started living a purposeful life. Another person's fame, fortune, or success doesn't help any of us attain our soul correction; therefore, when we gaze at other people's gifts in life, we fail to develop our own gifts in life, the needed tools in accomplishing what *we* need to do in this world.

For Helen Keller, blindness was not a handicap – it was a critical tool for her soul correction; otherwise, she would have never been so instrumental in implementing the use of Braille. One person's handicap is therefore another person's springboard to greatness. If Helen Keller would have been miserable, bitter, and jealous of those who see, she certainly would not have accomplished her mission in life.

The Gemorra in tractate Taanit tells the story of the generation's greatest sage, Rebbe Yehoshua ben Chananya:

> Rebbe Yehoshua was extremely ugly. Caesar's daughter once chided him and asked, "How is such magnificent wisdom in such an ugly vessel?"
>
> Rebbe Yehoshua smiled, then asked Caesar's daughter how her father stores his fine wines. "In simple ceramic jugs," she answered. He laughed and said that it's ridiculous that Caesar, the richest man in the world, should store his wine in simple earthenware jugs. She agreed, and transferred her father's best wine to solid gold vessels.
>
> A day or so later, Caesar asked for a glass of his favorite Cabernet. The wine was completely sour. Caesar summoned his royal wine master and demanded an explanation. "Your Majesty," shrugged the wine master, "the princess ordered me to transfer all the Cabernet into golden vessels!"
>
> Caesar sent for his daughter and demanded her explanation. "It's not my fault, father," she cried, "Rebbe Yehoshua ben Chananya told me to do it!"
>
> Caesar guards seized Rebbe Yehoshua ben Chananya and brought him to the royal court. Undaunted, Rebbe Yehoshua said, "Your daughter doesn't like ugly vessels, Your Majesty; but, wisdom and fine wine are similar, they are both preserved in ugly vessels."

Rebbe Yehoshua ben Chananya conveyed an important message – just as wine is best preserved in a simple earthenware vessel, so is Torah best preserved in a simple, not-so-beautiful individual. Such a person is far from pride, arrogance, and vanity. Gold – indicative of pride – sours fine wine. Rebbe Yehoshua ben Chananya was a man of complete emuna – he knew that his ugliness was by no means a deficiency, but an important quality necessary in accomplishing his mission on earth.

In light of the above, one person's deficiency is a valuable tool in another person's soul correction. If Rebbe Yehoshua ben Chananya would have been jealous of beautiful people, and if he would have wasted his time in pursuit of physical perfection, he would have become a bitter and frustrated individual that missed the opportunity of becoming one of the greatest minds of all time. When one pursues his or her true purpose in life, there's no room for jealousy!

Concentrate on your task

Concentrate on your task in life. Use your tools to the hilt. If you were born short, don't be jealous of the players in the NBA – it's not your job to play professional basketball! Take a good look at what you do best and develop the special tools that Hashem gave you.

If you're jealous of someone else, then you're not concentrating on your own task. Get back to work!

The test of poverty

People often ask why Hashem makes a person poor. The poor person most likely needs a soul correction that necessitates humility, emuna, trust in Hashem, and constant prayer. Poverty is the exact climate that helps certain people to acquire these wonderful characteristics. If they were rich, they'd probably never pray. Even more, they'd put their trust in their assets and not in Hashem.

The test of poverty is not easy; but, if a person is poor, then it's a clear sign that poverty is his or her personal path to getting close to Hashem. With eyes of emuna, such a person isn't jealous of someone else's wealth, nor does he or she resort to transgressions in trying to attain more money. With emuna, the poor person knows that his current situation is for his ultimate good.

Once again, as soon as the poor person becomes jealous of the rich neighbor, he is not concentrating on his own mission in life. If they were rich, they'd most certainly feel an abyss of spiritual emptiness, because they wouldn't be achieving their soul correction of emuna, trust in Hashem, and constant prayer.

The test of wealth

The challenge of a rich person is to develop generosity, humility, and trust in Hashem despite his or her wealth and power. As such, wealth is a more difficult test than poverty. It's much easier for a poor person to cast his or her hope to Hashem than it is for a rich person.

The wealthy must realize that Hashem gave them money and power for a purpose other than feeding their own bodily appetites. Hashem expects them to overcome natural human egotism and stinginess in order to perform acts of charity and lovingkindness; that is no simple task. The rich are expected to support such lofty causes as Torah learning and Jewish outreach, and not use Hashem's gifts for their own selfish pleasures.

Oftentimes, rich people obtained money illegally in a former life; in this life, they have the opportunity to correct by distributing sums to the needy. Chances are that they are simply returning to a needy person what they took from him unjustly in a former life. Therefore, a rich person should get used to giving as much and as often as possible.

The choice is not ours

It's ridiculous to be jealous of another person's success. Material and career success is up to Hashem, and not in the realm of our choices. So why be envious of someone else? Our only choice is whether to observe Hashem's commandments or not, to do good or the opposite, Heaven forbid.

Rabbi Yosef Chaim of Baghdad tells the story of the rich person who was envied by the whole town. The rich person feared that someone would give him an evil eye, so he decided to make a ridiculous investment that would cause him subsequent losses so that others wouldn't be jealous of him anymore. No matter how he invested his money, he still made a windfall. The rich man complained to his rabbi; the rabbi replied, "Success or failure is not up to you. Hashem decides!"

The opposite also holds true. Our great Spanish sage the Ibn Ezra tried everything to make money, but no matter what he did, he failed. "If I'm to be poor all my life, why work? I might as well learn Torah!" The Ibn Ezra dedicated his life to Torah, and was destined to write one of history's most significant commentaries on the Torah. Had he spent his life in commerce, subsequent generations wouldn't have benefited from the depth of his wisdom.

We know nothing!

Why look at others in envy? Despite the fact that you might be jealous of other people, you may be much closer to your soul correction than they are to theirs.

The son of an unassuming cab driver was accepted into a prestigious yeshiva after years of sacrifice and hard work. He became a classmate of the Rosh Yeshiva's son; while the former struggled to understand the difficult Talmudic lessons, the latter absorbed the material with almost no effort. The cab driver's son outpoured his broken heart to a wise man; the wise man said, "Don't be jealous of the Rosh Yeshiva's son. While you are fulfilling your purpose in life, he isn't scratching the surface of his potential. Be happy with your lot in life – your achievements are much greater than his!"

We don't know what Hashem knows. Therefore, we can't assess another person's situation because we know basically nothing about their task in life. When we don't look at others, we don't fall prey to jealousy.

True success

True success is being content with what we have in life. Rebbe Nachman of Breslev illustrates this principal in his famous tale of "The Clever and The Simple." There were once two friends, one very smart and the other very simple. Here's how Rebbe Nachman describes them:

> The simple one learned the trade of shoemaking. Because he was simple, he learned a long time until he was able to accept work, and he was not fully expert even so. He married a woman, and he lived off of his work. But because he was simple, he was not so talented in the work, and so his earnings were meager and limited. He did not even have time to eat, because he had to work constantly, since he could not do the work adeptly. So while he worked, while he hit with his hammer, and inserted and drew out the thick thread in the way of shoemakers, he would snatch a bite of bread to eat.
>
> **And he had the habit of being very happy all the time - he was filled with happiness always.**
>
> He had all types of food, all the drinks and all the clothing he wanted. He would say to his wife, "My wife, give me to eat!" She would give him a piece of bread and he would eat. After this, he would say, "Give me beans in sauce!" She would cut him another slice of bread, and he would eat. Then he would praise it: "How fine and tasty was that sauce!" And so he would ask her

to bring him meat and other fine foods, and in place of each item, she gave him a slice of bread, and he delighted very much from it. He would praise each food extravagantly, saying how well prepared and good it was, as if he was eating the actual food.

In truth, he really tasted in the bread the taste of each food he wanted, because of his simplicity and great happiness.

Likewise he would command: "My wife, give me beer to drink!" She would give him water. And he would praise the quality of the beer. "Give me honey!" She gave him water, and he would praise it as before. "Give me wine!" and so on. Each time she would give him water, and he would enjoy and praise that beverage as if he were really drinking it.

And so with clothing: He and his wife together shared one fur coat. He would say, "My wife, give me the fur coat!" when he needed to wear a fur coat, for example, to go to the market. And she would give it to him. When he needed to wear a suit to go in formal settings, he would say, "My wife, give me the suit!" She would give him the fur coat, and he would delight in it and praise it: "How fine is this suit!" When he needed a caftan, for example, to go to the synagogue, he would command, saying "My wife, give me the caftan!" And she would give him the fur coat, and he would praise it, saying "How fine is this caftan!" Similarly, when he needed to wear a formal overcoat, she would also give him the fur coat, and he would praise and delight in it as well: "How fine and beautiful is this overcoat", and so on. **And he was always filled only with joy and satisfaction.**

> When he would finish a shoe (and it can be assumed it had three ends, for he had not mastered the craft), he would take the shoe in his hand and praise it highly, and would take great delight in it. He would say, "My wife, how beautiful and wonderful is this shoe! How sweet it is! This shoe is as sweet as honey and sugar!"
>
> Then she would ask him, "If so, why do all the other shoemakers charge three gold pieces for a pair of shoes, and you take only a piece and a half?"
>
> He answered her, "What does it matter to me? **That is his affair, this is mine!"** And further: "Why must we talk about others? Why don't we make an estimate of how much direct profit I make from this shoe? The leather costs so much, the tar and the laces cost such and such, and the other materials like those cost that much, the filler costs that amount. Now, I make a direct profit of ten large coins. Why should I complain with a profit like that?"
>
> **And he was only joyful and satisfied all the time.**

Don't think for a moment that the simple one is stupid. He was realistic, fully aware of his imperfections and limitations. He knew that the shoes he produced were far from perfect, but in his complete trust of Hashem, he was happy with his lot in life. He wasn't jealous of anyone; when his wife mentioned another shoemaker that made more money than he did, the simple one answered with no sorrow at all, **"That is his affair, this is mine!"** He knew that his job in life was to perform his duties the best way he could and to be happy about it – nothing more!

On the other hand, his clever comrade was the exact opposite. Here's how Rebbe Nachman describes him:

Now the clever one was constantly filled with agony. For it became known that he was a magnificently intelligent man, a craftsman and a very great doctor. One nobleman came to him and asked him to make him a gold ring. He made the man a very wondrous ring, and engraved on it illustrations with incredible workmanship, and he engraved an image of a tree that was very impressive.

The nobleman came, and was not at all pleased with the ring. The clever one had much suffering from this, for he himself knew, that if this ring with the tree would be seen in Spain, it would be very honored and important. And so, another time, a high-standing nobleman came to him with an expensive precious stone that came from far away, and he brought him another stone with an engraving. He asked the clever one to copy the image from the illustrated stone onto the other one. And he copied it exactly, barring one mistake that no one else would be able to discern aside from himself. The noble came to take the stone, and was very pleased with it. But the clever man suffered intensely from the mistake. **"My wisdom is so great, and yet I made a mistake such as this!"**

Also from his work as a doctor he suffered. When he came to a sick person, and gave him a treatment, and he knew with certainty that if the man would only survive, he would be healed entirely, because the treatment was an amazing one. Then afterwards, if the man died, everyone would say he was at fault, and he suffered intensely from this. And thus, there were times when he treated a man and cured him, and everyone said, "It is just by chance." **And he was constantly filled with suffering**.

> One time he needed a garment, so he called upon a tailor, and toiled with him until he taught him to make the garment according to his desire, according to the style with which he was familiar. The tailor strived to make the garment according to his wishes, and succeeded with the exception of one lapel in which he erred. The clever one suffered exceedingly from this, for he knew that although here it was attractive enough, for people here were not versed in fashion, if he were in Spain with that lapel, he would be the butt of jokes and he would be looked on as a clown. And so he was constantly filled with agony.

Rebbe Nachman now describes the conversation between the clever one and the simple one:

> And the simple one would run and come to him joyfully, all the time. He always found him pained and full of suffering. He asked him, "Someone so wise and wealthy as you, why are you suffering all the time? You see, I am filled with joy all the time."
>
> However, he appeared in the eyes of the clever man as a joke, and as a lunatic. And the simple one said to him, "You see, the average man who mocks me is a fool. For if he is wiser than me, then on the contrary, he is a fool. So even a more clever man like you; what would you be if you were wiser than me?" Then the simple one said, "What would I not give for you to come to my level?"
>
> The clever one answered him, "That is possible, that I will come to your level, if I were to lose my intelligence, G-d forbid, or if I became sick, G-d forbid, and became insane. For what are you? A

> crazy man! But for you to come to my level, that is totally impossible - that you would become wise like me."
>
> The simple one answered him, "**With the Holy One, Blessed be He, anything is possible.** It could happen that within the wink of an eye I would come to your level."
>
> The clever one laughed at this a great deal...

In the continuation of the tale, Rebbe Nachman relates the turn of events that culminated in the simple one's appointment as a regional governor and ultimately as one of the king's closest ministers by virtue of his modesty, honesty, and impeccable character. "**With the Holy One, Blessed be He, anything is possible**."

From Rebbe Nachman's tale, we learn how emuna is the key to success in life, and not one's attributes and aptitudes. The more a person is happy with what he or she has, the more he or she succeeds, in this world and in the next.

Part 4 – Stinginess

Stinginess is a terrible trait and a sign of cruelty. The stingy person's love of money blinds him from seeing the needs of his fellow man, even those closest to him such as his wife and children. Therefore, a stingy person is disdained by others and seldom has peace at home.

There are several types of misers:

- Stingy with outsiders but generous with his own family;
- Stingy with his own family and generous with outsiders – these are the types that give charity for prestige and publicity;
- Stingy with everyone but lavish with himself;

- Stingy with everyone including himself – these are the types that hoard their money, and end up losing it or leaving it to others.

The good husband

One of the most tragic examples of stinginess is that of the stingy husband. Stinginess is a double expression of cruelty and insensitivity; the stingy husband is cruel to his wife and children and insensitive to their needs and feelings. Every household expenditure triggers his wrath.

There's no greater sorrow to a wife than a stingy husband. According to Kabbala, the health of a wife's soul depends on the abundance that her husband showers upon her. When the husband is poor, and lacks the means to provide his wife with plenty, she is saddened. But, when he has the means, and still doesn't give to her, she withers like a plant that's not watered. Even worse, when he says no to her needs, yet turns around and buys whatever amenities he desires for himself, she becomes his bitter enemy.

The Talmud teaches (*tractate Bava Metzia 59a*) that whoever honors his wife gets rich. If a man were smart, he'd cherish his wife, buy her whatever he can, and never criticize her about her expenditures. Just as honoring his wife brings him riches, being angry at her causes him to lose money.

Our sages also teach (*Hulin 84b*) that a man should forever eat and drink less than what he can afford, dress according to what he can afford, and to honor his wife **more** than what he can afford. This is the only mitzvah in the Torah that requires a person to spend more than what he has. Even for a mitzvah as important as honoring the Sabbath, the Gemorra says to avoid buying lavish food and drink if it means borrowing from others (*Pesachim 112a*)!

If a person can't afford to buy what his wife wants, then he should make a concerted effort to pray and ask Hashem to help him meet his wife's needs and to make her happy. If a man prays for his wife's happiness like he would pray for his own health, then Hashem will surely give him the ways and means to satisfy her.

If a wife makes a request from a husband, and he doesn't have the means to fulfill that request, he should never say no. Instead, he should promise her that with Hashem's help, he'll make every effort to fulfill her request as soon as he possibly can. The husband should complement his own efforts with prayer – the more the better. When Hashem sees that a person is sincere in his desire to honor his wife, Hashem will answer his prayers.

Money doesn't last

One of two things happens to money: Either the money is taken away from the person, or the person is taken away from the money. Therefore, one can't depend on one's money. We all know stories of rich people that ended up dying pauper's deaths; after spending a lifetime of accumulating money, they lost it. On the other hand, there are many cases of rich people that became so sick that they couldn't enjoy their money, and ultimately left this world and their money. A popular Hebrew expression laughs at those who sacrifice their health in search of money, then end up sacrificing their money in search of health. Either way, the money doesn't last.

Complete expense account

A person with emuna believes that Hashem will fulfill all the basic needs that we require in our service of Hashem – food, clothes, shelter, and the like. With emuna, we realize that as long as Hashem wants us to continue living on this earth, Hashem will pick up the tab for every needed expense. Hashem is the boss that provides a complete expense account.

Hashem enjoys when you're happy

A person with emuna also believes that just as Hashem provides for his needs today, Hashem shall continue to provide tomorrow. Therefore, he uses the money that Hashem gives him, especially in the service of Hashem. With emuna, a person realizes that Hashem gave him money to educate his children in Torah schools, to purchase a handsome pair of tefillin, and to buy his wife a new outfit for the holiday; Hashem doesn't send money to hoard in the bank. With emuna, one isn't afraid to put his hand in his pocket for a necessary expenditure and especially for a mitzvah such as charity, supporting Torah institutions, and Jewish outreach.

Without emuna, a person suffers every time he spends a cent.

Hashem, like a loving father, derives indescribable pleasure when His children spend money happily, such as when they enjoy lavish delicacies on Shabbat or when they build an exquisitely decorated Succah. When Hashem sees that His children trust in Him, and spend their money happily in the observance of His mitzvahs, He gives more and more. But, if Hashem sees that his children suffer every time they spend a cent, He is also disappointed.

Deductible expenses

Expenditures for mitzvahs are in effect "deductible" expenses. Our sages teach that even though one receives an annual allotment, expenditures for Sabbath, holidays, and Torah educations for our children are above and beyond one's annual allotment. Mitzvah expenditures are like milking a cow – the more you milk her, the more you get. As such, Hashem returns the money that we spend on mitzvahs.

Even more so, the Talmud teaches (*tractate Shabbos 119a*) that one who gives a tithe to charity will become rich. Hashem has compassion on those who have compassion on others.

A loyal trustee

With emuna, we understand that our money is basically not ours at all, but Hashem's. Hashem lets us invest the money He gives us in a way that earns dividends. For example, when we convert our money into mitzvahs and Torah learning, then the money becomes elevated from a material state to a spiritual state. Hashem considers that a wonderful use of the money, and is happy to give us more money since we've acted like a loyal trustee that knows how to invest properly.

Hashem gets no satisfaction from the stingy person that hoards money and fails to put it to use; He also is disappointed when someone squanders money on frills or uses money to violate the Torah's commandments.

> A poor person once came to the famed 18th century Chassidic master, Rebbe Avraham Yehoshua Heschel of Afta, known affectionately as "The Afta Rov". The poor man needed a dowry to marry off his lovely daughter who had come of age, but didn't have a cent to his name. He asked the rebbe for help; the rebbe wrote a personal note, sealed it in an envelope, and told the poor man to take it to a certain rich man in the big city.
>
> The poor man arrived at the rich man's mansion, and presented the rebbe's letter to him. The rich man read the letter, frowned, snarled, and then ripped the letter up. "Who does that rebbe think he is! What gall! I barely ever heard of him, and he has the nerve to send you here and demand three thousand rubles! Since when does he have the right to put his hand in my pocket?!? Where does he get off thinking that I have to listen to him?"
>
> Humiliated and degraded, the poor man left the rich man's mansion empty-handed. He returned to Afta, and told the rebbe about his unsuccessful

journey to the big city. The rebbe sighed deeply and said, "Go see Avremel - he's a pupil of mine that lives in a thatch-roofed cabin on the edge of town. Tell him that I said to give you five-hundred rubles." Five hundred was much less than three thousand, but to Avremel - a pious but poor Talmudic scholar - five hundred rubles was like five million rubles to the rich man.

The poor man found Avremel's cabin and relayed the rebbe's request. Avremel quickly put on his frayed gabardine and said happily, "Certainly my friend. You sit here and rest from your journey. My wife will give you food and drink. I'll be back in an hour or two." Avremel exchanged a few quiet words with his wife. Smiling, she took all her jewelry and silver ornaments and put them in a cloth rucksack. She blessed her husband with success and he left he house in the direction of the town center.

Avremel pawned his wife's jewelry, his Chanukah candelabra, his silver heirloom Kiddush cup, his silver snuff box and his wife's silver candlesticks. All in all, he put together a sum of 320 rubles. He then ran from merchant to merchant, telling them that he needed an urgent sum for a poor man to marry off his daughter. In an hour, he raised the additional 180 rubles. With joy in his heart, he raced home to present the poor man with the 500 rubles.

Everyone was delighted. The poor man blessed and hugged Avremel, and profusely thanked his wife. Avremel and his wife praised Hashem for enabling them to perform such a lofty mitzvah.

During the subsequent months, Avremel's luck took a sharp turn for the better. Inexplicably, good investments were literally forced on him. He began earning more money than he ever dreamed of, even though he barely picked his head up from his Talmudic studies. Before long, he became one of the richest men in the area.

The rich man from the big city wasn't so fortunate - his dealings plummeted, until he lost nearly everything he owned. Intuitively, his wife made the connection between her husband's misfortune and his refusal to heed the Rebbe from Afta. She urged her husband to go immediately to Afta and beg the rebbe's forgiveness. So he did…

The former rich man was ushered in to the rebbe. "Rebbe, please forgive me for my insolence!" the man cried pitifully.

"What insolence?" asked the Rebbe.

"The fact that I ridiculed the Rebbe's word, and refused to help the poor man as the Rebbe requested."

"Aha," nodded the rebbe. "There's nothing to forgive. You were given a task to do and you failed."

"How so?" asked the man.

"Let me explain," said the Rebbe. "My soul was destined to descend to this world as a rich man. I appealed before the Heavenly throne that riches will only distract me from devoting my life to Torah learning and the service of Hashem. My appeal was accepted on condition that I find another soul that would be willing to be a trustee over my riches. I appointed you. Your riches were actually mine, given to you for safe-keeping. So, when I asked that you give the poor man the three thousand rubles to comfortably marry off his daughter, I was asking for my own money. Your refusal showed that you were no longer a reliable trustee for my money, so you lost it. My pupil Avremel became the trustee instead of you."

"Rebbe, please take pity on me," cried the former rich man. "Please arrange for me a minimal stipend so that my wife and I won't starve to death!"

Avremel was more than happy to obey the Rebbe's request to send a monthly allotment to the former rich man from the big city. "After all," Avremel told himself, "The money's not mine - I'm only a trustee anyway!"

Summary: Additional emotions

Stinginess is a direct result from a deficiency of emuna. Emuna is the only way to uproot anger, sadness, depression, and jealousy as well. In like manner, emuna has the power to overcome any negative character or behavioral trait. Here's how in a nutshell:

Arrogance – with emuna, a person can't be arrogant, since he knows that all of his successes come from Hashem.

Gluttony – with emuna that Hashem sustains, a person doesn't eat any more than he or she needs.

Trust – with emuna, a person has the confidence that Hashem will always provide.

Flattery – with emuna, one need not fear or flatter any other human being in the world, no matter how apparently powerful or influential that person may be.

Slander – with emuna, one doesn't say a bad word about any other person. He or she leaves judging other people to Hashem.

Argumentative – when a person believes that all his or her trials and tribulations come from Hashem, he or she doesn't waste energy on arguments and disputes.

Patience – A person with emuna has patience with himself and with others, for he knows that everything in the world goes in accordance with Divine Providence and Hashem's timetable.

This chapter has been the foundation for personal character development and improvement. The underlying principles that we discussed at length in regard to sadness, anger, jealousy, and stinginess are capable of helping a person overcome any other negative trait. Once free of negative emotions, we begin to live sweet and fulfilling lives, in this world and in the next.

Chapter Six

Building Emuna

With Hashem's loving guidance, this chapter will teach us how to build emuna.

The Right Address

A person must ask Hashem for emuna.

Once, a soldier complained to the author about trepidations and worries. The author told him to strengthen his emuna. The soldier argued that he already had strong emuna.

The author elaborated: "You believe that there's a Creator of the world, but you don't believe that He personally takes care of you. When we have emuna in Divine Providence and recognize that everything Hashem does is for our very best, we don't worry."

The soldier then asked, "In that case, how do I build emuna?"

The author answered, "Ask Hashem to grant you emuna and to help you believe that everything He does is for the very best; pray for the awareness that there're no tribulations without transgressions. Ask Hashem to withhold severe soul corrections as long as you are trying your best to correct yourself."

"What, can I ask Hashem for emuna?"

"Do you have a better address?" asked the author. "We ask Hashem for all of our material needs, so why not ask for our spiritual needs too? Hashem won't give us material things that we don't need or that are detrimental to us, but He always gives us what our souls need. So, if you ask for emuna, you're sure to get it! Ask Hashem to help you believe that He's the address for everything – health, livelihood, material, your safety, and spiritual needs."

Every creation has a spark of emuna. Prayer, particularly personal prayer – speaking to Hashem in one's own words – has the ability of fanning that spark into a brightly-burning flame.

Rebbe Nathan of Breslev composed an entire collection of personal prayers. A close examination of these prayers show that they all rotate around a central theme, the request for emuna. When one builds emuna, all prayers are subsequently answered.

Even more noteworthy is the fact that Rebbe Nathan was a scholar and ordained rabbi, a kabbalist, and an individual of extreme piety. Despite his remarkable holiness, he never failed to ask Hashem for more and more emuna.

Personal prayer

Personal prayer is one's individual discourse with Hashem, in one's own language and one's own words. The wonderful attribute of personal prayer is that one needs no prescribed text, time, or place to speak to Hashem. Anywhere (except for places expressly forbidden in religious law, such as in the bathroom or shower) and anytime is opportune for personal prayer.

Personal prayer is the key to building emuna for the following reasons:

1. Speaking to Hashem on a daily basis instills emuna in a person's heart.

2. Having one's personal prayers answered greatly reinforces emuna.

3. Personal prayer is a cogent tool for personal improvement; by overcoming negative traits, one builds emuna and vice versa.

4. Hashem shines truth and emuna in the hearts of those who thank Him on a daily basis.

5. By confessing one's transgressions to Hashem daily in personal prayer, one attains the cognizance that everything Hashem does is for the very best.

Tangible emuna

Rabbi Avraham Yeshayahu Karelitz, the famed "Chazon Ish" of blessed and saintly memory, writes that a person attains tangible emuna by asking Hashem for every single need, from large to small, even the most mundane of requests.

For example, you're on the way to the shoe store; talk to Hashem while you're walking or driving, and say: "Hashem, please help me find the right pair of shoes at a price I can afford. Let them fit properly and be comfortable. Let them be attractive too, so I can wear them for Sabbath and the holidays." You'll be amazed to see how you find exactly what you want! Such prayer makes emuna tangible.

The Chofetz Chaim of blessed and saintly memory teaches that a person should speak to Hashem like a child speaks to a loving father, simply, sincerely, and in one's own words. Such prayers – earnest, heartfelt requests for mercy, understanding, and Divine assistance – are always heard.

Rebbe Nathan of Breslev writes (*Sichos HaRan, 233*), that Rebbe Nachman once spoke to one of his disciples about clothing. He said, "You must pray for everything. If your garment is torn and must be replaced, pray to G-d for a new one. Do this for everything. Make it a habit to pray for all your needs, large or small. Your main prayers should be for fundamental needs (of the soul) – that G-d help you in your devotion, that you be worthy of coming close to Him. Nonetheless, you should also pray even for trivial things."

Rebbe Nachman stresses, "G-d may give you food and clothing and everything else you need even though you do not ask for them.

But then, you are like an animal. G-d gives every living thing its bread without being asked. He can also give it to you this way. But if you do not draw your needs through prayer, then your livelihood is like that of a beast. For a human must draw all necessities of life from G-d only through prayer."

Rebbe Nathan once needed a button for his coat. Rebbe Nachman told him, "Pray to G-d for it" Rebbe Nathan was astonished to learn that one must even pray to Hashem for such seemingly trivial things. Seeing his surprise, Rebbe Nachman asked, "Is it beneath your dignity to pray to God for a minor thing like a button?"

To build emuna, we must pray for everything, even the most trivial things. By praying for the little things in life, we learn to take nothing for granted and build the emuna that everything comes from Hashem. The foundation of emuna is the cognizance that Hashem is the source of everything and that we are dependant on Him for all our needs – every breath and every heartbeat – every moment of our entire lives.

When people insist on believing in their own power and abilities, they expose themselves to tribulations that are designed to reveal their futility. Oftentimes, feelings of complacency invoke problems almost immediately. Here's an example: A person is smugly driving on the freeway in a new Mercedes feeling like he owns the world, and suddenly gets a flat tire. When he attempts to change the tire, he discovers that his spare is deflated. He must now call a tow service, waste time, and lose money – all because of a tiny nail on the highway – which is nothing other than an inanimate messenger from Hashem to show the man in the Mercedes his inherent futility.

One-stop shopping

The main manifestation of emuna is prayer.

Emuna brings a person to prayer. Praying to Hashem is like one-stop shopping - all your needs are under one roof. Hashem is the address for health, for livelihood, for success, or for sending a solution to a problem. The more one prays, the more one sees how remarkably those prayers are answered.

Hashem won't fulfill requests for material wealth or possessions unless they're beneficial for a person. But, requests for spiritual wealth – for more emuna, more understanding of Torah, or for assistance in fulfilling a mitzvah – are virtually always answered. The bulk of our prayers should focus on our spiritual needs, the nourishment of our souls.

The vessel of abundance

Prayer is the vessel, or receptacle, of Divine abundance. A person must be specific in prayer, and elaborate to Hashem exactly what he or she needs or wants.

People often wonder why we need prayer at all, for Hashem reads our hearts and minds and knows exactly what we need! Very true, but Hashem gives us the power to pray so that we'll seek Him and develop emuna. If our needs were fulfilled automatically, without ever having to ask for them, we'd never seek Hashem or emuna, and our souls would wither.

In order to know how to pray, we must learn about what we're praying for. The more specific a prayer, the better vessel of Divine abundance it becomes.

When learning about emuna, we should ask Hashem to help us internalize each stage of our learning. Once we've learned about the first stage of emuna, namely, that everything in the world is a product of Divine will, then we should incorporate it our prayers, as follows: "Hashem, help me believe that everything comes from You. Help me realize that my wife's yelling at me is none other than Your reprimand, so that I won't lose my temper and ruin the peace at home. Help me realize that my success at work today was a blessing from You, so that I'll thank you all the time...," and so forth.

After we've learned the second stage of emuna, namely, that everything Hashem does is for the very best, we can create a new receptacle of Divine abundance by praying to implement this too. A sample prayer in this case would be, "Hashem, help me realize that everything you do is for the very best, and even if I fail to understand how or why, help me believe strongly that everything that's happening in my life is for the very best." This principle should also be applied when we learn the third stage of emuna as well, that everything is a message from Hashem to accomplish a specific purpose.

Prayer designed to implement our learning is a cogent spiritual vessel. Hashem especially loves those prayers that are the outcome of our Torah learning, for they show that we are internalizing the Torah and applying it to our daily lives. Practical application of Torah, or living according to Torah, is the loftiest motivation of Torah learning. Hashem is ever so happy to answer our prayers to implement what we learn.

Rebbe Nachman of Breslev writes (*Likutei Moharan II:25*) that we strive to convert our Torah learning into prayers, and beg Hashem to teach us how to properly implement what we have learned. When a person truly desires to apply and internalize the Torah's lessons, Hashem readily answers those prayers; even more, Hashem derives indescribable joy from the prayers that stem from Torah learning.

According to Rebbe Nachman's teaching, by learning about emuna, then converting our learning into prayer, we're assured of acquiring more and more emuna, the secret to success and happiness in this world and in the next!

Additional Ways of Building Emuna

Crying out to Hashem

Rebbe Nachman of Breslev teaches (*Rebbe Nachman's Discourses, 146*) that when a person lacks emuna, he or she should cry out to Hashem. Such a cry doesn't have to be audible at all; a silent cry from deep down in the heart is very good. The fact that one cries out to Hashem is proof of the spark of emuna in their midst, for without that spark, they wouldn't cry out at all. The spark in turn becomes a glowing flame of emuna.

Speaking words of emuna

Anyone can recover from a breakdown of emuna by speaking words of emuna. When a person feels like he's clouded in darkness, and has difficulty feeling Hashem's presence, then he should speak words of emuna out loud, such as: "I believe in Hashem, that He's the One and Only G-d, and He protects me and watches over me every minute of the day my entire life, and He always listens to my prayers. Hashem loves me and cares about me."

One should continue to speak words of emuna in whatever area one needs help, as follows: "I believe that Hashem sustains all His creations. He will surely send me my livelihood;" or, "I believe that Hashem is the physician of all flesh. He will surely send me a cure." Before an important exam or negotiation, we enhance chances of success by saying, "I believe that success comes from Hashem. I've done my best to prepare, please Hashem, help me succeed!"

By speaking words of emuna, we arouse the spark of emuna within us, which kindles a bright flame of emuna that not only warms the soul and illuminates the darkness within us, but invokes Divine compassion.

As speaking words of emuna does wonders for the soul, we should consequently be careful to avoid saying anything that contains the slightest hint of heresy, even in a joke. Words of heresy or agnosticism extinguish the spark of emuna and render a person's soul cold and dark, Heaven forbid.

Self evaluation

By evaluating ourselves every day, we are reminded of our relationship with Hashem. Four wonderful things happen when we judge ourselves on a daily basis:

1. We remind ourselves of Hashem and of His commandments;

2. We make decisions to correct what needs correcting, and therefore don't accrue spiritual debts that lead to stern judgments;

3. Since Hashem doesn't allow double jeopardy, when we judge ourselves, the Heavenly Court is not allowed to judge us.

4. Daily self-evaluation reminds us that there is a Creator in the world; when we contemplate whether our actions are in accordance with His will, we contemplate Him. By thinking of Hashem, we enhance emuna.

Avoid reading philosophy books and works of heresy

We have often compared emuna to a flame or flickering candle in the heart. Emuna is difficult to acquire but simple to destroy. Emuna also resembles a fine crystal chandelier hand-crafted in months of tedious work. Yet, with one shove of the elbow, the chandelier can be pushed off the artisan's work table, and in the shortest moment, shatters into a million tiny slivers.

An old Jewish expression says that a fool throws a stone in the well that a hundred wise men can't remove. The power of the written word, especially the heretical written word, is that it penetrates the heart faster than a swift sword to destroy emuna.

When a person turns to philosophy or investigative books to search for logical arguments and proof of Hashem's existence, the result is confusion and an eventual breakdown of emuna. When our emuna is dependant on the strength of our intellect, then we are dangerously exposed to thoughts and opinions of those who know how to present stronger arguments than we do, and our emuna is liable to be destroyed, G-d forbid. For that reason, the way of true Jewish emuna is the way of our forefathers – the simple and uncomplicated belief in Hashem that has passed down in an unbroken chain from Abraham, Isaac, and Jacob to us.

We should avoid heretical input in every possible way – not only by avoid reading books that weaken emuna, but by avoiding radio, television, internet, and newspapers that are programmed and published by those who spread agnostic and atheistic views and ideas. If we would compare heretical input to non-kosher food for the soul, then we should note that forbidden thoughts enter soul via the ears, heart, eyes, and brain much faster than forbidden food enters the body.

Learning Torah

The light of Torah destroys the darkness of heresy.

People construe heresy, or *epikorsis*, as total denial of Hashem; that's not true. Oftentimes, so-called "religious" people harbor heretical ideas that resemble weeds in a garden. Learning Torah uproots these weeds.

Torah leads to emuna only when learned purely for the sake of performing Hashem's will and not for the sake of person gain. By learning Torah in order to implement Hashem's will, one attains emuna.

The light of Torah cleanses and illuminates the heart and soul, and makes them suitable receptacles for emuna. With emuna, the soul is an ideal vessel of Divine light.

"Shmirat Habrit", or guarding the holy covenant

Nothing destroys emuna like lewdness and licentiousness. The Torah tells of Err (*see Gen.38:7*), calling him "evil in the eyes of God". Rashi explains that Err would spill his seed so that his wife wouldn't become pregnant and her beauty would be preserved.

The Code of Jewish Law states (*Shulchan Oruch, Even HaEzer 23:1*), "It is forbidden to spill one's seed in vain, and this transgression is worse than all the sins of the Torah. As such, one may not thresh on the inside and sow seed on the outside. Those guilty of masturbation who spill seed in vain, not only have they done a heinous violation, but they are subject to excommunication." Even though today's religious courts no longer excommunicate people, when a person commits a transgression that is subject to excommunication, Hashem turns a deaf ear to that person's prayers.

The holy covenant means that we use our reproductive apparatus only in the performance of a mitzvah, which is either procreation, insuring marital bliss, or both. The guarding of the holy covenant, or ***Shmiras Habrit***, is probably the most conducive factor in attaining and preserving emuna.

Kedusha, or holiness of thought, speech, and deed, is the best way of guarding the holy covenant. The more we immerse ourselves in Torah and the less we expose ourselves to the influences of today's lewd and permissive society, the better we guard the holy covenant. Practically, one should marry at as early an age as possible, avoid looking at other women, and avoid looking at the media. Since the eyes are the window of the soul, seeing lewd and forbidden images immediately tarnishes the soul. For that reason, both the Torah and the Code of Jewish Law specifically and emphatically require us to avoid looking at any woman other than our mothers, wives, and daughters. Our sages teach *(see Rambam, Laws of Teshuva, 4:4)* that merely harboring the image of a strange woman in one's brain is tantamount to mental adultery.

Lewd thoughts and unclean speech lead to violations of the holy covenant, since they defile the brain and the mouth. The brain was designed for contemplating Torah and Hashem, and the mouth was designed for speaking Torah and praying. A mouth that has been contaminated with unclean and lewd speech can't pray properly; using such a mouth for prayer is like using one's toilet as a soup bowl. Even if the toilet were crystal clean and disinfected, who would want to eat from a toilet bowl? In like manner, Hashem doesn't want to hear the prayers of a mouth that's used for lewd and forbidden speech.

Masturbation and spilling one's seed lead to a sealing of the heart and the brain from Divine light. That's why emuna and debauchery are mutually exclusive. As we've learned earlier in this book, emuna is more conducive than anything else to a good income. Therefore, debauchery – the opposite of *Shmirat Habrit* – causes financial difficulties and destroys one's livelihood.

All the wonderful benefits of emuna that we've learned previously in this book are destroyed when one fails to guard the holy covenant. For example, emuna brings a person to spiritual awareness and to happiness. A breach of one's holy covenant destroys emuna and leads directly to sadness, depression, and other emotional problems.

Adultery, a flagrant breach of the holy covenant, goes against all the principles of Judaism and emuna. Nothing severs a person so fast from Hashem as adultery. As such, the wicked Bilaam advised Balak, the king of Moab, that if he couldn't overcome Israel by military means, then all he had to do was to tempt them with licentiousness.

The Zohar says that a person's principal test in the world is to overcome the lust for adultery. From a spiritual standpoint, adultery begins way before the forbidden act – as soon as a person *looks* at someone else's spouse or *contemplates* adultery in any way, the eyes and the mind become spiritually contaminated. Such contamination destroys the soul, Heaven forbid.

Our sages teach us that what the eye sees, the heart desires. Therefore, by guarding the sight of our eyes and by limiting our gaze to the permissible, we protect ourselves from falling into the trap of lustful desires. Lustful desires alone are enough to wreak havoc on the soul. Also, lustful desires are the spiritual opposite of the love of Hashem – one can't have both. A person can't have lustful desires and cling to Hashem simultaneously. Stop and think – is a lustful thought or desire worth being separated from Hashem?

The Land of Israel

The Gemorra teaches that one can't fully attain emuna outside the context of the Land of Israel. Therefore, one who truly desires emuna should pray to Hashem for the privilege of coming to Eretz Yisrael, and meanwhile, should long to be in the Land of Israel.

Clinging to Hashem

The Gemorra asks a question: It's a mitzvah to cling to Hashem, yet Hashem is like an all-consuming fire; so, who can cling to Him?

The Gemorra answers its own question and says, by clinging to Torah scholars and *tzaddikim* that teach the way of Hashem, one clings to Hashem.

Religious law requires us to cling to our wise men and to heed their words. A substantial portion of the Torah comes under the classification of "Oral Law," that which has been passed on from teacher to pupil in a generation after generation unbroken chain that dates back to Moses on Mount Sinai, who received the oral elaboration of the Torah directly from Hashem. Therefore, a person shouldn't think that it's sufficient to teach himself Torah – there's much room for error; one avoids error by clinging to a righteous scholar and learning from him.

In like manner, one cannot fully attain emuna without clinging to the righteous spiritual leaders of the generation, what we refer to as *emunat chachamim,* or belief in our sages. Without *emunat chachamim*, one cannot properly develop emuna in Hashem.

Studying the works of the true tzaddikim is highly conducive to emuna, for the writings of a true tzaddik arouse one's heart to seek Hashem and to cling to Him. Like all other holy books, a person should learn the works of a tzaddik with the help of one of the tzaddik's learned disciples to avoid confusion or misunderstanding. By establishing a relationship with the tzaddikim's disciples, one is able to cling to the tzaddik and subsequently enhance emuna.

Rebbe Nachman of Breslev writes in *Sefer HaMiddot* (under the subject "tzaddik"):

- The main perfection of the soul is contingent on getting close to tzaddikim.
- The proximity of tzaddikim is beneficial in this world and in the next.
- The coming of Moshiach depends on getting close to the tzaddik.
- Those who are close to the tzaddik in their lifetime will be close to him after they die.
- That which you hear from the mouth of the tzaddik is more beneficial than that which you learn in books.

- It's good to invest a lot of time in order to merit one hour of proximity to the tzaddik.

For all the above-mentioned reasons, one must search for a genuine, righteous tzaddik and spiritual guide. By clinging to such a person and by learning from him, one attains emuna.

Strengthening emuna

Rebbe Nathan of Breslev writes (*Rebbe Nachman's Discourses, 222*): "I heard that the Rebbe was once encouraging a man who was greatly confused about emuna. The Rebbe told him, 'It is written that all creation came into being only because of people like you. G-d saw that there would be people who would cling to our Holy faith, suffering greatly because of the confusion and doubts that constantly plague them. He perceived that they would overcome these doubts and remain strong in their beliefs. It was because of this that G-d brought forth all creation.'"

Rebbe Nathan adds, "This man was then greatly strengthened and unperturbed whenever he had these confusing thoughts. The Rebbe said many times that the creation was mainly for the sake of faith. Thus it is written, 'All His works are through emuna' (*Psalms 33:4*)."

Over two hundred years ago, Rebbe Nachman of Breslev warned of the great flood of atheism that will drown people in the spiritual and emotional perils that we're fighting against today. True to his words, the only way to save ourselves from modern society's perilous sea of denial and disbelief is to learn as much as we can about emuna, and to constantly reinforce it. More than anything, we should constantly pray to Hashem for more and more emuna and invest our principal efforts in attaining and strengthening emuna. **Our lives in this world and in the next depend on emuna.**

Collection of Thoughts from "Sefer HaMidot" about Emuna

Factors detrimental to emuna

- Hardening one's heart
- Violating the laws of Torah
- Jealousy, anger, and covetousness
- Disdain of Torah scholars
- Dishonesty and flattery

Factors conducive to emuna

- Modesty and humility
- Tearful prayer
- Silence
- Charity
- Sleeping in holiness.

Chapter Seven

Self-Correction

The most important prerequisite for self-correction is self awareness. The first thing we all need to know about ourselves is that each of us has a ***yetzer hara***, or evil inclination.

Many people are frustrated or intimidated by their evil inclination. We often hear, "If only I didn't have such a strong evil inclination…," or "Why did Hashem have to weigh me down with an evil inclination?"

The evil inclination is a necessary part of our spiritual anatomy just as two arms and two legs are necessary parts of our physical anatomy. Our principal task on earth is to correct ourselves by channeling the negative energy of the evil inclination into positive endeavors, such as Torah learning and the fulfillment of mitzvoth.

Teshuva, which literally means "returning," is the process of elevating and converting our animal drives into spiritual power. No other creation on earth is capable of transforming the material into the spiritual. As such, the Jew has a unique task on earth – with an animal body, he or she is capable of surpassing an angel and achieving lofty spiritual heights.

Self-correction, the refinement of the evil inclination, is a war with constant ups and downs. Like in a war, we win some battles and we lose some. The stronger a person gets, the stronger his or her evil inclination becomes as well. One wonders why – shouldn't the evil inclination be weakened in time? The answer is no. As a person makes spiritual gain, he or she meets harder opposition; this is for their ultimate good in order to enable them to make further spiritual gains and to increase their ultimate reward in the world to come. The same principal applies in professional athletics – the better an athlete becomes, the more difficult the competition he competes against.

One should never be discouraged by the evil inclination, just keep on fighting! A winning pitcher might easily shutout all of his opponents in the minor leagues, but then lose a few games when he moves up to the major leagues. Anyone knows that a 50-50 win-loss record in the major leagues is much more admirable than a 90-10 win-loss record in the minor leagues. Therefore, setbacks remind us that we have a job to do and that we're fighting tough adversaries. By striving against fierce resistance, we make formidable spiritual gain and refine our souls.

Hashem helps

After we've become aware that we each have an evil inclination, the second principal we need to know is that we are incapable of overcoming it unless Hashem comes to our aid. This necessitates us to seek Hashem's help.

The main way to overcome the evil inclination and to strengthen ourselves in spirituality is to pray to Hashem, asking for His help and guidance in avoiding sin and in making the right choices. Hashem helps those who seek His help.

Some people punish themselves, chastise themselves, or become totally disappointed with themselves when they do something wrong. That's a self-destructive mode, which leads only to depression and despair. If a boxer would become depressed when hit by his opponent, he'd soon be knocked out altogether. Each of us, even the greatest tzaddikim, has setbacks from time to time. Disappointment in ourselves doesn't accomplish a thing; asking for Hashem's help does!

Know your Evil Inclination

Once a person realizes that he has an evil inclination (EI), he must learn the way to fight against it. The EI's objective is to contaminate a person's soul with doubt and heresy, for as soon as a person's emuna is weakened, he becomes a slave to the EI. On the other hand, as long as a person constantly reinforces his emuna, the EI has no control over him. This is true freedom.

The EI is a master strategist. Rather than operating with a standard template, it uses a different approach with different people. The EI injects one person with total heresy and denial of Hashem, Heaven forbid. It attacks another person with partial heresy, such as a denial of the Oral Torah and of rabbinical law. A third person's EI causes him to be selective about the mitzvoth – he'll observe what seems to him logical, but will ignore and transgress any mitzvah that he doesn't understand or approve of. A fourth person might even be an Orthodox rabbi, yet the EI will try to contaminate his soul with a disbelief in the true tzaddikim.

Then again, there's a fifth person who has already repelled the four onslaughts of EI mentioned in the previous paragraph. This person has a strong belief in Hashem and in the Torah and strives to live his life according to Hashem's will. So, what can the EI do to a person like this?

The answer is simple: The EI attacks those who aspire for complete emuna with arrogance, self-persecution, or both. Now, let's learn how to combat this type of EI.

Rebbe Nachman of Breslev teaches us an important guideline in life (see Likutei Moharan II:110). The Rebbe says, "A person has a simple choice: if he wants – he does; if he doesn't want – he doesn't do." This notion is amazingly simple, but very deep.

Every time a person is faced with an option, he must do his best to make the right choice. Successful people use all the tools that Hashem puts at their disposal:

First, they have a strong desire to make the right choice.

Second, they cling to the emuna that Hashem will help them make the right choice.

Third, they learn as much as they can, seeking the advice of the Torah and of the great tzaddikim in making the right choice.

Fourth, they pray profusely to Hashem, asking Him to help them make the right choice.

The above four tools can be boiled down to one word – **emuna**. We have apparent free choice *before* we choose, but the moment after we make our choice, we must know that we made our particular choice because Hashem wanted us to do so. Remember the Rambam's first of the thirteen principles of emuna – Hashem did, does, and will do every single action. Consequently, one needn't boast about successes because Hashem enabled him to succeed. Conversely, one needn't persecute oneself about failing, for Hashem engineered the failure.

Here we have a very cunning EI that misleads a person into giving himself the credit for his successes and blaming himself for his failures by subtly removing Hashem from the picture. This in itself is another mode of choice, for a person must cling to emuna just as much "after the fact" as before the fact. The "a priori" emuna helps us make the right choices, but the "post facto" emuna saves us from the arrogance that might follow a success and the self-persecution that is liable to follow a failure.

Remember: Before the fact, do your best to make the best choice. After the fact, believe that this is Hashem's will and all for the best.

Omniscience and free choice

The classic dilemma of the Jewish faith is the seeming discrepancy between Hashem's omniscience and free choice. If Hashem knows what we're going to do, then how do we have free choice? If Hashem did, does, and will do every single action as we said previously, then that would make Hashem responsible for our sins as well. If a person can't lift a finger without Hashem enabling him to, then where's the free choice?

Let's remind ourselves of Rebbe Nachman's teaching: "A person has a simple choice: if he wants – he does; if he doesn't want – he doesn't do." Even though Hashem *knows* what we're going to choose, He doesn't *force* us to make a particular choice. If we were robots, then there's no context for a system of reward and punishment. Hashem allows us to choose between good and evil. That notwithstanding, Rebbe Nachman explains that the human intellect is incapable of fully comprehending the notion of omniscience and free choice (see Likutei Moharan I:21). A person who could fully grasp this notion would no longer be a person, but a much higher spiritual being. Higher spiritual beings don't have free choice, for the truth of Hashem is crystal clear to them.

Only mortal man has free choice. No matter how hard he might try, a man can't fully grasp the concept and compatibility of omniscience and free choice. If he stubbornly insists on understanding, he's liable to become totally confused. Even worse, he might even fall into the pit of heresy, Heaven forbid. King Solomon said (Proverbs 2:19), "Some searchers never come back, yet they fail to grasp the ways of life." In other words, we must recognize that there are spiritual laws that govern the universe that transcend human understanding. Where understanding leaves off, emuna must kick in.

When speaking about free choice, we'd be best advised to put the notion of Hashem's omniscience aside. Hashem's omniscience and free choice are two different resources that we utilize on different occasion, but like milk and meat, we never mix between the two.

Before the fact, we use our power of free choice.

After the fact, we draw on Hashem's omniscience, for everything is in his hands. Once again, this saves us from the two cunning EIs of arrogance and self-persecution.

When you're faced with making a choice, don't even think about Hashem's omniscience. Use the tools at your disposure to make the very best choice you can. Try your best and draw on your desire to do what's right, your Torah learning, your emuna, the advice of tzaddikim. Most of all, invest plenty of time and effort in praying that Hashem guide you in the right direction; the more one prays, the greater the chances of success.

Making the right choices

A person shouldn't think that the "game is thrown," in other words, that since everything is predestined from Above, it doesn't matter what we do. Some people say, "If Hashem wants me to be a righteous person, then let Him make me be righteous! Until then, I'll do what I want…"

"Do what I want…" – such a person is caught red-handed. That's the free choice, guaranteed by the Torah (Deut. 30:15): "Behold, I have given before you life and the good or death and the evil." Torah commands a person to make a choice. Torah gives us the option of choosing emuna and holiness which guarantee life in this world and in the next or choosing cigarettes, alcohol, substance usage, and promiscuity which destroy our bodies and our souls, Heaven forbid. King Solomon, the wisest of all men said that only a fool makes stupid choices then blames Hashem (see Proverbs 19:3).

We therefore must do our utmost to make the right choices and to avoid transgressing at all costs. Everyone will have to suffer the consequences and assume responsibility for bad choices. If we didn't have free choice, then we wouldn't be judged in the Heavenly Court for everything we do.

Once again though, even if a person made the worst mistake or transgression in the world, after the fact he should know that this was Hashem's will – and for the very best!

Dear reader, you're probably asking how committing a sin can possibly be for a person's ultimate good. Understand that Hashem helps each person attain his or her soul correction.

Suppose that a person must overcome a lust for sweets and overeating. Maybe Hashem will allow that person to eat something that wasn't kosher. For example, "Yankele" has a lust for chocolate, and grabs a bar of milk chocolate thinking that it's non-dairy. Along comes his wife, and says, "What are you doing? You just finished eating a meat meal!" and shows him that the chocolate contains dairy ingredients. Yankele's heart breaks; he realizes that if his lust for sweets were not so strong, he certainly would have been careful to check the label before he put it in his mouth and he wouldn't have violated the law that requires waiting six hours after eating meat before eating a dairy-derived substance.

Since Yankele has emuna, he realizes that Hashem engineered the mistake by taking advantage of his own free choice, all for the purpose of helping him realize what he must correct, namely, his lust for sweets and overeating.

Everything Hashem does is with precision Divine Providence, tailor-made for the individual needs of each soul and to facilitate its correction.

As such, everything is for the best! Our deficiencies are designed to direct us on the right path toward our individual soul correction.

Neutralizing the Evil Inclination

When a person arouses himself to do better and to seek Hashem with greater effort after a setback, he effectively neutralizes the Evil Inclination. The EI is nothing but heresy, so when a person realizes that even his temporary setback comes from Hashem and is definitely for his ultimate good, then he is applying the power of emuna which destroys the EI.

With emuna, a person doesn't torment himself or fall into despair and depression after a setback. He simply analyzes his setbacks, draws conclusions, and takes positive action to improve. This is a process of observation, evaluation, and implementation. Such a person makes constant growth by using the tools that Hashem gives him to climb higher and higher. Since he's constantly connected to Hashem – observing Hashem's messages, evaluating himself, and implementing the lessons he has learned from previous setbacks – he overcomes the EI; indeed, the EI has no power over him.

By not tormenting himself, the person with emuna actually uses his setbacks to climb higher. The setbacks keep him from becoming arrogant and arouse him to make even greater effort in his service of Hashem. For that reason, people with emuna wholeheartedly thank Hashem for their setbacks. Here's an example of such a prayer of thanks:

Master of the World, beloved Father in Heaven, thank You for Your wonderful and personal intervention in my life. Thank You for showing me my shortcomings by letting me make a mistake. Thank You for arousing me to make a greater effort to get close to you. I wouldn't have made this effort if I hadn't experienced the setback.

Knowing that our setbacks are for our ultimate benefit, we can fulfill a law in Judaism that many people have difficulty in observing, namely, that one is obliged to thank Hashem for the seemingly bad in the same manner that one thanks Hashem for the good (see Gemara, tractate Berachot 33b, and Shulchan Oruch, Orach Chaim 222:3).

We try our best to make the best choices in life. Before the fact, we do our best to succeed. But after the fact, we realize that our setbacks are also the product of Hashem's perfect precision Divine Providence, and everything Hashem does is for the very best.

Teshuva from love

A person who thanks Hashem for his failures and setbacks is immune from sadness, depression, and despair. He knows that Hashem is doing everything for the best to help him fulfill his potential and reach greater spiritual heights.

The Gemara says (tractate Yoma 86b) that if a person does teshuva from love (as opposed to teshuva from the fear of retribution), then his willful misdeeds that appear in his spiritual debits column become merits in his spiritual credits column. People ask how this can be – the answer is simple: when a person uses his misdeeds to see how utterly far away from Hashem he is, then these very misdeeds become a catalyst for teshuva. When one's misdeed triggers one's observation, self-evaluation, and subsequent teshuva, then that misdeed becomes a merit and a feather in his spiritual cap.

Furthermore, our sages said that a person doesn't thoroughly understand a law of Torah until he stumbles on that very law. The reason is that if a person has strong enough emuna not to lose heart from his misdeed or to persecute himself, then he can learn very much from his setback. Setbacks are an impetus to making a much stronger second effort. They also keep us from becoming arrogant and encourage us to increase our prayers in quality and quantity. With emuna, we can see that our setbacks in life are actually the silver lining of what appears to be a very dark cloud.

Truth

As long as a person doesn't reconcile himself to his human frailties and fails to understand that setbacks are a necessary part of personal and spiritual growth, he'll continue to fail time after time. If his arrogance doesn't allow him to acknowledge and accept his shortcomings, he'll never see the truth.

Rebbe Menachem Mendel of Kotsk comments on the episode of the forbidden fruit in the Torah portion of Breishit. Hashem asks Adam (see Genesis, ch. 3), "Where are you? Did you eat from the tree that I told you not to?" What does the first question have to do with the second? The Kotsker Rebbe explains that Hashem is telling Adam, "Look to where you've fallen. Rather than learning from your mistake, you blamed it on Eve!"

Hashem knows that we're human. He also knows that despite our best efforts, we still fall from time to time. Hashem doesn't ask us to be perfect; all He wants is that we use our setbacks and failures as a way to truthfully evaluate ourselves and as a catalyst for self-improvement.

Saying Thank You

A person can't truly make teshuva until he builds enough emuna to thank Hashem for his shortcomings. Living without emuna means living without Hashem. How can people do teshuva if they live without Hashem?

Thanking Hashem for our setbacks and shortcomings is a true indication of emuna and a springboard to prayer and personal improvement.

Meet your Creator

Remember, Hashem knows you intimately. He knows that you have an evil inclination and that you need His help to overcome it. Even if you've done the worse thing imaginable, Hashem doesn't want you poking around in the muck and the mire of the past. Go forward! Make a new beginning. You won't be effective until you kick into the positive mode.

Don't forget that Hashem loves you always. He's always ready to help you. He created you in order to shower His mercy and lovingkindness on you, more than you can ever imagine. His mercy and loving-kindness are infinite, and are at your disposal constantly, especially at life's most challenging times.

What does Hashem ask from us?

The Gemorra says (*tractate Avoda Zara 3a*), "Hashem doesn't complain about His creations." This means that Hashem doesn't make demands that a person is incapable of fulfilling. Hashem knows exactly who each of us is, and what we're capable of accomplishing in this world.

Cherished reader, it's not possible to demand that from this moment on, you shouldn't sin anymore, for at this stage of your life, there may be certain laws that are difficult for you to observe. But, you should at least ask for Hashem's forgiveness for not yet observing them! If you don't strive to fulfill the Torah's commandments, you never will!

Hashem wants each of us to make the first step in bettering ourselves. Once we make the effort, He comes to our assistance.

Teshuva is happiness

The only way to make teshuva is by being happy.

A sad and depressed person has no control over his or her thought processes. Without mental composure, one won't be able to attain emuna and to make teshuva. A sad and depressed person is like a prisoner of war, captured by the ruthless evil inclination. Depression and holiness are mutually exclusive. For that reason, the evil inclination wants a person to be constantly down in the dumps.

One asks, so how can I be happy? The answer is surprisingly simple: A person is happy when his or her soul is gratified, and the soul is gratified when the person performs Hashem's will. Since teshuva brings a person to perform Hashem's will, teshuva also leads to gratification of the soul and to happiness.

The 24 Heavenly Courts

There are 24 Heavenly Courts that judge a person every single hour of every single day. A person that does good deeds receives a positive verdict; the soul immediately reacts to a positive judgment in the Heavenly Court with optimism and happiness. The opposite also holds true; one who incurs an unfavorable verdict that resulted from a negative action feels sadness, pessimism, and a heaviness of the spirit.

Rosh Hashanah, the New Year of the Jewish calendar, is the annual Day of Judgment that determines whether a person will live or die, how much annual income he or she will have, and other general factors. This doesn't contradict the fact that a person is judged every hour of the day. For example, on Rosh Hashanah, it's decided that a person will earn two thousand dollars on January 8th; on the morning of January 8th, it's decided *how* that person will earn the money, whether in joy or in sorrow.

The following Chassidic story further explains the concept of daily and annual judgment:

> The Baal Shem Tov met an elderly water-carrier on the way, and asked him how he was. The water carrier smiled a semi-toothless smile, and praised G-d for giving him once more the strength to earn a respectable day's living.
>
> A few days later, the Baal Shem Tov met the same elderly water-carrier. This time, the old man barely moped along under his yoke and two buckets, as if he were carrying the entire world on his shoulders. With a long face, he complained

> to the Baal Shem Tov how difficult his lot in life was.
>
> The elderly man's extreme change of mood surprised the Baal Shem Tov. After a moment's contemplation, the Baal Shem Tov smiled and thanked the water-carrier. "My friend, you've just answered a difficult question I had while learning tractate Rosh Hashanah. The Mishna says that a person is judged on Rosh Hashanah, yet the Gemorra says that a person is judged every day and every hour. The question in my mind was, if a person is judged on Rosh Hashanah as to the outcome of the entire year, why be judged again every day and every hour?"
>
> The Baal Shem Tov then explained that the hourly and daily judgments determine the way a person will receive what's been predetermined in the beginning of the year; if one's actions are favorable, they receive their lot happily that particular hour. If their deeds are otherwise, then they get what they deserve with sadness, depression, or aggravation on that particular day and hour.

The day that the water-carrier was happy and optimistic was a day when his actions received a favorable judgment in the Heavenly Court. He didn't earn any more than he did on any other day, nor did he toil any less. Yet, he felt gratitude to Hashem and joy in his heart. A few days later, having apparently received an unfavorable judgment from the Heavenly Court for less than desirable deeds, his mood plummeted and his work became torture.

In any event, a person can change that which has been predetermined on Rosh Hashanah by teshuva, prayer, and charity.

Listening to the hints

The story of the Baal Shem Tov and the water carrier explains how our moods, situation, or circumstances can change from hour to hour. You've most probably experienced how you're getting along famously with your spouse or with your superior one hour, and then all of a sudden, out of the clear blue, you're being yelled at and chastised in a manner that logically makes no sense at all. When you take hourly judgments into consideration though, everything makes sense; last hour's favorable judgment simply became this hour's severe judgment.

Everything that saddens a person, even the tiniest cause of mild anguish such as a small itch, is the result of a Heavenly-Court decision.

The Gemorra teaches (*see tractate Arachin 16b*) that every tiny anguish in life comes under the heading of Heaven-sent tribulations, such as trying on a garment that doesn't fit properly or reaching in your pocket and pulling out a quarter when you wanted to pull out a nickel. By internalizing the knowledge that these moment-to-moment happenings in our life are the products of Heavenly-Court judgments, we greatly enhance our spiritual awareness, our emuna, and our connection to Hashem.

Hashem is righteous

Imagine that a son misbehaves and subsequently receives a punishment from his father. The mischievous son now blames his misfortune on his younger brother, and picks a fight with him. Now, the father is doubly perturbed: Not only has the mischievous son failed to correct his behavior, but he's now started a fight with his little brother, who had nothing to do with the punishment!

Many of us act like the mischievous son in the above example. Rather than tracing our tribulations to Hashem and to our own misdeeds, we look for a third party to pin the blame on or to vent our frustrations. Instead of making the right decision – teshuva, the only real solution to all our problems – we fall into traps of anger, frustration, and despair. What a shame.

Even worse, we fail to realize that Hashem is righteous. The feeling that Hashem's judgments are askew is what Rebbe Nathan of Breslevcalls, "spoiled justice." One who feels that Hashem's judgments are unfair develops a warped sense of justice that impairs honest self-evaluation and soul-searching.

Rebbe Nathan writes (*Likutei Halachos, Choshen Mishpat, Nezikin 5*), "One develops a warped sense of judgment from the mistaken notions of the world. Most people yell that Hashem doesn't deal fairly with them, and that their tribulations are beyond their capability of withstanding. They also say that they have no time to serve Hashem, because of the demands of making a living. They therefore believe that Hashem makes impossible demands."

The truth is that Hashem doesn't demand anything that a person is not capable of.

The key to inner peace is the internalization of the fact that Hashem is righteous and that His decisions are just. We achieve this by constantly reviewing the principles of emuna, namely, that Hashem runs the world, does everything for the best, and has a specific purpose for everything He does. Just as one believes that everything comes from Hashem, one must believe that all of Hashem's judgments are not only righteous, but merciful and compassionate as well. Since Hashem's Judgments are merciful and compassionate – even though they might not seem that way sometimes – they are *always* for our ultimate personal benefit. The trials and tribulations that Hashem sends us are designed to bring us closer to Him.

Hashem's magnificent mercy

One doesn't become a tzaddik overnight. Yet, many people shy away from making teshuva since they're afraid of "paying the price" for past sins. Sooner or later, everyone will be making teshuva; does that mean that they all will have to go through an odyssey of torture as a process of atonement?

The answer is no. There's a way to beat the rap. Hashem doesn't allow double jeopardy. Therefore, when we judge ourselves, the Heavenly Court is not allowed to judge us.

The Zohar teaches that where there's judgment below, there can't be judgment above. In other words, when we judge ourselves, the Heavenly Court is not allowed to judge us. Practically speaking, this means that when we regularly confess our wrongdoings to Hashem, seek forgiveness, and resolve to improve, then Hashem doesn't allow the Heavenly Court to judge us; Hashem judges us himself.

There's a vast difference between Hashem's judgments and those of the Heavenly Court – whereas the Heavenly Court judges in exacting, hair-splitting precision by the letter of the law, Hashem's judgments are merciful and forgiving. When the Heavenly Court tries the case, the defendant is almost always found guilty. **When Hashem tries a case, the defendant is always declared innocent.**

So, if we want to avoid suffering and tribulations, we should set aside sixty minutes a day for self-evaluation and personal prayer, where we judge ourselves in front of Hashem. If we find ourselves guilty of wrongdoing, all we have to do is confess, ask for forgiveness, and commit to do better. The Heavenly Court subsequently is not allowed to touch the case and to try us even for the worst crime, providing that we've confessed to Hashem and are truly making Teshuva at our own initiative. Where there's judgment below, there can't be judgment above.

Serving Hashem with a smile

A person that spends an hour a day in personal prayer and self-evaluation is bound to win a favorable verdict on the critical annual judgment day of Rosh Hashanah.

Our sages teach that we should make teshuva at least one day before we die. The Midrash asks, "Who knows when they're going to die?" The logical answer is that we should make teshuva right now, for today might be our last day. That way, we're making teshuva our entire lives!

Imagine that a person was caught red-handed in crime. The police bring him in front of a judge for arraignment. The judge then says that he's willing to give the criminal an opportunity to judge himself before the court judges him. The criminal knows that if the case reaches the court, he's liable to be punished with years of imprisonment. Yet, if he judges himself, he's off the hook!

Sounds like a fantasy, doesn't it? What judge would allow a criminal to judge himself?

Hashem.

Hashem, in his unfathomable mercy, allows us to judge ourselves before our case reaches the Heavenly Court. Not only do we avoid punishment, but we get rewarded for our teshuva!

Here's another example that actualizes the above concept: A driver goes through a red light. In his rear-view mirror, he sees flashing red and blue lights; a siren wails up and down, and a state trooper with an iron jaw and cold-steel glare motions the driver to pull over to the side of the road.

The state trooper gets out of the patrol car, walks up to the driver's-side window, and prepares to throw the book at the delinquent driver. As he approaches, the state trooper hears the driver mumbling,

"Hashem, I've deliberately violated the traffic laws and have gone through a red light. I'm really sorry for doing something so irresponsible, endangering myself and other drivers as well. Please forgive me; I promise to do my utmost so this never happens again as long as I live."

The state trooper hears the confession, the remorse, the apology, and the decision to improve, and his iron jaw becomes a warm smile. "Mister, I was planning to haul you into court, get your license revoked, and ask the judge to nail you with the maximum penalty. But, I hear you rehabilitating yourself. You don't need to lose your license and to pay a six-hundred dollar fine. Wait a second…"

Pulling out a checkbook with "State of New Jersey" engraved on it, the state trooper writes the driver a check for one hundred thousand dollars, blesses him with a continued safe trip, and lets him go!

If the physical world behaved according to the state trooper's standards, would there be anyone on earth that wouldn't make teshuva? A person would have to be totally daft to leave his or her misdeeds uncorrected! Yet, the spiritual world runs exactly according to the state trooper model; when we make teshuva for a misdeed, not only do we avoid punishment, but we're handsomely rewarded!

In light of the above, an hour a day of personal prayer and self-evaluation is the opportunity of a lifetime. Teshuva is the greatest gift that a loving G-d can bestow on mankind!

Anyone that spends sixty minutes a day in personal prayer and self-evaluation keeps his or her spiritual ledger free of debits. With only credits to one's name, a person becomes a worthwhile vessel for Divine light. When Hashem illuminates His splendid Divine light on our souls, we feel deeply happy. As such, with an hour a day of personal prayer and self-evaluation, we can serve Hashem with a smile.

Practicality of personal prayer

Every person, man or women, young or old, should spend an hour a day in teshuva, which is basically personal prayer and self-evaluation. Pick the hour that's most convenient for you; many prefer early in the morning or late at night. Preferably, one should choose a place devoid of other people such as a solitary room, a park, or a field. The most important thing is to feel comfortable with no outside interference, so you can freely pour your heart out to Hashem.

A good warm-up is to begin by thanking Hashem for the wonderful blessings He gives you – your health, your livelihood, and the clothes on your back. Don't take anything for granted. Next, tell Hashem everything that has transpired in your life since the last time you spoke to Him – don't skip any details, especially the things that make you happy and the things that upset you. Thank Hashem for helping you do your good deeds, and confess your misdeeds while judging yourself in the process. Implement a four-part teshuva process that consists of confession, remorse, asking forgiveness, and commitment to improve. Finally, ask Hashem for anything and everything you want.

Personal prayer is a guarantee for a happy and meaningful life.

The four steps of Teshuva

The four-part teshuva process is too important for us to suffice with the above-mentioned reference in passing. It's vital to memorize and internalize the four steps of teshuva, so that if we need to make teshuva right away for a misdeed, we don't have to wait until our daily hour of personal prayer.

Teshuva can be done anywhere, except in the bathroom, shower, or in an unclean place. One can implement the four steps of teshuva in the office, on the subway, or while peeling potatoes in the kitchen.

The four steps of Teshuva are:

1. **Confession** – telling Hashem what we've done wrong.

2. **Remorse** – we should feel sorry for going against Hashem's will.

3. **Asking forgiveness** – we ask Hashem's forgiveness like a child would ask forgiveness from a loving parent.

4. **Commitment** – we commit to do our utmost to improve in the future, and not to slide back to our old ways.

Daily teshuva is the best preventive medicine in the world for suffering and tribulations, and a guarantee of happiness.

Remember this important rule: **The Evil Inclination isn't interested as much in the transgression as he is in the sadness and depression that immobilize a person after the transgression**. With teshuva, we disarm and neutralize the Evil Inclination. Rather than sinking into despair, we use our misdeed as raw material that can be refined with teshuva and converted into a steppingstone to getting closer to Hashem.

Four guidelines in judging ourselves

Four important guidelines show us the way to make our own self-evaluations work best. **Hashem wants teshuva, not depression**. We should always ask ourselves: What does Hashem want, that I should despair and become depressed because I committed a sin? Wouldn't He prefer that I reinforce my spiritual self and make teshuva? Of course!

1. **Hashem wants us to implement the four steps of teshuva**, as listed above.

2. **Hashem doesn't give us a test that we can't pass**. Therefore, we can't blame our misdeeds on anyone or anything else.

3. **With prayer, we can accomplish anything**. So, even if it's difficult for us to commit to doing better in an area that we tend to transgress, we should pray to Hashem to help us become stronger and to observe the particular mitzvah that we're having trouble with.

4. **Remember, we don't deserve anything**! We can't take Hashem's forgiveness for granted, but literally beg Hashem to forgive us for our wrongdoing and to help us in the future.

Let's make Teshuva!

The above four guidelines for judging ourselves are in effect a blueprint for making teshuva.

Many people attempt to make teshuva and then become disappointed because their efforts don't turn them into tzaddikim overnight. Then, they become disheartened and disillusioned, and are liable to fall down altogether. By sticking to the four guidelines for judging ourselves, we're assured steady, gradual, and sure-footed spiritual progress that will lead to our full soul correction and happiness in this world and in the next.

Sometimes, a negative character trait, such as a bad temper, hampers teshuva. Even worse, when we first begin making teshuva, our bad habits and traits actually surface; this is a gift from Hashem, who shows us what we need to correct.

With the aid of the four guidelines for judging ourselves, we can also rectify and improve negative habits and traits. In the following elaboration, we'll use anger for an example, but you can apply the guidelines to improving anything you want, as follows:

1. **Hashem wants teshuva, not depression** – Every time our bad attribute trips us up, we ask ourselves, does Hashem want me to be depressed because I lost my temper (*or plug in whatever you might have done wrong*)? Wouldn't He prefer that I reinforce

my spiritual self and make teshuva? Of course! The fact that I'm aware of my problem and trying my best to correct it is already 50% of the solution!

2. **Hashem doesn't give us a test that we can't pass** – if Hashem is testing my temper, that means that I have the ability to overcome it. How?

3. **With prayer, we can accomplish anything** – Since I'm already aware of the problem, if I turn to Hashem and ask Him to help me, I am sure to make considerable improvement. The more I pray, the more I learn about emuna, and the harder I try, the more I'll overcome my bad temper (*or other negative trait*).

4. **Remember, we don't deserve anything** – we must approach Hashem with humility, and not with demands for instant gratification. When we speak to Hashem modestly, and ask Him for a gift, our prayers become much more cogent. For example: "Hashem, my terrible temper is a barrier that prevents me from serving You properly and performing Your commandments; please give me the emuna to realize that everything comes from You and is all for my ultimate welfare, so that nothing in the world will upset me. I know that I'm not deserving of such a gift, but I want to serve You better with all my heart." It won't take long for prayers like these to be answered.

Start walking!

A group of friends once made a trip together. On the way to their destination, they saw someone standing with a backpack on a desert crossroads. Seven days later, on their way home, they encountered the same person with the backpack standing on the same desert crossroads in the hot sun. The group of friends asked the backpacker, "Why are you standing here?"

> "I want to go to Jerusalem," responded the backpacker. "I'm waiting for a ride."
>
> "How long have you been waiting?" they asked.
>
> "More than a week," he answered.
>
> They laughed. "Jerusalem's only a two-day walk from here. If you'd have started walking, you could have been there and back four times already!"

Many of us want to change, yet we expect it to happen automatically, with no effort on our part. Life doesn't work that way. An old Hebrew expression says, "Even a journey of a thousand kilometers begins with a first step."

The first step toward teshuva, self-correction, and character perfection is establishing a daily 60-minute session of personal prayer and self-evaluation. Once we take the first step on the road to spiritual gain, Hashem helps us the whole way. King David describes Hashem's constant guidance along the journey to self improvement when he says to Hashem (*Psalms 73:23*), "You held my right hand."

Our most important personal prayers are requests for enhanced emuna and that Hashem should open our eyes to what we need to correct. Such requests coupled with daily self-evaluation and teshuva invoke a marvelous illumination of the soul that brings a person to true happiness and inner peace.

Praying for prayer

Prayer, especially personal prayer, doesn't come easy. Since prayer brings a person so very close to Hashem, and one's entire soul correction is dependant on prayer, the evil inclination tries everything in its power to impede prayer. Once a person decides to invest his or her daily 60 minutes in personal prayer, the evil inclination will present a long list of obstacles and impediments. Therefore, we should pray to Hashem that He help us pray; particularly, we should ask Hashem to enable us to speak to Him in personal prayer every day.

Once we succeed in establishing our personal prayer session, it's a good idea to devote the first few minutes in praying for prayer, as follows: "Hashem, please give me the words to express myself. Help me think clearly and verbalize my thoughts. Help me thank You for all the wonderful gifts You give me daily, and help me evaluate myself and make teshuva properly. More than anything, please give me the faith that You are with me and that You listen to my prayers."

Any worthwhile endeavor begins with prayer. Adding prayer before whatever we do gives life an indescribable sweetness. With prayer, a person is granted a passport to success.

The secret of the good life

Rebbe Nathan of Breslevsaid, "Wherever I see deficiency, I see lack of prayer!"

Rebbe Nathan's above remark is the secret of a good life: Since lack of prayer is the cause of deficiency, with prayer, we can attain literally anything and fulfill all of our needs, both material and spiritual. Yet amazingly, most people don't pray at all! They claim that they lack the time for prayer. Earlier in this book, we told the story of the disheveled and ragged prince sleeping on the park bench; when one of the King's ministers found him and asked why he doesn't turn to his all-powerful father for assistance, the prince answered that he didn't have the time…

The fortunate person that discovers the secret of the good life can't go for a day without prayer. Indeed, those who discover the power of prayer can't go for a few hours without feeling a thirst for prayer. The more one prays, the more one attains proximity to Hashem. The closer we are to Hashem, the more He illuminates our souls. The more He illuminates our souls, the happier we feel. That's the secret of the good life in a nutshell.

A Word of Conclusion

Practice makes perfect. Now that you've gone through this book a first time, try reviewing it again from cover to cover. The more you internalize the principles of emuna, the easier you'll be able to apply them in everyday life.

Emuna is the axis around which the world rotates. As we strengthen our cognizance that Hashem runs the universe, does everything for our ultimate good, and has a specific purpose in everything He does, namely, to assist us to correct our souls and to cling to Him, we find ourselves happier and more successful in everything we do.

May Hashem bless you always and help you attain all your heart's wishes for the very best, amen.

Glossary

Amalek (Biblical) – evil grandson of Esau; nickname for the Yetzer Hara, the evil inclination

Baal Teshuva (Hebrew) – spiritually awakened Jew

Brit mila (Hebrew) – ritual circumcision

Chassid (Hebrew) – literally "pious person", but alludes to the disciples of the Chassidic movement, founded by Rabbi Yisroel Baal Shem Tov in the early 18th Century CE

Chattan (Hebrew) – bridegroom

Chuppa (Hebrew) – marital canopy

Dinim (Hebrew) – the spiritual forces of severe judgments that are created by a person's misdeeds.

Emuna (Hebrew) - the firm belief in a single, supreme, omniscient, benevolent, spiritual, supernatural, and all-powerful Creator of the universe, who we refer to as God

Emunat Chachamim (Hebrew) - the belief in our sages

Epikoris (Greek) – skeptic, heretic

Epikorsis (Greek) – heresy, skepticism

Gemorra (Aramaic) – The 2nd-5th Century CE elaborations on the Mishna, which serve as the foundation of Jewish law

Geula (Hebrew) – the redemption process of the Jewish people

Hashem (Hebrew) - literally means "the name," a substitute term for The Almighty so that we don't risk using God's name in vain.

Hitbodedut (Hebrew) – personal prayer

Kabbala (Hebrew) - Jewish esoteric thought

Kedusha (Hebrew) - holiness

Mishna (Hebrew) – The oral elaboration of the Torah as given from Hashem to Moses, finally codified by Rabbi Akiva, his pupil Rabbi Meir, and his pupil Rabbi Yehuda HaNassi, 1st-2nd Century, CE

Mitzvah (Hebrew) – a commandment of the Torah; good deed.

Mitzvoth (Hebrew, pl.) – literally, the commandments of the Torah; good deeds

Moshiach (Hebrew) – Messiah

Onaat Devarim (Hebrew) – a broad term for verbal abuse which includes several Torah prohibitions against causing anguish to a fellow human being

Pidyon Nefesh (Hebrew) – literally "redemption of the soul"; a monetary donation that is given to a tzaddik as atonement for a person's soul

Sandek (Hebrew) - godfather

Shabbat (Hebrew) – Sabbath, day of rest

Shalom Bayit (Hebrew) – literally "peace in the home", marital bliss

Shmirat Habrit (Hebrew) – literally "guarding the covenant"; male holiness in thought, speech, and deed, particularly the use of one's reproductive organs only in the performance of a mitzvah

Shmirat Eynayim (Hebrew) – "guarding the eyes," or refraining from looking at forbidden objects, particularly at a woman other than one's wife

Shulchan Oruch (Hebrew) – Code of Jewish Law, compiled by Rabbi Joseph Caro of Tzfat, late 16th Century CE

Tallit (Hebrew) – prayer shawl

Talmud (Hebrew) – Jewish oral tradition, comprised of the Mishna and the Gemorra

Tanna (Aramaic) – Mishnaic sage, 1st – 2nd Century CE

Tefillin (Aramaic) - phylacteries

Teshuva (Hebrew) – literally "returning," the term that refers to the process of atoning for one's misdeeds

Tfilla (Hebrew) - prayer

Tikkun (Hebrew) – correction of the soul

Tikkunim (Hebrew) – plural for tikkun

Tzaddik (Hebrew) – extremely pious and upright person

Tzaddikim (Hebrew) – plural for tzaddik

Tzedakka (Hebrew) – charity

Yetzer Hara (Hebrew) – evil inclination

Yetzer Tov (Hebrew) –inclination to do good

Yir'at Shamayim (Hebrew) – literally "the fear of Hashem," a term for sincere piety

Zohar (Hebrew) - the 2nd-Century C.E. esoteric interpretation of the Torah by Rebbe Shimon Bar Yochai and his disciples

The author wishes to express his gratitude to all those whose comments and corrections contributed to the publication of this edition, and particularly to Eliezer Friedman for his tireless efforts and assistance. May Hashem bless you all with both material and spiritual abundance, amen.

לעילוי נשמת

צבי בן זלמן יהודה

מלכה דבורה בת הרב דוד שלמה הכהן

צבי בן הרב יהושע

לאה בת שמחה בונים

משה בן ברוך יצחק

מייכלא בת משה דב

ת.נ.צ.ב.ה.

Did you enjoy this book?

If so, please help us spread the message of emuna around the world. Send your contributions to:

Chut Shel Chesed

POB 50226

Jerusalem, Israel

Dear reader!

The book You have just finished reading has changed the lives of many. Please note that this book is the outcome of a wonderful enterprise that is dedicated to the goal of spreading Jewish wisdom and emuna to hundreds of thousands of people around the globe.

We turn to you, dear reader with a request to become a partner in this enterprise by contributing to our efforts in spreading emuna around the world.

For your convenience please fill in the form on the back and send it to us.

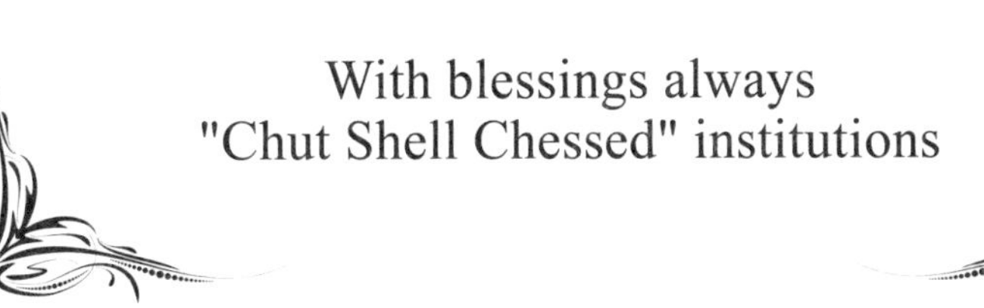

With blessings always
"Chut Shell Chessed" institutions

"Chut Shell Chessed"
p.o. 50226
Bucharim mail box office
Jerusalem zip code: 91050
Israel

Attach here

Support The Important Work of "Chut Shel Chessed"

Thank you for supporting "Chut Shel Chessed".

Recommended Operation Support Levels:

$ 15.60 (30¢/week) ☐

$ 26.00 (50¢/week) ☐

$ 39.00 (75¢/week) ☐

$ 52.00 (1.00$/week) ☐

Other Amount: $ _______

Recommended Support Levels:

$ 100

$ 250

$ 500

$ 1000

Please include your email address,
We will keep you informed about

E-mail address: ______________________________

Name: ______________________________

Street address: ______________________________

City, State, Zip: ______________________________

Phone: (_____) ______________________________

Contribute by Credit Card:

Credit Card Type:

☐ Visa ☐ MasterCard ☐ Discover ☐ American Express

Credit Card #: ______________________________

Expiration: ______________ (Month / Year)

Cardholder Signature: __________________________

Contribute by check :

send a check to the address listed on the back of this card

Attach here